Voices of Conscience

VOICES —OF— CONSCIENCE

Poetry from Oppression

**Edited by
Hume Cronyn
Richard McKane
Stephen Watts**

First published 1995 by IRON Press
5 Marden Terrace Cullercoats
North Shields Northumberland
NE30 4PD. Tel: 0191 2531901

Typeset by David Stephenson in 10pt Palatino

Printed by Peterson Printers
12 Laygate South Shields Tyne & Wear

Cover and book design by Peter Mortimer

ISBN 0 906228 53 0

Edited by Hume Cronyn, Richard McKane
and Stephen Watts

IRON Press books are distributed by
Password Books Ltd
23 New Mount Street
Manchester M4 4DE
Tel: 0161 953 4009
Fax: 0161 953 4001

Contents

Fascism and Genocide in Europe

Fascism (Mainly pre-1945)

The Holocaust

European Communism: Post-1945

Soviet Republics

South-East Asia/Pacific Rim/Australia

South Asia

Latin America/The Caribbean

Cuba

The Caribbean

Britain/Ireland/USA

Britain/Ireland

FOREWORD

This anthology brings together some of the often quite extraordinary, rooted and liberating poetry that has been written in the face of state-inflicted terror - or terrorism as it should surely be named. There has always been terror, violence inflicted on individuals, groups and cultures by other individuals and groups and cultures. It would be difficult to think of a culture (including the western democracies) that has not used terror for its own purposes at the very least to deracinate oppositions. This use has often been invoked or crudely activated by governments against their own citizens or minorities within their power. While the experiences under the Nazis, under the totalitarian communisms of the Soviet Union and elsewhere, within the apartheid state of South Africa and in Latin America are well known and still highly profiled, there are equally repressive regimes in many other parts of the world. We have attempted to include poetries from countries where the practices of oppression, irrespective of political leanings, are rife.

We have tried to bring together poetry that does not avoid what has happened, poetry that names the violences of state terror and that bears witness in often extraordinary fashion. We have also tried to give some emphasis to the poetry of breakthrough beyond the confines of torture and to bring to people's notice poetry that is not well-known in an English-speaking world but whose richness and courage and harsh experience could be supportive of our own language and our own poetries.

With the exception of an extract from *The Ballad of Reading Gaol* which was written in 1898, and is a sort of wilde card to the whole book, the anthology consists entirely of poetry written in the twentieth century. We have arranged it in broad geographical-political sections, but chronologically the range is from poets killed in the Armenian massacres of 1915 (a systematic policy of atrocity and killing which is correctly recognised as the first holocaust of the century) to the work of poets imprisoned or tortured in 1980s. We have not attempted to be entirely systematic or tried to cover the whole geographical and political spread of prison poetry. However we have tried to include many voices across a wide spectrum and we have been unhappy not to be able, for various reasons, to include a number of poets and to leave certain areas under- or unrepresented.

Imprisonment, torture and oppression are not isolated events (even though one of their intentions is to isolate and erode the political prisoner), but are fundamentally linked to other experiences and processes.These include exile, the oppression of women in society , psychiatric abuse in prisons, the status of asylum, the violation of the human rights of refugees, and indeed the abuse of civil liberties in any society. We have included a smaller number of poems addressing some of these linked issues. Most of the poetry here is a poetry of the imprisoned, but it is pointless to see this in isolation from its causes, or its repercussions.

There is no ordinary or immediate language in which pain and torture can be named and objectively discussed. It is one of the extraordinary achievements of certain poets to have found a language in which pain *can* be named, gone beyond and objectively described, so the traumas of being tortured are evoked without the effect being only one of numbing shock. This is one of the fundamental attributes of language that poetry gives access to. Thus Reza Baraheni having been grossly tortured and having seen and heard others being tortured by SAVAK, describes this in words that, while making us flinch and turn away, bring before us in objective, accessible language those experiences – as in his poem 'Barbecue':

– would the man whose buttocks are roasted like to sit down?

- no, never! I would rather die than sit down!

he sleeps on his heart and on his knees
he arches his back
and purrs with pain
the puss and blood stick his ass to his shorts and to his pants

– doesn't the man whose back is burnt want to undress?

– no, never! I'd rather die than undress! They undressed
me once! Isn't that enough? In a quarter of an hour you
could roast a cow on that bed!
I burn, burn, burn, burn forever!

One danger in an anthology of this sort is too much emphasis on the poet as victim. We wanted to avoid this as the dominant impression because most of the poets have written for other reasons as well. There is the poet as survivor, in word, spirit or body. And some who have died in prison or who were disappeared still live on in their words (Vasyl Stus, Osip Mandelstam, Alaide Foppa) or as testament in the survival of others. Some poets are aware of being witness for a culture (Mitta Vasleye, U Sam Oeur et al.), or involved with struggle as combatant, as with Javier Heraud or Otto Rene Castillo, Jose Maria Sison or Mila Aguilar. But at the heart of it all there is the matter of pain. The banal matter of pain in one sense, as Hannah Arendt might have put it. Pain inflicted by intention and often by craft and most frequently by organised (or disorganised) government action, or to put it bluntly – by various forms of state terrorism. Thus, pain not come upon by chance or accident.

If one core of the book is suffering and survival, and another is struggle and anger, then a third is the poetry of non-partisan testimony. If language can be both a spiritual and a political structure erected against the paranoias and barbarisms of dictatorship it is also the house of healing where political power may be reclaimed. Political poetry of both a partisan and non-partisan nature can be effective, and we have included some partisan poetry: One problem with much of this poetry is the difficulty of translation, given that its commitments are very precisely melted in to its language. Thus the fiery poetry written by Nazrul Islam in the 1920s and '30s (at a time when he was imprisoned in Bengal under British colonial rule) is particularly difficult to put into an English that adequately represents its power and rooted balance. This is a political and cultural problem that should be faced. However we have had to exclude his poetry (and thus also its very pertinent cultural anger) because we did not feel available translations did justice to the culture of his language – a volatile and difficult one to translate.

If the language and poetry of non-partisan testimony (a poetry we as editors would want to admit to loving) perhaps dominates the anthology, we hope that many voices come through, some without doubt partisan and angry. There is no balance within barbarism or brutality and the range of voices that cope with and oppose torture cover a wide spectrum. We have included some poets for their strong individualit or for their unique reaction to particular circumstances. This in turn has led to some uneasy inclusions: the quatrains that Ho Chi Minh wrote in classical Chinese to relate his experience in Chinese jails seemed to us to say things in a way that no other poet has. Ho himself later presided over a regime (admittedly in the context of a brutal war.) that oppressed many of its writers and much of its culture. We have included, in addition to Ho's, some quatrains by Nguyen Chi Thien, who was imprisoned under Ho, not so much to attempt any balance (barbarism has no balance) but because both poets suffered imprisonment and gave voice to their suffering. Reactions to evil and brutality come through many and varied voices: we have tried to gather together a range of poems, without simplifying issues where they are complex and without excluding disparate voices.

Anyone who has seen the extraordinary book *Surviving Beyond Fear (edited by Marjorie Agosin)* will realise the extent to which women, and children, have been subjected to detention and torture. Agosin and Alicia Partnoy experience and write of such terrors, as does Maria Eugenia Brava Calderera. Alaide Foppa, a feminist and a lyrical poet, was herself disappeared and undoubtedly murdered on her return to Guatemala. We have included poems by two modern Greek women poets: Victoria Theodorou and Rita Mpoumi-Pappas wrote poems of labour camp detentions and executions during the Greek Civil War , and , almost as if in echo of that, is a poem by the Turkish poet Gulten Akin coming from her work as a barrister defending women detained in human rights cases. Rachel Korn and Edith Bruck were both in Nazi concentration camps, Nelly Sachs fled Nazi Germany. Irina Ratushinskaya and Natalya Gorbanevskaya were both sent to Soviet prisons and labour camps, and in both cases were subjected to severe torture and abuse. Anna Akhmatova in 'Requiem' recounts her pain and the pain of other women who are not put in prison but whose lives are deeply affected by the imprisonment and murder of very close relatives. There are regimes that specifically use this form of pressure on women, to the point where it in itself becomes a form of torture. A further elaboration of this, well documented from Latin America and elsewhere, is when women are forced to look-on while husbands /lovers/fathers/sisters/or dear friends are subjected to or threatened with torture. We have included poems by women that reflect these realities.

We have included a number of poets who have not been imprisoned or censored, such as Gyula Illyes whose great poem 'One Sentence on Tyranny' is very pertinent. This poem was not written in 1956 or in reaction to the Soviet repression in Hungary in that year, but in the early 1950s after which it was put in the poet's drawer. Nor was Illyes imprisoned, or notably harrassed by the communist regime in Hungary, or grossly censored when the poem was published. But the scope of this poem and its words place it at the core of the anthology:

> Where there's tyranny
> there is tyranny,
> not just in gun barrels,
> not just in jails,
> ....
> not just the interrogation,
> it's in the declaration,
> in the rapturous moan,
> like the fly in the wine,
>
> because even in your dreams
> you're not alone, it's even
> in the marriage bed, and earlier
> in the desire

Adrienne Rich has not been imprisoned in the particular stark and terrifying ways that so many poets in this anthology have been. And indeed there are other fine women poets in the USA (Muriel Rukeyser for instance) who have been imprisoned. But we have included Rich's poem 'North American Time' for the relevance of her lines

> I am thinking this in a country
> where words are stolen out of mouths
> as bread is stolen out of mouths
> where poets don't go to jail
> for being poets, but for being
> dark-skinned, female, poor.

The cover painting is by Arshile Gorky, who grew up in Armenia with his family, and suffered greatly before managing to leave for exile in America. *'The Artist And His Mother'* (1926-1942) is in fact a memory of his own mother and himself and was taken in part from a photograph from his childhood. A painting of very Armenian colours and culture, it evokes the memory of pain and loss.

It has not been possible to put all diacritical marks in the text. In particular there are no accents for Nepali and Vietnamese names. In the text and in the biographical notes certain poets (Korean, Chinese, Vietnamese, and Cambodian in particular) appear under their first names, as is the usual practice in those languages. It should also be noted that a few poets may appear to some people to be in an anomalous section: it is always difficult to use exact, universally accepted categories in a book such as this, but there have always been reasons of cultural or political affiliation for our decisions. We have also usually kept to American spellings where the translators have used them. Although the editors have made every effort to contact all the copyright holders, or their representatives, in a very few cases these efforts proved fruitless. We decided, however, in the interests of the book, to publish the work.

We would like to thank many people; the poets, publishers and translators who gave their permissions freely and who in not even one instance said no. Some wrote warm and appreciative letters for which we were, in the throes of compiling, very grateful. Particular thanks should go to Ronan Bennett, Mary Aylward at Green Ink, Anthony Rudolf, Daniel Weissbort, Katherine Gallacher, John Cayley, Brian Holton, and Mandy Garner at the PEN Writers In Prison Committee for suggestions and support. Many thanks to Peter Mortimer of IRON Press for readily agreeing to publish the book and for his immense support and involvement in helping to see it through, even as it grew to three times its planned size. And for their endless patience and access our printers Peterson Ltd. Thanks finally to the kitchen table (and those who sat round it!), to the moths and the library and the reticent pipe. And to everyone else who helped us in the huge task of seeing this book into print.

Hume Cronyn, Richard McKane, Stephen Watts,
June 1995

Fascism and
Genocide
in Europe

BERTOLT BRECHT

When Evil-doing Comes Like Falling Rain

Like one who brings an important letter to the counter after office hours: the
counter is already closed.
Like one who seeks to warn the city of an impending flood, but speaks another
language. They do not understand him.
Like a beggar who knocks for the fifth time at a door where he has four times
been given something: the fifth time he is hungry.
Like one whose blood flows from a wound and who awaits the doctor: his
blood goes on flowing.

So do we come forward and report that evil has been done us.

The first time it was reported that our friends were being butchered there was
a cry of horror. Then a hundred were butchered. But when a thousand
were butchered and there was no end to the butchery, a blanket of
silence spread.

When evil-doing comes like falling rain, nobody calls out 'stop!'

When crimes begin to pile up they become invisible. When sufferings become
unendurable the cries are no longer heard. The cries, too, fall like rain
in summer.

Translated from the German by John Willett

BERTOLT BRECHT

To Those Born Later

I

Truly, I live in dark times!
The guileless word is folly. A smooth forehead
Suggests insensitivity. The man who laughs
Has simply not yet had
The terrible news.

What kind of times are they, when
A talk about trees is almost a crime
Because it implies silence about so many horrors?
That man there calmly crossing the street
Is already perhaps beyond the reach of his friends
Who are in need?

It is true I still earn my keep
But, believe me, that is only an accident. Nothing
I do gives me the right to eat my fill.
By chance I've been spared. (If my luck breaks, I am lost.)

They say to me: Eat and drink! Be glad you have it!
But how can I eat and drink if I snatch what I eat
From the starving, and
My glass of water belongs to one dying of thirst?
And yet I eat and drink.

I would also like to be wise.
In the old books it says what wisdom is:
To shun the strife of the world and to live out
Your brief time without fear
Also to get along without violence
To return good for evil
Not to fulfil your desires but to forget them
Is accounted wise.
All this I cannot do:
Truly, I live in dark times.

II

I came to the cities in a time of disorder
When hunger reigned there.
I came among men in a time of revolt
And I rebelled with them.

So passed my time
Which had been given to me on earth.

My food I ate between battles
To sleep I lay down among murderers
Love I practised carelessly
And nature I looked at without patience.
So passed my time
Which had been given to me on earth.

All roads led into the mire in my time.
My tongue betrayed me to the butchers.
There was little I could do. But those in power
Sat safer without me: that was my hope.
So passed my time
Which had been given to me on earth.

Our forces were slight. Our goal
Lay far in the distance
It was clearly visible, though I myself
Was unlikely to reach it.
So passed my time
Which had been given to me on earth.

III

You who will emerge from the flood
In which we have gone under
Remember
When you speak of our failings
The dark time too
Which you have escaped.
For we went, changing countries oftener than our shoes
Through the wars of the classes, despairing
When there was injustice only, and no rebellion.

And yet we know:
Hatred, even of meanness
Contorts the features.
Anger, even against injustice
Makes the voice hoarse. Oh, we
Who wanted to prepare the ground for friendliness
Could not ourselves be friendly.

But you, when the time comes at last
And man is a helper to man
Think of us
With forbearance.

Translated from the German by John Willett, Ralph Manheim, and Erich Fried

C. P. Cavafy

Waiting For The Barbarians

What are we waiting for, assembled in the forum?

> The barbarians are due here today.

Why isn't anything happening in the senate?
Why do the senators sit there without legislating?

> Because the barbarians are coming today.
> What laws can the senators make now?
> Once the barbarians are here, they'll do the legislating.

Why did our emperor get up so early,
and why is he sitting at the city's main gate,
on his throne, in state, wearing the crown?

> Because the barbarians are coming today
> and the emperor is waiting to receive their leader.
> He has even prepared a scroll to give to him,
> replete with titles, with imposing names.

Why have our two consuls and praetors come out today
wearing their embroidered, their scarlet togas?
Why have they put on bracelets with so many amethysts,
and rings sparkling with magnificent emeralds?
Why are they carrying elegant canes
beautifully worked in silver and gold?

> Because the barbarians are coming today
> and things like that dazzle the barbarians

Why don't our distinguished orators come forward as usual
to make their speeches, say what they have to say?

> Because the barbarians are coming today
> and they're bored by rhetoric and public speaking.

Why this sudden restlessness, this confusion?
(How serious people's faces have become.)
Why are the streets and squares emptying so rapidly,
everyone going home so lost in thought?

    Because night has fallen and the barbarians have not come.
    And some who have just returned from the border say
    there are no barbarians any longer.

And now, what's going to happen to us without barbarians?
They were, those people, a kind of solution.

Translated from the Greek by Edmund Keeley and Philip Sherrard

Paul Éluard

Liberty

On my schoolboy's copy-books
On my desk and on the trees
On sand and snow
I write your name

On all pages read
On all blank pages
Stone blood paper or ash
I write your name

On the gilded images
On the arms of warriors
On the crown of kings
I write your name

On the jungle and the desert
On nests on gorse
On the echo of my childhood
I write your name

On the wonders of the nights
On the white bread of the days
On seasons betrothed
I write your name

On all my rags of blue
On the pond musty sun
On the lake living moon
I write your name

On the fields on the horizon
On the wings of birds
And on the mill of shadows
I write your name

On every whiff of daybreak
On sea on ships
On the raging mountain
I write your name

On the foam of clouds
On the toil of storm
On the dense and tasteless rain
I write your name

On gleaming shapes
On bells of colour
On physical truth
I write your name

On awakened paths
On roads spread out
On overflowing squares
I write your name

On the lamp that kindles
On the lamp that dies
On my houses joined together
I write your name

On the fruit cut in two
By the mirror and my room
On my bed empty shell
I write your name

On my greedy loving dog
On his pricked up ears
On his awkward paw
I write your name

On the threshold of my door
On familiar things
On the surge of blessed fire
I write your name

On all accordant flesh
On the foreheads of my friends
On every hand held out
I write your name

On the window of surprises
On attentive lips
High above the silence
I write your name

On my devastated shelters
On my perished beacons
On the walls of my fatigue
I write your name

On absence without desire
On barren solitude
On the steps of death
I write your name

On health returned
On vanished risk
On hope without remembrance
I write your name

And by the power of a word
I begin my life again
I was born to know you
To name you

Liberty.

Translated from the French by Gilbert Bowen

MIGUEL HERNÁNDEZ

Lullaby Of The Onion

(Lines for his son, after receiving a letter from his wife in which she said that all she had to eat was bread and onions.)

An onion is frost
shut in and poor.
Frost of your days
and of my nights.
Hunger and onion,
black ice and frost
huge and round.

My son is lying now
in the cradle of hunger.
The blood of an onion
is what he lives on.
But it is your blood,
with sugar on it like frost,
onion and hunger.

A dark woman
turned into moonlight
pours herself down thread
by thread over your cradle.
My son, laugh,
because you can swallow the moon
when you want to.

Lark of my house,
laugh often.
Your laugh is in your eyes
the light of the world.
Laugh so much
that my soul, hearing you,
will beat wildly in space.

Your laugh unlocks doors for me,
it gives me wings.
It drives my solitudes off,
pulls away my jail.
Mouth that can fly,

heart that turns to
lightning on your lips.

Your laugh is the sword
that won all the wars,
it defeats the flowers
and the larks,
challenges the sun.
Future of my bones
and of my love.

The body with wings beating,
the eyelash so quick,
life is full of color
as it never was.
How many linnets
climb with wings beating
out of your body!

I woke up and was an adult:
don't wake up.
My mouth is sad:
you go on laughing.
In your cradle, forever,
defending your laughter
feather by feather.

Your being has a flying range
so high and so wide
that your body is a newly
born sky.
I wish I could climb
back to the starting point
of your travel!

You laugh, eight months old,
with five orange blossoms.
You have five tiny
ferocities.
You have five teeth
like five new
jasmine blossoms.

They will be the frontier
of kisses tomorrow,

when you feel your rows
of teeth are a weapon.
You will feel a flame
run along under your teeth
looking for the centre.

My son, fly away, into the
two moons of the breast:
the breast, onion-
sad, but you, content.
Stay on your feet.
Stay ignorant of what's happening,
and what is going on.

Translated from the Spanish by Robert Bly

Attila József

A Breath Of Air!

Who can forbid my telling what hurt me
    on the way home?
Soft darkness was just settling on the grass,
    a velvet drizzle,
and under my feet the brittle leaves
tossed sleeplessly and moaned
    like beaten children.

Stealthy shrubs were squatting in a circle
    on the city's outskirts.
The autumn wind cautiously stumbled among them.
    The cool moist soil
looked with suspicion at streetlamps;
a wild duck woke clucking in a pond
    as I walked by.

I was thinking, anyone could attack me
    in that lonely place.
Suddenly a man appeared,
    but walked on.
I watched him go. He could have robbed me,
since I wasn't in the mood for self-defence.
    I felt crippled.

They can tap all my telephone calls
    (when, why, to whom.)
They have a file on my dreams and plans
    and on those who read them.
And who knows when they'll find
sufficient reason to dig up the files
    that violate my rights.

In this country, fragile villages
    – where my mother was born –
have fallen from the tree of living rights
    like these leaves
and when a full-grown misery treads on them
a small noise reports their misfortune
    as they're crushed alive.

This is not the order I dreamed of. My soul
  is not at home here
in a world where the insidious
  vegetate easier,
among people who dread to choose
and tell lies with averted eyes
  and feast when someone dies.

This is not how I imagined order.
  Even though
I was beaten as a small child, mostly
  for no reason,
I would have jumped at a single kind word.
I knew my mother and my kin were far,
  these people were strangers.

Now I have grown up. There is more foreign
  matter in my teeth,
more death in my heart. But I still have rights
  until I fall apart
into dust and soul, and now that I've grown up
my skin is not so precious that I should put up
  with the loss of my freedom.

My leader is in my heart. We are
  men, not beasts,
we have minds. While our hearts ripen desires,
  they cannot be kept in files.
Come, freedom! Give birth to a new order,
teach me with good words and let me play,
your beautiful serene son.

Translated from the Hungarian by John Bátki.

ATTILA JÓZSEF

The Seventh

If you set out in this world,
better be born seven times.
Once, in a house on fire,
once, in a freezing flood,
once, in a wild madhouse,
once, in a field of ripe wheat,
once, in an empty cloister,
and once among pigs in a sty.
Six babes crying, not enough:
you yourself must be the seventh.

When you must fight to survive,
let your enemy see seven.
One, away from work on Sunday,
one, starting his work on Monday,
one, who teaches without payment,
one, who learned to swim by drowning,
one, who is the seed of a forest,
and one, whom wild forefathers protect,
but all their tricks are not enough:
you yourself must be the seventh.

If you want to find a woman,
let seven men go for her.
One, who gives his heart for words,
one, who takes care of himself,
one, who claims to be a dreamer,
one, who through her skirt can feel her,
one, who knows the hooks and snaps,
one, who steps upon her scarf:
let them buzz like flies around her.
You yourself must be the seventh.

If you write and can afford it,
let seven men write your poem.
One, who builds a marble village,
one, who was born in his sleep,
one, who charts the sky and knows it,
one, whom words call by his name,
one, who perfected his soul,

one, who dissects living rats.
Two are brave and four are wise;
you yourself must be the seventh.

And if all went as was written,
you will die for seven men.
One, who is rocked and suckled,
one, who grabs a hard young breast,
one, who throws down empty dishes,
one, who helps the poor to win,
one, who works till he goes to pieces,
one, who just stares at the moon.
The world will be your tombstone:
you yourself must be the seventh.

Translated from the Hungarian by John Bátki

Czeslaw Milosz

Dedication

You whom I could not save
Listen to me.
Try to understand this simple speech as I would be ashamed of another.
I swear, there is in me no wizardry of words.
I speak to you with silence like a cloud or a tree.

What strengthened me, for you was lethal.
You mixed up farewell to an epoch with the beginning of a new one,
Inspiration of hatred with lyrical beauty,
Blind force with accomplished shape.

Here is the valley of shallow Polish rivers. And an immense bridge
Going into white fog. Here is a broken city,
And the wind throws the screams of gulls on your grave
When I am talking with you.

What is poetry which does not save
Nations or people?
A connivance with official lies,
A song of drunkards whose throats will be cut in a moment,
Readings for sophomore girls.
That I wanted good poetry without knowing it,
That I discovered, late, its salutary aim,
In this and only this I find salvation.

They used to pour millet on graves or poppy seeds
To feed the dead who would come disguised as birds.
I put this book here for you, who once lived
So that you should visit us no more.

Warsaw, 1945

Translated from the Polish by the author

CZESLAW MILOSZ

from The World

The Sun

All colors come from the sun. And it does not have
Any particular color, for it contains them all.
And the whole Earth is like a poem
While the sun above represents the artist.

Whoever wants to paint the variegated world
Let him never look straight up at the sun
Or he will lose the memory of things he has seen.
Only burning tears will stay in his eyes.

Let him kneel down, lower his face to the grass,
And look at light reflected by the ground.
There he will find everything we have lost:
The stars and the roses, the dusks and the dawns.

Warsaw, 1943

Translated from the Polish by the author

Jorge de Sena

Letter To My Children On The Shootings of Goya
(Goya's 'Third of May' in the Prado, Madrid)

I do not know, my children, what world will be yours.
It is possible, for all things are possible, that it may be
the one I desire for you. A simple world,
where all things will have only the difficulty that stems
from there being nothing that is not simple and natural.
A world in which all things are permitted,
according to your taste, your craving, your pleasure,
your respect for others, others' respect for you.
And it is possible that it may not be this one, it may not even be this one
that interests you for living. All things are possible,
even when we struggle, as we ought to struggle,
for whatever seems to us liberty and justice,
or more than any of those a faithful
dedication to the honor of being alive.
Some day you will know that greater than humankind,
countless is the number of those who thought this way,
loved their fellow man for what in him was unique,
unusual, free, different,
and they were sacrificed, tortured, beaten,
and hypocritically handed over to secular justice,
to be liquidated with supreme piety and without bloodshed.
For being faithful to a god, to a thought,
to a country, a hope, or often even
to the unanswerable hunger that gnawed their vitals,
they were quartered, flayed, burned, gassed,
and their bodies heaped up as anonymously as they had lived,
or their ashes scattered so that no memory of them might remain.
At times for being of a race, at other times
for being of a class, they all expiated
the errors they had not committed or had no consciousness
of having committed. But it also happened
and it happens that they were not killed outright.
There were always infinite methods of prevailing,
annihilating gently, delicately,
by mysterious ways as they say God's ways are mysterious.
These shootings, this heroism, this horror,
were one happening among a thousand in Spain
over a century ago and which because of its violence and injustice

offended the heart of a painter named Goya,
who had a very large heart, filled with fury
and love. But this is nothing, my children.
Merely an episode, a brief episode,
in this chain of which you are a link (or will not be)
of iron and sweat and blood and some semen
on the way to the world I dream for you.
Believe that no world, nothing, nobody,
is more valuable than a life or the joy of having it.
This is what matters most – that joy.
Believe that the dignity of which they will tell you so much
is nothing but that joy which comes
from being alive and knowing that not even once
will anybody be less alive or suffer or die
in order that a single one of you may resist for a little longer
the death which belongs to all and will come.
That you will know all this serenely,
without guilt toward anyone, without terror, without ambition,
and above all without detachment or indifference,
ardently I hope. So much blood,
so much pain, so much anguish, some day
– even if the tedium of a happy world harasses you –
cannot be in vain. I confess that
many times, thinking of the horror of so many centuries
of oppression and cruelty, I hesitate momentarily
and inconsolable bitterness submerges me.
Will they be in vain or not? But, even if they are not,
who resuscitates those millions, who restores
not only life but all that was taken from them?
No Last Judgment, my children, can give them
that instant they did not live, that object
they did not come to enjoy, that gesture
of love that they would make "tomorrow."
And therefore, the same world we may create
it behooves us to hold carefully, like a thing
that is not only ours that is granted to us
for us to guard respectfully
in memory of the blood that flows in our veins,
of our flesh that belonged to others, of the love that
others did not love because they were robbed of it.

Translated from the Portuguese by Jean R. Longland

NIKOLA VAPTSAROV

Last Words Found In His Pockets

(To My Wife)

I'll come sometime to see you in your sleep,
a visitor from far-off, unexpected.
Don't leave me standing in the street outside –
don't slide the bolt against me.

Softly I will enter, quietly sit down,
forcing my gaze through the dark to see you.
And when at last I am satisfied
I will kiss you, I will leave you.

(Unaddressed)

All this makes the sense it must. My people,
first firing squads –   then worms.
With you, whom we have loved,
with you we stand through this storm.

The fight is ruthless, fierce.
Is, as they put it, epic.
I'm fallen. Another takes my place.
What does one death matter?

Note: Nikola Vaptsarov was executed for his participation in the anti-Nazi Resistance.
This is his last known work.

Version of the Bulgarian by William Pitt Root

EDITH BRÜCK

Equality, Father

Equality, father! Your dream has come true.
I glimpse you dimly, still see you walking
next to Roth the man of property who refused us
a little cottage cheese for the holidays,
Klein the shoemaker who wouldn't resole your only shoes
on credit, Goldberg the butcher
with his trimmed goatee who dragged you
into court for selling meat without a licence,
Stein the teacher who gave us Hebrew lessons
in expectation of a heavenly reward and directed us
like a demoniac conductor
breaking dozens of pointers over the heads
of your children, illiterate in Hebrew, destined to hell.
And you, the poorest, most recognizable
by those skinny buttocks! The most agile,
most exploitable in forced labor.
Forward, father! You've been tried by every eventuality,
armed with experience
you know the front lines, rifles, trenches,
the daily struggle even in good times.
You know prison, the hard plank in the dark cell
where you picked off lice, licked your wounds,
unrolled cigarette butts.
You know the taste of blood in your mouth
from a rotten tooth
from a Fascist's fist
from a bullet you caught defending the homeland
you stubbornly believed was yours.

You know death lurking in ambush
the meanness of men
the power game
the bosses' exploitation.
You know the whole gamut of humiliation
the dark street with menacing shadows
ravenous wolves and skittish horses
on sleepless nights during your solitary trips
in the illusion of business deals
doomed to fail
the promises not kept

except for Jehovah's wrath!

Forward, father! You know the marches,
the cold, hunger! Hold your head high!
you no longer have to hide from your creditors:
they're all there, naked!

Ah, you turn toward me? Don't you know me?
I've grown up, my breasts are firm,
the down on my skin is pure and soft
like mama's when they brought her to you
as a bride. Take me, father!
I'll give you pleasure, not children,
love, not obligations,
love not reproaches,
love undreamed of by you,
imagined by me. Run:
It is the time of the Apocalypse!
Let us commit a mortal sin
worthy of death.

Translated from the Italian by Ruth Feldman

EDITH BRÜCK

Why Would I Have Survived?

Why would I have survived
if not to symbolize
guilt, especially in the eyes
of those who are close to me?
Of all their guilts
one, the greatest, would be
repentance
for having hurt
me, who endured so much.
I, who am different
from the rest and carry within me
six million dead
who speak my language,
who ask man to remember,
man, whose memory is so short.
Why would I have survived
if not to bear witness
with my life
with my every gesture
with my every word
with my every look.
And when will this mission be
accomplished?
I'm tired of my
accusing presence,
the past
is a double-edged
weapon
and I'm bleeding to death.
When my hour comes
I'll leave behind
perhaps an echo
for man, who forgets
and remembers and starts again...

Translated from the Italian by Anita Barrows

PAUL CELAN

Death Fugue

Black milk of daybreak we drink it at sundown
we drink it at noon in the morning we drink it at night
we drink and we drink it
we dig a grave in the breezes there one lies unconfined
A man lives in the house he plays with the serpents he writes
he writes when dusk falls to Germany your golden hair Margarete
he writes it and steps out of doors and the stars are flashing he whistles his
    pack out
he whistles his Jews out in earth has them dig for a grave
he commands us strike up for the dance

Black milk of daybreak we drink you at night
we drink in the morning at noon we drink you at sundown
we drink and we drink you
A man lives in the house he plays with the serpents he writes
he writes when dusk falls to Germany your golden hair Margarete
your ashen hair Shulamith we dig a grave in the breezes there one lies
    unconfined

He calls out jab deeper into the earth you lot you others sing now and play
he grabs at the iron in his belt he waves it his eyes are blue
jab deeper you lot with your spades you others play on for the dance

Black milk of daybreak we drink you at night
we drink you at noon in the morning we drink you at sundown
we drink and we drink you
a man lives in the house your golden hair Margarete
your ashen hair Shulamith he plays with the serpents

He calls out more sweetly play death death is a master from Germany
he calls out more darkly now stroke your strings then as smoke you will rise
    into air
then a grave you will have in the clouds there one lies unconfined

Black milk of daybreak we drink you at night
we drink you at noon death is a master from Germany
we drink you at sundown and in the morning we drink and we drink you
death is a master from Germany his eyes are blue
he strikes you with leaden bullets his aim is true
a man lives in the house your golden hair Margarete

he sets his pack on to us he grants us a grave in the air
he plays with the serpents and daydreams death is a master from Germany

your golden hair Margarete
your ashen hair Shulamith

Translated from the German by Michael Hamburger

Paul Celan

Tenebrae

We are near, Lord,
near and at hand.

Handled already, Lord,
clawed and clawing as though
the body of each of us were
your body, Lord.

Pray, Lord,
pray to us,
we are near.

Askew we went there,
went there to bend
down to the trough, to the crater.

To be watered we went there, Lord.

It was blood, it was
what you shed, Lord.

It gleamed.

It cast your image into our eyes, Lord.
Our eyes and our mouths are so open and empty, Lord.
We have drunk, Lord.
The blood and the image that was in the blood, Lord.

Pray, Lord.
We are near.

Translated from the German by Michael Hamburger

PAUL CELAN

Psalm

No one moulds us again out of earth and clay,
no one conjures our dust.
No one.

Praised be your name, no one.
For your sake
we shall flower.
Towards
you.

A nothing
we were, are, shall
remain, flowering:
the nothing-, the
no one's rose.

With
our pistil soul-bright,
with our stamen heaven-ravaged,
our corolla red
with the crimson word which we sang
over, O over
the thorn.

Translated from the German by Michael Hamburger.

PAUL CELAN

Corona

Autumn eats its leaf out of my hand: we are friends.
From the nuts we shell time and we teach it to walk:
then time returns to the shell.

In the mirror it's Sunday,
in dream there is room for sleeping,
our mouths speak the truth.

My eye moves down to the sex of my loved one:
we look at each other,
we exchange dark words,
we love each other like poppy and recollection,
we sleep like wine in the conches,
like the sea in the moon's blood ray.

We stand by the window embracing, and people look up from the street:
it is time they knew!
It is time the stone made an effort to flower,
time unrest had a beating heart.
It is time it were time.

It is time.

Translated from the German by Michael Hamburger

Robert Desnos

Epitaph

I lived in those times. For a thousand years
I have been dead. Not fallen, but hunted;
When all human decency was imprisoned,
I was free amongst the masked slaves.

I lived in those times, yet I was free.
I watched the river, the earth, the sky,
Turning around me, keeping their balance,
The seasons provided their birds and their honey.

You who live, what have you made of your luck?
Do you regret the time when I struggled?
Have you cultivated for the common harvest?
Have you enriched the town I lived in?

Living men, think nothing of me. I am dead.
Nothing survives of my spirit or my body.

Translated from the French by Kenneth Rexroth

JERZY FICOWSKI

The Seven Words

> *'Mummy! But I've been good! It's dark!' – words of a child being*
> *shut in a gas chamber at Belzec in 1942, according to the statement*
> *of the only surviving prisoner; quoted in Rudolf Reder,* Belzec *(1946)*

Everything was put to use
everyone perished but nothing was lost
a mound of hair fallen from heads
for a hamburg mattress factory
gold teeth pulled out
under the anaesthetic of death

Everything was put to use
a use was found even for that voice
smuggled this far in the bottom of another's memory
like lime unslaked with tears

and belzec opens sometimes right to the bone
and everlasting darkness bursts from it
how to contain it

and the protest of a child who was who was
though memory pales
not from horror
this is how it has paled for thirty years

And silences by the million are silent
transformed into a seven-figure sign
And one vacant place is calling calling

Who are not afraid of me
for I am small and not here at all
do not deny me
give me back the memory of me
these post-Jewish words
these post-human words
just these seven words

Translated from the Polish by Keith Bosley with Krystyna Wandycz

JERZY FICOWSKI

I did not manage to save ...

I did not manage to save
a single life

I did not know how to stop
a single bullet

and I wander round cemeteries
which are not there
I look for words
which are not there
I run

to help where no one called
to rescue after the event

I want to be on time
even if I am too late

Translated from the Polish by Keith Bosley with Krystyna Wandycz

JERZY FICOWSKI

The Assumption Of Miriam From The Street In The Winter Of 1942

snowflakes were teeming down
the sky was collapsing in shreds

so she was being assumed
she passed unmoving
whiteness after whiteness
mild height
after height
in an elijah's chariot
of degradation

above the fallen angels
of snows
into a zenith of frost
higher and higher and
hosanna
lifted
right to the bottom

Translated from the Polish by Keith Bosley with Krystyna Wandycz

Jerzy Ficowski

The Silence Of The Earth

Time here is reckoned only by the woodpecker,
the cuckoo tells out the hours.

This way once people passed crying,
the juniper tugged at their cloak flaps.

For years those shot have lain here
in the deep silence of the earth.

They do not break the branches of the trees,
faces do not sprout from boughs,
eyes do not burst from buds.

A cry does not shatter the veins of wood,
the earth does not tear up the grasslands,
does not fling off its sheets of wild thyme.

The lime-trees do not shut off their fragrance,
the grains are not afraid to grow,
the roads do not run off into the fields.

The roadside stones do not whine,
the smooth air does not crumble,
the wind breathes no sigh.

And they utter not a word
nor a leaf nor a sandgrain

who are devoured by the roots of the pines.

Translated from the Polish by Keith Bosley with Krystyna Wandycz

ERICH FRIED

Paradise Lost

When I had lost
my first country
and when in my second country
and in my place of refuge
and in my third country
and in my second place of refuge
I had lost everything
then I set out

to look for a land
that was not poisoned
by any memories
of irreplaceable losses

So I came to Paradise
there I found peace
Everything was whole and good
I lacked for nothing

Then a sentry
with a flaming sword
said: 'Get away
Here you have lost nothing'

Translated from the German by Stuart Hood.

KATSETNIK 135633

Melech Shteier (Poem For Burning)

When Melech Shteier
went for burning
in the crematorium
the *Shekhina* disappeared
from poetry.
The stalls in the markets
were closed.

A funeral procession
is passing by,
Sabbath of Sabbaths,
may God preserve us.
The wife of the rabbi
has died.
No classes today.

Radioactive rain is falling
on thirsty ground,
becoming confetti.
Never again
shall Rodin sculpt
hands in prayer.
God has broken
the model of Himself,
His image, His likeness.

When Melech Shteier
went naked
to the crematorium
He who is on high
remained indebted to him.
Melech Shteier, by mistake,
out of habit, lifted
his hands to his spectacles
(they were already on
the heap at the entrance
to the crematorium).

Like a baby
he looked up to

heaven, I swear,
like a baby,
his eyes lifted up
to the One whose name
I am unfit to mention.
Am I not worthy
to mention God's name?
But I am worthy
to reclaim
from Him my poem
which together
with Melech Shteier
went naked
to the crematorium.

Translated after the Hebrew by Anthony Rudolf

Katsetnik 135633

At The Moment's End

Eli, Eli, be my Angel of Death
Give me death by Your hand
Silence
And not by the hand of a man

Not by choking, not by fire,
Not by the hand of a man

Like a beaten horse dragging
Under its loaded cart
I shall bring down
My forehead to the earth
I shall see Your face and not Your back

And it was morning, and it was evening,
the eighth day.
Eli, Eli, at the twenty-fifth hour,
On the day of judgment –
Let chaos
Come forth from Your hand
As it was in the beginning
So at the end
In the fourth Sephira

Do not forgive them, Father
For they know what they have done to me

And you regret Your creation

At the moment of the end, oh Eli,
Not by the hands
Of a man in Your image, in Your likeness,
Come down that I may see You
And You alone
At the end of the moment

Translated after the Hebrew and Yiddish by Anthony Rudolf

RACHEL KORN

A New Dress

Today for the first time
after seven long years
I put on
a new dress.

But it's too short for my grief,
too narrow for my sorrow,
and each white-glass button
like a tear flows down the folds
heavy as a stone.

Stockholm, 1947

Translated from the Yiddish by Ruth Whitman

PRIMO LEVI

Shemà

You who live secure
In your warm houses,
Who return at evening to find
Hot food and friendly faces:

Consider whether this is a man,
Who labors in the mud
Who knows no peace
Who fights for a crust of bread
Who dies at a yes or a no.
Consider whether this is a woman,
Without hair or name
With no more strength to remember
Eyes empty and womb cold
As a frog in winter.

Consider that this has been:
I commend these words to you.
Engrave them on your hearts
When you are in your house, when you walk on your way.
When you go to bed, when you rise.
Repeat them to your children.
Or may your house crumble,
Disease render you powerless,
Your offspring avert their faces from you.

10 January 1946

Translated from the Italian by Ruth Feldman and Brian Swann

Primo Levi

'Gedale's Song'

Do you recognize us? We are the ghetto sheep,
Shorn for a thousand years, resigned to injury.
We are the tailors, the copyists, and the cantors
Withered in the shadow of the Cross.
Now we know the forest paths,
We have learned to shoot and we're right on target.
    If I am not for myself, who will be for me?
    If not like this, how? And if not now, when?
Our brothers have risen to the sky
Through the ovens of Sobibór and Treblinka,
They have dug themselves a grave in the air.
Only we few have survived
For the honor of our submerged people,
For revenge and witnessing.
    If I am not for myself, who will be for me?
    If not like this, how? And if not now, when?
We are the sons of David, and the stubborn ones of Massada.
Each of us carries in his pocket the stone
That shattered Goliath's forehead.
Brothers, away from the Europe of graves:
We will climb together toward the land
Where we shall be men among other men.
    If I am not for myself, who will be for me?
    If not like this, how? And if not now, when?

Translated from the Italian by Ruth Feldman

PRIMO LEVI

Song Of Those Who Died In Vain

Sit down and bargain
All you like, grizzled old foxes.
We'll wall you up in a splendid palace
With food, wine, good beds and a good fire
Provided that you discuss, negotiate
For our and your children's lives.
May all the wisdom of the universe
Converge to bless your minds
And guide you in the maze.
But outside in the cold we will be waiting for you,
The army of those who died in vain,
We of the Marne, of Montecassino,
Treblinka, Dresden and Hiroshima.
And with us will be
The leprous and the people with trachoma,
The Disappeared Ones of Buenos Aires,
Dead Cambodians and dying Ethiopians,
The Prague negotiators,
The bled-dry of Calcutta,
The innocents slaughtered in Bologna.
Heaven help you if you come out disagreeing:
You'll be clutched tight in our embrace.
We are invincible because we are the conquered,
Invulnerable because already dead;
We laugh at your missiles.
Sit down and bargain
Until your tongues are dry.
If the havoc and the shame continue
We'll drown you in our putrefaction.

14 January 1985

Translated from the Italian by Ruth Feldman

DAN PAGIS

Written In Pencil In The Sealed Railway-Car

here in this carload
i am eve
with abel my son
if you see my other son
cain son of man
tell him that i

Testimony

No no: they definitely were
human beings: uniforms, boots.
How to explain? They were created
in the image.

I was a shade.
A different creator made me.

And he in his mercy left nothing of me that would die.
And I fled to him, floated up weightless, blue,
forgiving – I would even say: apologising –
smoke to omnipotent smoke
that has no face or image.

Translated from the Hebrew by Stephen Mitchell

MIKLÓS RADNÓTI

Fragment

I lived on this earth in an age
When man fell so low he killed with pleasure
And willingly, not merely under orders.
His life entangled, trapped, in wild obsession,
He trusted false gods, raving in delusion.

I lived on this earth in an age
That esteemed informers, in an age whose heroes
Were the murderer, the bandit and the traitor.
And such as were silent - or just slow to applaud –
Were shunned, as if plague-stricken, and abhorred.

I lived on this earth in an age
When any who spoke out would run for it –
Forced to lie low and gnaw their fists in shame.
The folk went mad and, drunk on blood, filth, hate,
Could only grin at their own hideous fate.

I lived on this earth in an age
When a curse would be the mother of a child
And women were glad if their unborn miscarried.
The living – with poison seething on his plate –
Would envy the grave-dweller the worms eat.

....

I lived on this earth in an age
When poets too were silent: waiting in hope
For the great Prophet to rise and speak again –
Since no-one could give voice to a fit curse
But Isaiah himself, scholar of terrible words.

19 May 1944

Translated from the Hungarian by Clive Wilmer and George Gömöri

MIKLÓS RADNÓTI

A La Recherche...

You too, past gentle evenings, are being refined into memory!
Bright table, once adorned by poets and their young women,
Where in the mud of the past, now, do you slide away to?
Where is the night when friends, sparkling with wit and gusto,
Still drank their fine hock gaily from bright-eyed slender glasses?

Lines of poetry swam around in the lamplight, brilliant
Green adjectives swayed on the metre's foaming crest and
Those who are dead now were living, the prisoners still home, and all of
Those dear friends who are missing, the long-ago-fallen, wrote poems.
Their hearts are under the soil of Flanders, Ukraine and Iberia.

There were men of a kind who gritted their teeth, ran into gunfire
And fought – only because they could do nothing against it,
And while, sheltered by the filthy night, the company
Slept restlessly around them, they'd be thinking of rooms they had lived in –
Islands and caves to them inside this hostile order.

There were places they travelled to in tight-sealed cattle wagons;
They had to stand, unarmed and freezing, in the minefields.
There was also a place they went to, guns in their hands and willing,
Without a word: they saw their own cause in that struggle.
And now the angel of freedom guards their deep dream nightly.

There were places...No matter. Where are the wise, wine-drinking parties?
Their call-up papers flew to them, fragmentary poems multiplied,
And wrinkles multiplied, too, around the lips and under
The eyes of young women with lovely smiles: girls who in bearing
Were sylph-like grew heavy during the silent years of the war-time.

Where is the night, the bar, the table under the lime-trees?
And those still alive, where are they – those herded into the battle?
My hand still clasps their hands, my heart still hears their voices;
I recall their works – I perceive the stature of their torsos
Which appear to me, silent prisoner, on the wailing heights of Serbia.

Where is that night? That night will never more come back to us,
For whatever has passed on, death alters its perspectives.
They sit down at the table, they hide in the smiles of women,
And shall sip wine from our glasses: they who now, unburied,
Sleep in far-away forests, sleep in distant pastures.

Lager Heideman 17 August 1944

Translated from the Hungarian by Clive Wilmer & George Gömöri

Miklós Radnóti

Forced March

A fool he is who, collapsed,   rises and walks again,
Ankles and knees moving   alone, like wandering pain,
Yet he, as if wings uplifted him,   sets out on his way,
And in vain the ditch calls him   back, who dare not stay.
And if asked why not, he might answer   – without leaving his path –
That his wife was awaiting him,   and a saner, more beautiful death.
Poor fool! He's out of his mind: now, for a long time,
Only scorched winds have whirled   over the houses at home,
The wall has been laid low,   the plum-tree is broken there,
The night of our native hearth   flutters, thick with fear.
O if only I could believe   that everything of worth
Were not just in my heart –   that I still had a home on earth;
If only I had! As before,   jam made fresh from the plum
Would cool on the old verandah,   in peace the bee would hum,
And an end-of-summer stillness   would bask in the drowsy garden,
Naked among the leaves   would sway the fruit-trees' burden,
And She would be waiting, blonde   against the russet hedgerow,
As the slow morning painted   slow shadow over shadow, –
Could it perhaps still be?   The moon tonight's so round!
Don't leave me friend, shout at me: I'll get up off the ground!

15 September 1944

Translated from the Hungarian by Clive Wilmer & George Gömöri

Nelly Sachs

A Dead Child Speaks

My mother held me by my hand.
Then someone raised the knife of parting:
So that it should not strike me,
My mother loosed her hand from mine.
But she lightly touched my thighs once more
And her hand was bleeding –

After that the knife of parting
Cut in two each bite I swallowed –
It rose before me with the sun at dawn
And began to sharpen itself in my eyes –
Wind and water ground in my ear
And every voice of comfort pierced my heart –

As I was led to death
I still felt in the last moment
The unsheathing of the great knife of parting.

Translated from the German by Ruth and Matthew Mead

NELLY SACHS

O The Chimneys

And when this my skin has been destroyed, without my flesh I shall see God.
— Job19:26*

O the chimneys
On the cleverly devised abodes of death,
As Israel's body drew, dissolved in smoke,
Through the air –
As a chimney-sweep a star received it
Turning black
Or was it a sunbeam?

O the chimneys!
Roads to freedom for Jeremiah's and Job's dust –
Who devised you and stone upon stone built
The road for refugees from smoke?

O the abodes of death
Invitingly arranged
For the host of the house who was once a guest –
O fingers
Laying the threshold
Like a knife between life and death –

O chimneys,
O fingers,
And Israels's body in the smoke through the air!

*The Hebrew reads literally "from my flesh," apparently meaning "released from..." Christian interpreters have generally taken the phrase to mean "looking out from..." – the exact opposite. The translation given above is from the German version quoted by the poet. - Translator.

Translated from the German by Keith Bosley

ABRAHAM SUTZKEVER

For A Comrade

Murdered comrade
at the barbed wire —
you still press this scrap
of food to your heart.
Forgive my hunger
and forgive this daring —
I must bite into your
bloodstained bread.

Nameless comrade
now I know your name —
let this stained morsel
comfort you too.
As the healing light
sustains our people,
together with the bread
you enter me.

Silent comrade,
absorbing you I live.
Demand of the world a reckoning
through every fibre of mine.
If I fall as you fell
at the barbed wire
let another swallow my word
as I, your bread.

Vilna Ghetto
December 30 1941

Translated from the Yiddish by Seymour Mayne

ABRAHAM SUTZKEVER

A Cartload Of Shoes

The wheels hurry onward, onward,
What do they carry ?
They carry a cartload
Of shivering shoes.

The wagon like a canopy
In the evening light ;
The shoes – clustered
Like people in a dance.

A wedding, a holiday ?
Has something blinded my eye ?
The shoes – I seem
To recognise them.

The heels go tapping
With a clatter and a din,
From our old Vilna streets
They drive us to Berlin.

I should not ask
But something tears at my tongue
Shoes, tell me the truth
Where are they, the feet ?

The feet from those boots
with buttons like dew –
And here, where is the body
And there, where is the bride ?

Where is the child
To fill those shoes
Why has the bride
Gone barefoot ?

Through the slippers and the boots
I see those my mother used to wear
She kept them for the Sabbath
Her favourite pair.

And the heels go tapping:
With a clatter and a din,
From our old Vilna streets
They drive us to Berlin .

Translated from the Yiddish by Hillel Schwartz & David G. Roskies

DAVID VOGEL

Days Were Great As Lakes

Days were great as lakes
And clear
When we were children.

We sat a long time on their banks
And played,
Or went down to swim
In the fresh water.

And sometimes we wept
In our mother's apron,
For life was filling us
Like jugs of wine.

In Fine, Transparent Words

In fine, transparent words
Like silk scarves
I wrapped my life,

And when I unfasten them now
I can't recognize
My old passions.

All the old lures are laid out
In the market place,
And I have no wish
To buy anything.

Now as evening spreads
Our backs are bent low.
Even a little joy
Is too heavy for us to bear.

Translated from the Hebrew by A.C. Jacobs

Rita Mpoumi-Pappas

Krinio

Aim straight at my heart
it has served me well up to now.
to make it easy for you
I've sewn this black piece of cloth
right in the middle of my breasts.

I don't know what your fire will be like
– poor beardless soldiers – they've got you up
at dawn on my account
I've never held a gun – I don't know

I see your eyes wide open
– you can't help all this –
your hands want to touch me
before they pull the trigger – I understand

You probably still have the nicknames
of your boyhood
and who knows, we might've played together in the streets

Go on, spare me the morning frost
I'm almost naked
dress me in your fire
smile at me boys
cover my body with your gaze

I've never been covered by a lover
not even in dream ...

Translated from the Greek by Eleni Fourtouni

RITA MPOUMI-PAPPAS

Maria R.

Well then, it's all over. The case
my future prospects
the anxiety about the outcome of the trial

Yesterday they announced my sentence:
"Death!"

I don't have to bother about it anymore.
Now I can even say that I got through it
successfully.
I expected it to be drawn-out, exhausting,
and tragic.

Nothing like that.
The whole thing lasted five minutes.
Their docket is crowded with
the names of comrades
waiting to be convicted.

I'm suddenly filled with peace, my friends!
Even joy. It looks like some of the men
will get out – you know I've a weakness for them
I'm glad I stuck to my guns. I feel it's right
for our struggle.

So, I'm on "death row!"
It seems like a funny thing – even if it is
dead serious – I'm not big enough for it.
Even so, it makes me proud, stubborn.
It makes me a rock.

And I'll spit on their decision –
this scrap of paper that kicks me
out of life at 19 – I'll step on it like
the stub of their cigar
before I go.

Translated from the Greek by Eleni Fourtouni

YANNIS RITSOS

Awaiting His Execution

There, stood against the wall, at dawn, his eyes uncovered,
as twelve guns aimed at him, he calmly feels
that he is young and handsome, that he deserves to be clean shaven,
that the pale pink distant horizon becomes him –
and, yes, that his genitals retain their proper weight,
somewhat sad in their warmth – that's where the eunuchs look,
that's where they aim; – has he already become the statue of himself?
Himself looking at it, all nude, on a bright day
of the Greek summer, in the square above – looking at it standing upright
himself behind the shoulders of the crowd, behind the hurrying gluttonous
      tourist women,
behind the three made-up old women wearing black hats.

11 November 1969

Translated from the Greek by Nikos Stangos

YANNIS RITSOS

Soldiers And Dolls

Maps, pins, lamps, crushing engines, uphill slope, night,
wheels in wheels, intrigues; they shout, they run; – where to stay? –
One calls up after the other – who is the enemy? Who is the friend? –
Smoke everywhere; nothing can be seen; – there is the belfry, they say;
yes, you say, without seeing; they aim, you aim. The women
are left behind alone, far, in shapeless houses, without beds;
they make dolls from army coats with bullet holes,
or holes burned by the cigarettes of soldiers who fell asleep or died
	in the snow –
soft dolls, filled with bran; they paint their hands,
their faces, their feet red with dye for Easter eggs;
they give them to children to play with; they don't play; they hang them
from the tree in the yard, they use them as targets for their slings until sunset.

2 November 1969

Translated from the Greek by Nikos Stangos

YANNIS RITSOS

From The Blackened Pot

IT WAS a long road here. Very long, my brother.
The handcuffs weighed down the hands. In the evenings
when the small light bulb shook its head saying, 'Time's up,'
we were reading the history of the world in obscure names,
in some dates scratched with the nail on the prison walls,
in some childish drawings by those condemned –
a heart, an arrow, a boat that tore through time with certitude,
in some verses left half-finished for us to complete,
in some verses ended so we would not come to an end.
It was a long road to here – a difficult road.
The road is yours now. You hold it
the way you hold your friend's hand and count his pulse
on this scar left by the handcuffs.
A normal pulse. A sure hand. A sure road.

BEFORE the cripple beside you goes to bed he removes his leg;
he leaves it in the corner – a hollow wooden leg –
you must fill it the way you fill a flower pot with earth to plant flowers,
the way the darkness fills with stars,
the way poverty fills little by litle with thought and love.

We have decided that one day all men are to have two legs,
a happy bridge from eyes to eyes,
from heart to heart. This is why anywhere you sit,
among the sacks on the decks departing for exile,
behind the prison bars of the transit station,
close to death that does not say 'tomorrow'

among thousands of crutches of bitter maimed years
you say 'tomorrow' and you sit serene and sure
the way a just man sits facing other men.

THESE RED spots on the walls could also be blood –
all the red in our days is blood –
it could also be from the sunset striking the opposite wall.
At sundown all things redden before they fade out
and death is closer. Beyond the railings
are the children's cries and the train whistle.

Then the cells become narrower
and you must think of the light on a plain of wheat
and the bread on the table of the poor
and the mothers at the windows smiling
for you to find a little space to stretch your legs.

At those hours you clasp your comrade's hand
there comes to be a silence full of trees,
the cigarette cut in half goes around from mouth to mouth
like a lantern searching through a forest – we find the vein
that reaches into the heart of spring. We smile.

WE SMILE deep down inside us. We hide this smile now.
An illegal smile – the way the sun has also become illegal
and truth illegal. We hide the smile
the way we hide in our pockets the photograph of our beloved,
the way we hide the idea of freedom in the bottom of our hearts.
All of us here now have one sky and the same smile.

Tomorrow they may kill us. They can't
take away from us this smile and this sky.

WE KNOW that our shade will remain on the fields,
on the brick courtyard wall of the humble house,
on the walls of the large houses to be built tomorrow,
on the apron of the mother stringing fresh beans
at the cool courtyard door. We know it.
Blessed be our bitterness.
Blessed be our brotherhood.
Blessed be the world being born.

ONCE we were very proud, my brother,
because we were not at all sure.
We used to say big words,
we placed many gold stripes on the arms of our verse,
a tall plume waved on the forehead of our song,
we made a noise – we were afraid, this is why we made a noise –
we covered our fear with our shout,
we struck our heels on the pavement –
wide-open strides, clangorous strides
like those parades with the empty canons,
parades that people stare at through doors and windows
and that no one applauds.

THE WIND has subsided. Silence. In the corner of the room
a pensive plow waits for the plowing.
The water boiling in the pot can be heard more clearly.

Those waiting on the wooden bench
are the poor, our own people; the strong
are the peasants and the proletarians –
their every word is a glass of wine,
a crust of black bread,
a tree beside the rock,
a window open to the sunlight.

They are our own Christs, our own saints.
Their stout shoes are like wagons of coal,
their hands are security –
tanned hands, hard hands, calloused
with worn-down fingernails, with wild hairs,
with the thumb as wide as the history of man,
the broad span of the hand like a bridge over the precipice.

Their fingerprints are not just impressions on the prison registers;
they are preserved in the archives of history,
their fingerprints are dense railroad tracks
that traverse the future. And my own heart,
my comrades, is nothing more than a clay, blackened pot
that does its work well – nothing more.

WELL THEN, my children, now I am thinking like the grandfather who tells
    fairytales
(and don't get angry that I call you 'my children';
I am older perhaps only in years –
in nothing else –
and tomorrow you will call me 'my child,' and I will not get angry
because as long as youth exists in the world I will be young,
and you must call me 'my child,' my children) –
so, my children, now I am thinking
of finding a word that will match the stature of freedom:
neither taller, nor shorter –
the sufficient and the abundant are false,
the scant is shy,
and I have no intention of taking pride
in anything more, in anything less than man.

We will find our song. We're doing fine. What do you say, comrade?
Fine. Fine.

The dandelion leaves are boiled. Not enough olive oil. No matter.
There is more than enough appetite and heart. It is time.

HERE IS a brotherly light – hands and eyes are simple.
Here it's not a matter of my being over you or you over me.
Here everyone is over himself.

Here is a brotherly light running like a river along the high wall.
We hear this river even in our sleep.
And when we are asleep, our one arm hanging outside the blanket
becomes wet in this river.

Two drops alone of this water are enough for you to sprinkle
the face of the nightmare, and it vanishes like smoke beyond the trees.
And death is nothing more than a leaf falling to feed
a leaf that is rising.

NOW through its leaves the tree looks you straight in the eye,
the root points out to you its whole journey,
you look the world straight in the eye – you have nothing to hide.
Your hands are clean, washed with the stout soap of the sun;
you leave your hands exposed on the comradely table;
you entrust them to the hands of your comrades.

Their movement is simple, full of precision.
And even when you remove a hair from your friend's jacket
it is as if you are removing a page from the calendar
accelerating the rhythm of the world.
Even though you know that you have to weep much more
before you teach the world to laugh.

ONLY a pot then. Nothing more.
A blackened clay pot,
boiling, boiling and singing,
boiling on the fire of the sun and singing.

Concentration camp for political detainees,
Kontopouli, Lemnos, December 1948 - February 1949

Translated from the Greek by Rae Dalven

TAKIS SINOPOULOS

Deathfeast

Tears scorched me as I wrote alone, what was I, speaking like this with

year upon year quickening the lost faces, and from the windows came

glory, dull golden light, benches and tables all about

the windows mirroring the underworld. And then came
Porporas, and Kontaxis, and Markos, and Gerasimos,
dismounting one after the other,
dark hoarfrost on the horses and the day
slanting through the quiescent air, Bilias came and Gournas
gypsies imprinted on the dusk, and Fakalos, they held
mandolins, flutes, guitars,
the soul leapt at the sound, the house smelt everywhere
of rain and wood, and when,
only when they'd lit a great blaze to warm themselves,
then only did I call them.

There came Sarris, and Tsakonas,
Farmakis, Toregas, and

Face pox-scarred, bitter, clawed the ground with his nails by the castle
at Akova, he bled, spoke of pain and debauchery, so dark was he that I
became afraid, ran stumbling off down the hill.

We took the low road, ashes everywhere, iron, burnt earth, a black X
painted on the doors told death had passed that way, days and nights
and the machine guns reaping

and you would hear oh! and nothing more. And many

came. Before them came Tzannis, Eleminoglou, Papparizos, followed
by Lazarithis, and Flaskis, and Constantopoulos – no one can say in
which church they were sung, in what ground buried.

Then I pulled him out of the ditch, as I held him he gave up the ghost in
my arms, and some weeks later his wife smelling of grass, at noon deep
in the garden telling her of his death, the full dark body whimpered on
my chest, at night the forests and the roots would glow, for years the
voice would not die and.

Moon, moonlight, close days, winter building itself a tower of stone, sunless and hard, I heard

the first knock and the second knock, at dawn they smashed down the doors and dragged us out breathless, "wait here," and what a day was dawning!

There came old men and children.

How could they survive in such ragged clothes,
how could the children grow up in such horror?
The old men creaking, taller than their bodies.
And the children
clutching the axe, the knife, the hatchet
contempt and menace in their eyes, nor did they speak.

Ditches, wastelands, mothers in black wailing, whom did you kill, whom did you kill, how many have we killed?

So much blood and then we came across Louka's hands in the gully, and others severed at the wrist

after months on the run, here today, tonight elsewhere

murderers, narks, thieves and fornicators, soldiers, policemen, house-holders and shopkeepers

and many others riding on time's back and from among them

ruin's daughters stepped out, hunger and fever, set up
against the wall, an ill wind blew. And there came

Fanni and Litsa sweet-apple trees, Dona came and Nana, slim as the wheat, Eleni's maidenhair still green,

laurels, myrtles, wild vines
small lost rivers.

And one morning

that morning when I woke the tree had turned all green, I loved it so much that it rose to the sky.

And birds arrived, birds of sunlight and joy, filling the place with colours and feathers, perwits and felderels and other such fantastic species, skimmers and calicocks and morrowdims, and,

gifts of the Lord, merry birds, constant slashes in the blue sky. And
among them came

Yannis Makris, Petros Kallinikos, Yannis the lame.

We sat on the embankment, Rouskas took out his pocketknife and cut
down the young grass.

And mist over the plain. And you could hear spring coming, a door
whose wood smelt of the sky.

Then came the days of forty-four
and the days of forty-eight.
And from the Morea up to Larissa
deeper yet into Kastoria,
a black pestilence on the map,
Greece's breath rasping –
we held a count that Easter in deserted Kozani,
how many stayed on high, how many travelled on
stone, branch and hill,
down the dark river.

Prosoras came holding his broken rifle,
Alafouzos, and Bakrisioris, and Zervos
approached the gathering. Look, I shouted, and we looked:
a flood of light, the fruitful sun a monument
to the obscure dead. The years have passed, I told them,
our hair's turned grey.
Tzepetis came, and Zafoglou and Markoutsas
they settled themselves on the bench
and Constantinos nursed his foot at the end.

The voices gradually grew calm.

Gradually, as they had come, they disappeared,
took to the valley, scattering in the wind.

For the last time I watched them, called to them.
The fire sank to the ground and from the windows came –

How just a single star can make night navigable.

How in the empty church is the unknown dead anointed
his body laid to rest among the flowers.

Translated from the Greek by John Stathatos

VICTORIA THEODOROU

Picnic

3.

Here I lived with the other women prisoners
the canvas is rotten – and the ropes
not a trace left of the wall and the ditch
but the poles have sprouted. I know them
one of them's oak the other poplar
it's all written down on their leaves
and the leaves don't lie

Once again I see the snake near the wells
slithering from olive tree to olive tree
blocking the water
I see Saint George, monster killer, indifferent
inside this chapel, his spear made of paper
unmoved in his icon all those years
by the child's thirst
by the need of the bleeding mothers
Torrents have washed me, purified me
more merciful and consistent than health officers
deadly bacilli and dysentery germs have feared me
the earth innoculated me

Four winters
forbidden any fires for fear we'd flash signals
to the guerilla-filled mountains
How did we survive this?

Translated from the Greek by Eleni Fourtouni

European Communism: Post-1945

HORST BIENEK

The Silos Of Torment

Unlamented
We are shovelling
In the silos of torment
Where the guilt of the living,
The guilt of the dead
But not the guilt of those who were killed
Has been stored for ages.

Unlamented
We are shovelling
In the silos of torment,
Measuring the guilt:
Now to eternity.
Collecting it, classifying it, stowing it
Into the labyrinth of categories of guilt
Which are marked with magic ciphers.

Unlamented
We are shovelling
In the silos of torment
And our bent bodies
Straighten up only for seconds
When with lifeless hands
We write sphinx-like digits on the walls.
(Registries of sorrow).

And stooping we no longer see
How new numbers are always
Being inscribed by unknown hands,
How deadly nets,
Woven from plus and minus,
Appear on the walls,
Coordinates, nomograms,
Formulae, prayers,
Mathematical equations of guilt and pain,
Calculations of sin and repentance,
Parallelograms of torment.

And sometimes one of us
Puts down his shovel

Walks out thirstily
And does not come back.

But we are still shovelling
Unlamented
In the silos of torment,
To which we have been banished
By the Commissars of Reason.

Translated from the German by Ruth and Matthew Mead

HORST BIENEK

Our Ashes

Barbed-wire
     is the cloak of saints
whoever is covered by down
or darkness
     is living in sin
Only when the lamp blinds your eyes
can you deny your guilt
only when you are interrogated
     remain silent

No one speaks of the
forty days on bread and water
     (who painted the Tintorettos
     on the wall of your cell?)
No one speaks of the path
to the latrine-pits
     no one helps you carry
     the latrine-buckets
and carrying them
     you broke down
          more than thrice

No one came
     but a bird of black smoke
and later the murderers
     appeared punctually
they bore the sun
wounded / pierced / bleeding
   on their bayonets
     to the black wall*
     Walk
said a voice
     five paces to the wall
     and do not turn round
          when you hear the shots
What will happen
     when the cry crucifies the sky
what will happen
     when the wind destroys the memory
what will happen

when the sun-fish leaps in the veins
and quick-lime deletes our faces?

The answer has
          been given
but which of us
which of us has heard it?
          Who among us, the living,
          can say
                    he has heard it
          who has seen it –
which of us?

We have chlorine in the eyes
and sand in the ears
and eternity
          grows silently in our bodies

When will our ashes speak?

black wall : the wall against which shootings were carried out in Auschwitz.

Translated from the German by Ruth and Matthew Mead

ION CARAION

Hallucination

They took me and shot me.
One more bed free.

Watch and listen:
never was so much solitude as this.

Through sleep's thistle,
the Mother of God walks barefoot.

At The Rotten Sea

We shall torture you, we shall kill you and we shall laugh
then we will be killed and others will laugh
we are old enough and shrewd enough
not to care
everything is truth, even the lie
everything is lie, even truth –
darkness begets itself.

Translated from the Romanian by Marguerite Dorian and Elliott B. Urdang

Ion Caraion

Nobody's Who I Have

Where are they taking you, sir?
To the garden, sleep.
To do what, sir?
To shoot me, sleep.
Because they have bullets, sir?
Because they have time, sleep.
Where will they bury you, sir?
Under the snow, sleep.
Are you scared, sir?
It turns my stomach, sleep.
Who shall be informed, sir?
The hells, sleep.
Have you relations, sir?
I own nobody, sleep.
Will it be all right, sir?
It will be evening, sleep.
Have a cup, sir?
What's it cost, sleep?
Don't bother, sir.
Of poisons, sleep...
You don't want the cup, sir?
Smashed into splinters, sleep!
Shall we grieve for you, sir?
Don't bother, sleep.
Good night, sir!
Sleep with me, sleep!
I sleep by myself, sir.
I die by myself, sleep.
Good death, sir!
Good night, sleep!

Translated from the Romanian by Marguerite Dorian and Elliott B. Urdang

ION CARAION

The Porch With Mud Saints

when the rains caught us in the fields and soaked us to the skin
when we gathered bindweed, cowflop, plums, crickets and twigs
when we went fishing, to plant trees or to the hunt
when kerosene dealers from Moldavia brought salt
when we skinned foxes, or hares, when we killed snakes
when we caught Old Lisper, the goat and Tzica in the grass
when waters overflowed, when we gathered hay, when wolves, or boars
(which was it?) broke into Cuculetze's garden between the pond and the road
when we pickled mushrooms, split chubs, or plucked the wild geese
shot toward fall, when flocks of chickens fell beneath the axe
– weddings were coming – vats of brandy began to steam
sending the village reeling, and the women's full bulging thighs
would fill with children like combs with honey
when we made fences of brambles and the milk began to hope
when we climbed birches for nests and cherry trees for resin
when haystacks caught fire like the city of Pompei
when fountains dried up, the dogs died,
the dear departed men and women stayed unburied
when the war came, took the cattle and men away
when icicles gored like stalactites
when the mountain-men were found on all fours grazing
meek, slavering through wild garlic groves,
grown mad with hunger, forgetting how to speak,
                                        a viper
was pulled from the withers of Zimb's cow or from its back
it had sucked and we heard nests of mice squeaking in the living lard of the
      pigs
as in the loft where ledgers, tobacco sheaves, vultures' beaks,
boar tusks, claws of hawks and bears were kept,
when mice in flocks went in and out like shuttles of years
threshing the glooms of Amulius' legend
when in the valley's maw, the poplar blob shed glaucous tears
tree-hole and distance, hamlet big as a hat
and rainmaking gypsies leaped with every shot on the hill
when night-long the murder of ideal progression flowed
when walking was annulled, when things stopped, when beings stopped
when genesis called back its seeds,
its sense and secrets and its brewing clay,
confounding, thrusting them in nightmares' graves
and the great dark set in...

Translated from the Romanian by Marguerite Dorian and Elliott B. Urdang

Blaga Dimitrova

Blinded, they march on ...

Blinded, they march on, the soldiers of Tsar Samuil,
And when in summer we stretch on this lazy shore,
having shed our history, having washed away the blood
on our memory in the sea, and anchored
                    the rusty shadows of their chains
at the bottom, when we forget our origins,
where we come from, whether we had, perhaps, arrived...

They march on, the blinded soldiers of Tsar Samuil,
through the deep snowdrifts of centuries,
they continue, led by one man left with one eye
for each hundred blinded, searching for narrows
to tomorrow. They keep falling and getting up hand in hand,
                    leaning on each other.
They keep marching on in the laughter with which we
                    disguise our fears.
They keep marching on in our dreams at dawn,
                    before we start on a journey.

They march and persist – to open our eyes
and make us look through the black emptiness
of their pupils that mirror our blindness,
                    how we mark time,
how we carry Vasilii in ourselves:
a shoulder touches your shoulder –
do you trust it?
A voice next to your ear – isn't it treacherous?
And a footstep next to yours –
where might it lead you?

Blinded, they march on the soldiers of Samuil.
They march on, blinded.
They march on.
They.

Note: In 1014, the Bulgarian king, Samuil, was defeated at Belasitsa by the Byzantine emperor Basil II (Vasilii), who ordered the 15,000 captured Bulgarian soldiers to be blinded. One man of each hundred was left with one seeing eye to lead the blinded men back to their king. Vasilii's epithet remains 'Bulgaroktonos', Murderer of Bulgarians.

Translated from the Bulgarian by Ludmilla Popova-Wightman

MAK DIZDAR

The Blue River

No one knows where it is
We know little but it is known

Behind the mountain behind the valley
Behind seven behind eight

And even farther and even worse
Over the bitter over the torturous

Over the hawthorne over the copse
Over the summer heat over the oppression

Beyond foreboding beyond doubt
Behind nine behind ten

And even deeper and even stronger
Through silence through darkness

Where the roosters do not sing
Where the sound of horn is not heard

And even worse and even madder
Beyond sense beyond God

There is one blue river
It is wide it is deep

A hundred years wide
A thousand years deep

About the length do not even think
Jetsam and flotsam unmending

There is one blue river

There is one blue river
We must cross the river.

Translated from the Serbo-Croat by Vasa Mihailovich

ZBIGNIEW HERBERT

The Trial

During his great speech the prosecutor
kept piercing me with his yellow index finger
I'm afraid I didn't appear self-assured
unintentionally I put on a mask of fear and depravity
like a rat caught in a trap an informer a fratricide
the reporters were dancing a war dance
slowly I burned at a stake of magnesia

all of this took place in a small stifling room
the floor creaked plaster fell from the ceiling
I counted knots in the boards holes in the wall faces
the faces were alike almost identical
policemen the tribunal witnesses the audience
they belonged to the party of those without any pity
and even my defender smiling pleasantly
was an honorary member of the firing squad

in the first row sat an old fat woman
dressed up as my mother with a theatrical gesture she raised
a handkerchief to her dirty eyes but didn't cry
it must have lasted a long time I don't know even how long
the red blood of the sunset was rising in the gowns of the judges

the real trial went on in my cells
they certainly knew the verdict earlier
after a short rebellion they capitulated and started to die
one after the other
I looked in amazement at my wax fingers

I didn't speak the last word and yet
for so many years I was composing the final speech
to God to the court of the world to the conscience
to the dead rather than the living
roused to my feet by the guards
I managed only to blink and then
the room burst out in healthy laughter
my adoptive mother laughed also
the gavel banged and this really was the end

but what happened after that – death by a noose
or perhaps a punishment generously changed to a dungeon
I'm afraid there is a third dark solution
beyond the limits of time the senses and reason

therefore when I wake I don't open my eyes
I clench my fingers don't lift my head
breathe lightly because truly I don't know
how many minutes of air I still have left

Translated from the Polish by John Carpenter and Bogdana Carpenter

Zbigniew Herbert

Damastes (Also Known As Procrustes) Speaks

My movable empire between Athens and Megara
I ruled alone over forests ravines precipices
without the advice of old men foolish insignia with a simple club
dressed only in the shadow of a wolf
and terror caused by the sound of the word Damastes

I lacked subjects that is I had them briefly
they didn't live as long as dawn however it is slander
to say I was a bandit as the falsifiers of history claim

in reality I was a scholar and social reformer
my real passion was anthropometry

I invented a bed with the measurements of a perfect man
I compared the travellers I caught with this bed
It was hard to avoid – I admit – stretching limbs cutting legs
the patients died but the more there were who perished
the more I was certain my research was right
the goal was noble progress demands victims

I longed to abolish the difference between the high and the low
I wanted to give a single form to disgustingly varied humanity
I never stopped in my efforts to make people equal

my life was taken by Theseus the murderer of the innocent Minotaur
the one who went through the labyrinth with a woman's ball of yarn
an imposter full of tricks without principles or a vision of the future

> I have the well-grounded hope others will continue my labour
> and bring the task so boldly begun to its end

Translated from the Polish by John Carpenter and Bogdana Carpenter

VLADIMÍR HOLAN

To The Enemies

I've had enough of your baseness, and I haven't killed myself
only because I didn't give myself life
and I still love somebody because I love myself.
You may laugh, but only an eagle can attack an eagle
and only Achilles can pity the wounded Hector.
To be is not easy . . . To be a poet and a man
means to be a forest without trees
and to see . . . A scientist observes.
Science can only forage for truth:
forage yes, take wing no! Why?
It's so simple, and I've said it before:
Science is in probability, poetry in parables,
the large cerebral hemisphere
refuses the most exquisite poem by clamoring for sugar . . .
A rooster finds rain repulsive, but that's another story,
it is night, you might say: sexually mature,
and the young lady's breasts are so firm
you could easily break
two glasses of schnapps on them, but that's another story.
And imagine a ship's beacon,
a sailing beacon: but that's an entirely different story.
And your whole development from the stele for man
to the stele of a lichen: but that's an entirely different story!
A cloud is going to vomit, but there's not even a gas leak at your place,
you cannot be, you can't even be
strangled by snake scales,
what God conceived, he wants to be felt,
children and drunkards know this,
but they aren't brazen enough to ask
why a mirror fogs when a menstruating woman looks into it,
and poets, from love of life, do not ask
why wine moves in the barrels
when she passes by . . .

And I've had enough of your impudence
that permeates everything it wanted to contain
but couldn't embrace.
But a holocaust will come
that you couldn't have dreamed of
having no dreams,

what God conceived, he wants to be felt,
a holocaust will come, children and drunkards know it,
joy could come about only through love,
if love were not passion,
happiness could come about only through love,
if happiness were not passion,
children and drunkards know it . . .
In order to be, you would have to live,
but you won't because you don't live,
and you don't live because you don't love,
because you don't even love yourself, let alone your neighbour.
And I've had enough of your vulgarity,
and I haven't killed myself only because
I didn't give myself life
and I still love somebody because I love myself . . .
You may laugh, but only the female eagle can attack the male eagle
and only Briseis the wounded Achilles.
To be is not easy . . . Only shitting is easy . . .

Translated from the Czech by C. G. Hanzlicek & Dana Hábová

Gyula Illyés

One Sentence On Tyranny

Where there's tyranny
there is tyranny,
not just in gun barrels,
not just in jails,

interrogation cells,
the sentry's calls
challenging the night,
there is tyranny not

just in the smoke-dark burnt
flaming prosecutor's indictment,
not just in confessions,
in Morse wall-taps in prisons,

not only in the chilly
verdict: the judge's "guilty,"
there is tyranny
not only in the soldierly,

crackling, "tens-hut!",
in "fire!", in the drumbeat,
in the way that
they drag corpses to the pit,

not only in the news
in fearful whispers
passed through furtively
half-opened doors, not only

in the hushing finger
dropped on the mouth,
there's tyranny not only
in the sturdy

bar-solid faces, the
wordless shrieks of woe
struggling in those bars,
in the mute tears'

torrents magnifying
the silence,
in the glassy pupils,

there's tyranny not just in
the standing ovation
of roared hurrahs,
of songs and cheers,

where there's tyranny
there is tyranny
not just in the unremitting
booms of palms applauding,

in the trumpet, the opera house,
the lying, strident, sonorous
stones of statues,
in colors, galleries of pictures,

in each separate frame,
it's in the brush and paint,
not only in the soft glide
of car noises at night

and the way
it stops at the door;

where there's tyranny
it's everywhere,
in everything as
not even your old god was;

there's tyranny in
the kindergartens,
in the fatherly counsel,
the mother's smile,

in the way the child
answers a stranger;

not only in barbed wire,
in book-phrases more
deadly stupid-making
than barbed wire; it's there

in the good-bye kiss
as the wife says
when will you be home dear,
it's there

in the street, the customary
how-are-you's, the abruptly
softer grip, the slack
of the handshake,

there as your lover's face
turns suddenly to ice,
because it's with you
in the rendezvous,

not just the interrogation,
it's in the declaration,
in the rapturous moan,
like the fly in the wine,

because even in your dreams
you're not alone, it's even
in the marriage bed, and earlier
in the desire,

because what you think lovely
he's had already; it's he
who lay with you in bed
when you thought you loved,

on the plate, in the glass,
the mouth, the nose,
in cold, in twilight,
indoors and out,

as if the window were open
and a dead-flesh stink blew in,
as if somewhere gas
were escaping into the house,

if you talk to yourself it's he
who puts the question to you,
you're not free even
in your own imagination,

and the Milky Way: a zone
where border searchlights pan,
a whole fieldful of mines;
every star a spy hole,

the teeming celestial tent:
a single labor camp;
because tyranny speaks
from fever, the torture rack,

the priest who hears your confession,
the ringing of bells, the sermon,
from parliament, from church,
all those theatrical stages;

you shut your lashes, open them,
you're under observation;
like illness, like memory,
it keeps you company;

the rumbling train wheels whisper
a prisoner, you're a prisoner,
beside the sea, on the mountain,
it's this that you breathe in;

lightning flashes, it's there
in each unexpected murmur,
it's there in the light,
the jolt of the heart;

in tranquility, in this
shackled tediousness,
in the pelting downpour,
these sky-high bars,

the incarcerating snowfall
white as a cell wall,
that eyes you through the eyes
of your dog, and because

it's in all you aspire to,
it's in your tomorrow,
in all that you think,
every move you make,

as a river bed is cut,
you follow it, create it;
it's you spy from this circle?
he's in the mirror, watchful,

he sees you, escape's absurd,
you're the prisoner, also the guard;
it seeps into the fabrics
of your clothes, your tobacco's

aroma, it eats into
your marrow bones; you'd
have ideas, but those
that come to are his,

you'd look, but what you see
he's conjured up for you,
and a forest fire, lit
since you didn't stomp it out

when you tossed a match to the ground,
flames up now all around;
so his eyes are on you, sleepless,
in factory, field, and house,

and you don't feel anymore
what even bread and meat are,
what it is to desire, to love,
to open your arms, to live,

so the servant himself forges
and wears his own manacles;
if you eat, you're feeding him;
it's for him you beget children,

where there's tyranny everyone
is a link in the same chain;
it flows and festers from you,
you yourself are tyranny;

like moles in the sun, we walk
blind in the pitch-dark,
as restless in the closet
as we are in a desert;

because where there's tyranny
everything's vanity,
song, like this one faithful,
any art at all,

because from the beginning
he's been standing at your grave,
it's he who says who you've been,
even your dust serves him.

Translated from the Hungarian by Bruce Berlind with Mária Körösy

ÁGNES NEMES NAGY

To Freedom

You cathedral, you! Pure astonishment!
All those lovely-eyed frilly angels!
From here below their soles are gigantic,
but their heads are narrow as needles.

The theatrical set high on the cupola
– large pillars, a painted fiery sky between them – :
what good is it if you exist and I don't believe in you?
If I believe in you and you don't exist, what then?

Leftover God! You drag me this way, that way.
I'm through chasing you like a fool, I'm sick of you.
A few friends starved to death the other day.
I say this because evidently you don't know.

What straw did they bite into finally?
What sort of mouths, what sort of skulls?
You could have provided perhaps a pot of peas,
you could have worked a few puny miracles.

I wish I could see their mouths again,
their tepid chins that came unhinged –
I'd like to be in Rome marveling at the gardens,
and to gorge on rich food, go on an eating binge.

Give bananas! Meat! Be the world's udder!
Give Naples at night, Switzerland in the morning.
You, of all my wishes the faithless lover,
give air vibrating over the meadows!

Give airship! An image of paradise! Trust!
Crash through the law! Give yourself! Then
the speculators won't eat so much,
then the dead may rise again!

– One peony stands on the table,
its beauty compacted, like that of a gem.

Translated from the Hungarian by Bruce Berlind

György Petri

To Imre Nagy

You were impersonal, too, like the other leaders,
bespectacled, sober-suited; your voice lacked
sonority, for you didn't know quite what to say

on the spur of the moment to the gathered multitude. This urgency
was precisely the thing you found strange. I heard you,
old man in pince-nez, and was disappointed,
not yet to know

of the concrete yard where most likely the prosecutor
rattled off the sentence, or
of the rope's rough bruising, the ultimate shame.

Who can say what you might have said
from that balcony? Butchered opportunities
never return. Neither prison nor death
can resharpen the cutting edge of the moment

once it's been chipped. What we can do, though, is remember
the hurt, reluctant, hesitant man
who nonetheless soaked up
anger, delusion
and a whole nation's blind hope,

when the town woke to gunfire
that blew it apart.

To Be Said Over And Over Again

I glance down at my shoe and – there's the lace!
This can't be gaol then, can it, in that case.

Translated from the Hungarian by Clive Wilmer and George Gömöri

György Petri

Cemetery Plot No.301*

Let everything stay as it is!
With the carcasses from the Zoo?
Why, yes. Was their fate any different?
Was hanging any kinder than putting to sleep?
I cannot forget (when I say this,
I don't mean to threaten: it's the way I am:
I'm not able to forget).

On the other hand, what would I wish
for myself if I'd been – ha-ha! – hanged?
if I were to come back as a Stone Guest?
I'd wish at long last to be left in peace.
I shit on reverence. To these men
more mercy should've been shown when they were alive
(they should've been left alive). Now it's too late.

Against death there is no *remedium*.
No compensation for widows,
orphans, nations. I'm not interested
in the hangman's mate and his belated tears.
My eyes are dry. I need them for looking with.

Though actually there isn't much
to see – only, in the dusk
everything gets sharper:
a female body, a branch,
the downs of your face. I don't want
anything. Just to keep looking, no more.

[1989]

*When Imre Nagy and his colleagues were hanged, their bodies were immediately dumped in a cemetery adjacent to the prison. Their grave, unmarked, was plot no.301. In June 1989, on the 31st anniversary of their deaths, the bodies were exhumed, coffined, given the full honours of a state funeral and reburied in plot no.301, now suitably memorialised. It was found, when the graves were first opened, that the bones of animals from a nearby zoo had been buried along with them.

Translated from the Hungarian by Clive Wilmer and George Gömöri

JÁNOS PILINSZKY

Passion Of Ravensbrück

He steps out from the others.
He stands in the square silence.
The prison garb, the convict's skull
blink like a projection.

He is horribly alone.
His pores are visible.
Everything about him is so gigantic,
everything is so tiny.

And this is all.
       The rest –
the rest was simply
that he forgot to cry out
before he collapsed.

Translated from the Hungarian by János Csokits and Ted Hughes

János Pilinszky

Harbach 1944
to Gábor Thurzó

At all times I see them.
The moon brilliant. A black shaft looms up.
Beneath it, harnessed men
haul a huge cart.

Dragging that giant wagon
which grows bigger as the night grows
their bodies are divided among
the dust, their hunger and their trembling.

They are carrying the road, they are carrying the land,
the bleak potato fields,
and all they know is the weight of everything,
the burden of the skylines

and the falling bodies of their companions
which almost grow into their own
as they lurch, living layers,
treading each other's footsteps.

The villages stay clear of them,
the gateways withdraw.
The distance, that has come to meet them,
reels away back.

Staggering, they wade knee deep
in the low, darkly-muffled clatter
of their wooden clogs
as through invisible leaf litter.

Already their bodies belong to silence.
And they thrust their faces towards the height
as if they strained for a scent
of the far-off celestial troughs

because, prepared for their coming
like an opened stock-yard,
its gates flung savagely back,
death gapes to its hinges.

Translated from the Hungarian by János Csokits and Ted Hughes

VASKO POPA

Imminent Return

In a cell of Beckerek Prison
I spend the day with a Red Army man
Who'd escaped from a prison camp

Any moment the door may open
And he'll be taken out
And shot in the yard

He asks me to show him
The quickest way
To Moscow

With breadcrumbs on the floor
I build the towns he'd pass

He measures the distance with his finger
Claps me on the shoulder with his great hand
And rocks the whole prison with his shout

You're not far my beauty

Translated from the Serbo-Croat by Anne Pennington

Vasko Popa

The Cherry Tree In The House Of Death

For Ion Marcoviceanu

Little Jovica Agbaba got hold of
A handful of cherries
And smuggled them into the camp

He counted them out and divided them
Into three equal parts

We ask him where he puts the stones

He swallows them
So as to fill himself more quickly

We stare at the red fruit
On the branches of the cherry tree
Growing out of his belly

And all three suddenly
Burst out laughing

Translated from the Serbo-Croat by Anne Pennington

Vasko Popa

Wolves' Tenderness

We're lying in the grass
On Wolf-Meadow above Vrsac

They say
The wolves were killed here
Every last one

Only their name
Was left alive

An animal tenderness reaches us
From under the alert grass

And stirs our lips
And limbs and blood

We love each other without a word
My young she-wolf and I

Translated from the Serbo-Croat by Anne Pennington

Vasko Popa

United Apples

For Breyten Breytenbach

In Capetown in South Africa
The prison warder plays with his keys
And leers into the poet's face

Just you listen scum
You don't keep to the rules

For lunch you refuse
To eat an apple
And then for days on end
You draw it and write poems about it

Either you obey in future
Or I'll rip
Your father's apple out of your throat

Translated from the Serbo-Croat by Francis Jones

TADEUSZ RÓZEWICZ

The Survivor

I am twenty-four
led to slaughter
I survived.

The following are empty synonyms:
man and beast
love and hate
friend and foe
darkness and light.

The way of killing men and beasts is the same
I've seen it::
truckfuls of chopped-up men
who will not be saved.

Ideas are mere words:
virtue and crime
truth and lies
beauty and ugliness
courage and cowardice.

Virtue and crime weigh the same
I've seen it:
in a man who was both
criminal and virtuous.

I seek a teacher and a master
may he restore my sight hearing and speech
may he again name objects and ideas
may he separate darkness from light.

I am twenty-four
led to slaughter
I survived.

Translated from the Polish by Adam Czerniawski

Tadeusz Rózewicz

In The Midst Of Life

After the end of the world
after death
I found myself in the midst of life
creating myself
building life
people animals landscapes

this is a table I said
this is a table
there is bread and a knife on the table
knife serves to cut bread
people are nourished by bread

man must be loved
I learnt by night by day
what must one love
I would reply man

this is a window I said
this is a window
there is a garden beyond the window
I see an apple-tree in the garden
the apple-tree blossoms
the blossom falls
fruit is formed
ripens

my father picks the apple
the man who picks the apple
is my father

I sat on the threshold
that old woman who
leads a goat on a string
is needed more
is worth more

than the seven wonders of the world
anyone who thinks or feels
she is not needed
is a mass murderer

this is a man
this is a tree this is bread

people eat to live
I kept saying to myself
human life is important
human life has great importance
the value of life
is greater than the value of all things
which man has created
man is a great treasure
I repeated stubbornly

this is water I said
I stroked the waves with my hand
and talked to the river
water I would say
nice water
this is me

man talked to water
talked to the moon
to the flowers and to rain
talked to the earth
to the birds
to the sky

the sky was silent
the earth was silent
and if a voice was heard
flowing
from earth water and sky
it was a voice of another man

1955

Translated from the Polish by Adam Czerniawski

ALEKSANDER WAT

Before Breughel The Elder

Work is a blessing.
I tell you that, I - a professional loafer!
Who bedded down in so many prisons! Fourteen!
And in so many hospitals! Ten! And innumerable hotels!
Work is a blessing.
How else could we deal with the lava of fratricidal love toward our
    fellow men?
With those storms of extermination of all by all?
With brutality that has no bottom, no measure?
With the black-and-white era which does not want to end,
endlessly repeating itself da capo like a record
forgotten on a turntable
spinning by itself?
Or perhaps someone invisible watches over the phonograph?
Horror!
How, if not for work, could we live in the paradise of social hygienists
who never dip their hands in blood without antiseptic gloves?
Horror!
How else could we cope with death?
That Siamese twin sister of life
who grows together with it – in us, and is extinguished with it
and surely for that reason is ineffective.
And so we have to live without end,
without end. Horror!
How, if not for work, could we cope with ineffective death
(Don't scoff!)
which is like a sea,
where everyone is an Icarus, one of nearly three billion,
and besides, so much happens all around us
and everything is equally unimportant, yes, unimportant
although so difficult, so inhumanly difficult, so painful!
How then could we cope with all that?
Work is our rescue.
I tell you that – I, Pieter Breughel, the Elder (and even I,
your modest servant, Wat, Aleksander) – work is our rescue.

Translated from the Polish by Czeslaw Milosz & Leonard Nathan

Soviet Republics

EGHISHE CHARENTS

From Dantesque Legend*

Dedicated to Mihran Markarian, Stepan Ghazarian and Ashod Millionchian,
my martyred friends who fell on December 25, 1915 on the battlefield.

IV

And then the day we entered a village
which was at the shore of the small sea.
It had been destroyed. Here and there
a few houses still smoked.
While the water, blue and crackling,
clapped in with its old rhythm.

Like children glazed with smiles,
snapping in rings, with no cares,
the waves flew forward
with sweet screams telling us
a thousand tales of children's games,

while the ruined old village,
mysterious as a dead father,
slept its black sleep, silent
as a cemetery, uncomprehending
the mischief of lively, lucky waves.

Then I saw it, –
a green circle of vineyards
lush as a lewd, pagan woman
obediently spreading its autumn
harvest to any passer-by.

Two of us entered the sea of grapes
which were ripened by the sun's fire
to the tune of that snapping sea.

For a minute we forgot the burning
of our chests, dusty feet,
destruction and ruin.
We gave ourselves to thirsty nature,
reached out to the grapes,

until we saw there among the vines a body
of an old man, strangled,
fallen under bloodied grapes,
becoming one of the shadows,
with eyes fixed on us forever.

My friend fell. His lips murmured:
Water.
Slowly, dazedly, I stumbled toward
the vineyard well.
I hung over it. First I wanted
to see the water in the bottom.
Nothing. Only a rope hanging. I took it.

Let it down into the bottomless pit
and heard the distant splash
then pulled the taut rope.
The pail hit a stone somewhere.
Another minute and suddenly
as if spirits rose to dance about me

I looked, stiff-eyed, into the clear
water of the pail in which also
half disintegrated parts of a body
rocked calmly.
Barely controlling the scream in
my throat I left the well,

like a drunken waverer
pursued by ghosts. Both of us ran then
seeing neither vineyard nor sea
where the devil, with his poisons, slept.

V

And finally one day, exhausted by the road
we stopped to rest at the threshold of the Dead
City. We looked into musty, misted streets
of the Dead City where terror glided, flew
into our faces and into our fever-struck,
devil-struck hearts.

Nothing breathed in the Dead City.
The windows of the deserted buildings
stared darkly like eyes without pupils.

No, sockets without eyes. And we dared not return
their stare.

I don't know why we entered a house.
The wide holes of the windows gaped
like sunless, dug-out eyes.
At the threshold a cat's body.
Who would have killed it?

We entered, and saw the broken bed,
a woman fallen, drenched in blood. Naked.
The blood-stained mouth holding a laugh,
open like a hole, smelling of fear.
Her hips, the dry bloodied breasts
told us: rape.

The lid of my skull disappeared then
as if my brain were not mine
and sky and ground danced together.
Someone said: Let's get out of here.
But where could we go so that those naked
hips and those breasts could not find me?

We stayed there that night
in the ruined houses of the Dead City.
Terrifying visions crowded us
jumping, dancing like crippled,
maimed bodies in a feverish circle
dance of the dead.

In one of the houses of the Dead City,
my eyes propped open, in the candleless
dark, I lay, terrified and sleepless.
Before me the dead bayed
groaning, moaning around their fires.

Their dead bodies with blue legs
yellow breasts, swollen and blood-
spattered buttocks,
danced, staggering before
my terror-filled eyes
in the grave-pit dark.

They sang, moaned, cackled,
almost as if in joy.
Mixed with weeping, in

cold and horrible hollow tones
that gnawed at my hearing

and in my agitated brain their song
seemed to be transformed into
a sad knowledge that I too did not exist
that I was part of some hot, distant dream
in which my soul was being borne away
with no will to resist.

I flew like a ghost
leaping as they did, until another sound
joined their careless song
and I realized it was the sea
I heard, roaring in the dark.

Like joyful children under a red moon which
shone like a sun, the dead danced
chanting crazily about Asdghig,

saying Asdghig existed still,
there under the waves.
Let the storm roar over the world.
What does she care? She stays immortal,
undeniable, unblemished, virginal
on her divine shore.

Then the circle dance of the dead
lunatics ran on, their cackling song
rang of crisis and wrongs
and their blood bright legs stained
the darkness where they leaped.

Fusing their love, illusions and
their death, they rocked and swayed
over the excited canvas of my brain
condensed and faded until darkness filled
my eyes and I lost them in
a dreamless sleep.

During the 1915 massacres Charents joined the Armenian volunteer army which went from the Caucasus to fight the Turks who had destroyed Van.

Translated from the Armenian by Diana Der Hovanessian

EGHISHE CHARENTS

For Avedik Issahakian*

No matter how far I go
improving draft by draft
my art and my heart
must bow to your craft.

All my life, my impossible
aim was to finish
a song to charm children
that old men could cherish,

just as all hearts quicken
with the tempo of yours.
The heart of your nation
beats in your words.

Oh for such a song
affectionate and small
that would endure
inscribed on my walls,

so that generations to come
could say with a smile
my warmest poem
was for you (in your style).

1937

*Written on a handkerchief in prison 54 days before he died after listening to a song by Issahakian
sung by another prisoner. The handkerchief and a postscript were smuggled to Issahakian and are
now in the Charents museum in Erevan.*

Translated from the Armenian by Diana Der Hovanessian

SIAMANTO

The Dance

Her blue eyes, drowned in tears,
the German witness to the horrors tried
to describe the ashfields where Armenian life had died:

"This untellable thing I'm trying to say
I saw with my pitiless human eyes
from the hellish window of my safe house.
While I gnashed my teeth in terror and frustration
my eyes stayed open and pitiless.
I saw a garden city change into ash heaps.
Corpses piled to the tops of trees.
And from the waters, from the springs,
from the brooks and from the roads,
the roar of your blood.

It is the voice of that blood that still speaks
in my heart. Don't be disgusted,
but I have to tell this story
so that people understand the crimes
men do to men. Let all the hearts of the world hear.
That morning with death's shadows was a Sunday,
the first useless Sunday to rise over those bodies.

I had been in my room all night, tending,
from evening until morning, a girl I knew
stabbed by knives. I bent over her agony
wetting her death with my tears.
Suddenly I heard from a distance
a black mob of men, whipping, leading twenty girls.
Twenty young women, pushed into my vineyard
while the men sang lewd songs
'When we beat the drum, you dance!'

And their whips began to crack ferociously
against the flesh of the Armenian women
who longed for death. Twenty
of them, hand in hand, began their dance.
Tears flowed from their eyes, as if from wounds.
And I envied the dying girl
who could not see, but who cursed

with her harsh breathing, the universe,
poor beautiful Armenian girl
giving wings to her dove white soul,
while I shook my fists in vain against
the mob below. 'You must dance, faithless heathen
beauties. Dance, with open breasts, to death,
smiling at us without complaints!

Fatigue is not for you. Nor modesty.
All the way to death, dance, with lust, with lewdness.
Our eyes are thirsty for your forms and for your deaths.

Twenty handsome girls fell to the ground exhausted.
'Stand up' the roar thundered behind the snakelike
whirling swords. Someone brought a bucket
then, of kerosene. Oh, human justice
I spit at your forehead. Then they
doused those twenty brides, shouting
'You must dance. And here's a fragrance
Arabia does not have.' And with a torch,
set on fire the naked flesh.

The charred corpses rolled toward death
through the dancing. From my fright
I shuttered the window as if against
a hurricane. And asked the dead girl in the room,
'How shall I dig out these eyes of mine. How?'"

1909

Translated from the Armenian by Diana Der Hovanessian

SIAMANTO

A Handful Of Ash

(a)

Alas, you were a great and beautiful mansion,
And from the white summit of your roof,
Filled with star-flooded night hopes,
I listened to the Euphrates, racing below.

(b)

I learned with tears, with tears I learned of the ruins,
Of your broad walls battered down, stone by stone,
Onto your fragile border of flowers in the garden . . .
On a terror-filled day, a day of slaughter, of blood.

(c)

And charred is the blue room
Inside whose walls, on whose rugs
My childhood delighted,
And where my life grew, where my soul grew.

(d)

That gold-framed mirror is shattered, too,
In whose silver depth my dreams,
My hopes, my loves and my burning will
Stood reflected for years, and my musings.

(e)

And in the garden the spring song is dead,
The mulberry and the willow there, they have been blasted, too,
And the brook that flowed between the trees –
Has it gone dry? Tell me, where is it? Has it gone dry?

(f)

O I often dream of the cage
From which my grey partridge, mornings
And at sunrise, fronting the rose trees,
Would rise, as I did, and start its own distinct cooing.

(g)

O my homeland, promise that after my death
A handful of your holy ashes
Will come to rest, like an exiled turtledove,
To chant its song of sorrow and tears.

(h)

But who will bring, tell me, who is to bring
A handful of your precious ashes,
On the day of my death, to put into my dark coffin
And mingle with my ashes, ashes of a singer of the homeland?

(i)

A handful of ash with my remains, my native home –
Who is to bring a handful of ash from your ashes,
From your sorrow, your memories, your past,
A handful of ash to scatter on my heart?

Translated from the Armenian by Aram Tolegian

DANIEL VAROUJAN

Sowing

Like a Colossus straddling the sunset
the sower plants the seeds
over the naked land spread at his feet
without boundary, without fence.

His deep apron is packed, filled
with star-grained wheat. And
last year's fallow fields wait
for the wide palm spreading light like a dawn.

Plant, ploughman, plant, for the table.
Let the motion of your arm have no bounds
or confinement. Tomorrow this wheat
will fall to bless your grandchild's head.

Plant, ploughman, plant, for the hungry poor.
Let your palm never rise half full.
Today's poor will pour oil tomorrow
into the church lamp for your harvest.

Sow, ploughman, sow, for the sacred host,
the wafer of God. Let seeds of light flood
through your hand. Tomorrow the body of Christ
will ripen in each milky spike.

Sow, sow the horizon with stars,
with waves, with dew.
And should the birds steal the grains,
God will replace them with pearls.

Fill the tilled field, flood the ploughed land.
Let golden light flow from the earth's breast.
And as the day ends let it lengthen
the shadows of your arm toward the star-seeded skies.

1921

Translated from the Armenian by Diana Der Hovanessian

Anna Akhmatova

Terror, rummaging through things in the dark

Terror, rummaging through things in the dark,
aims a moonbeam at an axe.
A sinister thud from behind the wall –
what's there, rats, a ghost, or a thief?

It splashes like water in the claustrophobic kitchen,
counts the shaky floorboards
it flashes past the attic window
with a glossy, black beard,

then silence. How evil and crafty is terror,
it hid the matches and blew out the candle.
I'd rather the gleam of the rifle
barrels aimed at my breast,

rather lie down on the unpainted scaffold
on the green square
and for my life blood to flow out
to the groans and screams of joy of the crowd.

I press the smooth crucifix to my breast:
O God, bring peace back to me.
The sweet smell of decay wafts
in a swoon from the cool sheet.

Tsarskoye Selo, 27-28 August 1921

Translated from the Russian by Richard McKane

ANNA AKHMATOVA

The Seventh (Incomplete) Northern Elegy

And I have been silent, silent for 30 years.
For countless nights
silence surrounds me like arctic ice.

It comes to blow out my candle.
The dead are silent too – but that is understandable,
and less terrifying...

My silence is heard everywhere,
it fills the hall at my trial
and it could outshout the very roar
of rumours, and like a miracle
leave its imprint on everything.
My God, it takes part in everything!
Who could cast me in such a role?
O Lord, let me, even for just a moment,
become a little bit more like everyone else.

Didn't I drink hemlock?
Why then did I not die
right then as I ought to have done?

My own dream does not light on those persons
nor do I give them my blessing,
no, not to those who seek out my books,
who stole them, who even had them bound,
who carry them as though they are secret chains,
who remember their every syllable by heart.
But I do give it to those persons who dared to write
my silence on a banner for all to see,
who lived with it and believed it,
who measured the black abyss...

My silence is in music and song
and in a chilling love,
in partings, in books,
        in what is more unknown
than anything in this world.

Even I am frightened by it sometimes

when it squeezes me with its full weight,
breathing and moving in on me.
There's no defence, there's nothing faster.
Who knows how it turned to stone;
and how its flames
burnt the heart? Whatever happens
everyone is so cosy with it, so used to it.
You are all happy to share it with me.
And yet it is always my own.

It almost wolfed my soul.
It deforms my fate.
But one day I shall break the silence,
in order to call death to the pillory.

1958-1964

Translation from the Russian by Richard McKane

ANNA AKHMATOVA

From Requiem: Poems 1935-1940

Instead of a Foreword

During the terrible years of the Yezhov Terror I spent seventeen months in the prison queues in Leningrad. One day someone 'identified' me. Then a woman with lips blue with cold who was standing behind me, and of course had never heard of my name, came out of the numbness which affected us all and whispered in my ear – (we all spoke in whispers there):

'Could you describe this?'

I said, 'I can!'

Then something resembling a smile slipped over what had once been her face.

[1 April 1957]

III.

No, this is not me – someone else suffers.
I couldn't stand this: let black drapes
cover what happened,
and let them take away the lamps...
   Night.

IX.

Already madness has covered
half my soul with its wing,
and gives me strong liquor to drink,
and lures me to the black valley.

I realized that I must
hand victory to it,
as I listened to my delirium,
already alien to me.

It will not allow me to take
anything away with me,
(however I beseech it,
however I pester it with prayer):

not the terrible eyes of my son,
the rock-like suffering,
not the night when the storm came,
not the prison visiting hour,

nor the sweet coolness of hands,
nor the uproar of the lime trees' shadows,
nor the distant light sound –
the words of last comfort.

[4 May 1940]

Epilogue

2.

The hour of remembrance has drawn close again.
I see you, hear you, feel you:

the one they could hardly get to the window,
the one who no longer walks on this earth,

the one who shook her beautiful head,
and said: 'Coming here is like coming home.'

I would like to name them all but they took away
the list and there's no way of finding them.

For them I have woven a wide shroud
from the humble words I heard among them.

I remember them always, everywhere,
I will never forget them, whatever comes.

And if they gag my tormented mouth
with which one hundred million people cry,

then let them also remember me
on the eve of my remembrance day.

If they ever think of building
a memorial to me in this country,

I consent to be so honoured,
only with this condition: not to build it

near the sea where I was born:
my last tie with the sea is broken,

nor in the Tsar's Garden by the hallowed stump
where an inconsolable shadow seeks me,

but here, where I stood three hundred hours
and they never unbolted the door for me.

Since even in blessed death I am terrified
that I will forget the thundering of Black Marias,

forget how the hateful door slammed,
how an old woman howled like a wounded beast.

Let the melting snow stream
like tears from my bronze eyelids,

let the prison dove call in the distance
and the boats go quietly on the Neva.

[March 1940]

Translated from the Russian by Richard McKane

OSIP MANDELSTAM

Eyelashes sting with tears

Eyelashes sting with tears as a sob wells up in the chest.
I sense the storm is imminent but I am not afraid.
Someone wonderful hurries me to forget something,
I feel I'm being smothered yet I want to live to the point of dying.

At the first sound I rise from the bunks,
looking around me with wild and sleepy eyes,
thus a prisoner in a rough coat sings a convict song
as the strip of dawn rises over the labour camp.

March 1931

Translated from the Russian by Richard and Elizabeth McKane

Osip Mandelstam

The flat is quiet as paper

The flat is quiet as paper,
empty, without any ornaments.
One can hear the moisture bubbling
in the radiators.

Everything is in order.
The phone sits still like a frozen frog.
Our possessions, who have seen it all,
want to be on the move again.

And the cursed walls are thin,
and there's nowhere left to run,
and I'm forced to entertain someone,
like a fool playing a comb.

More brazen than a Komsomol cell
more brazen than a student song,
I teach bird calls
to the executioners perched on the school bench.

I read rationed books,
and catch fragments of demagogue speeches,
and sing a menacing lullaby
to the child of the *kulak*.

Some realist writer,
comber of the collective farm's speeches,
someone with blood in his ink
deserves such a hell.

After the purges are boiled away,
some honest traitor
is left like salt around the edges,
a good family man who will take a swipe at a moth like me.

How much torture and anger
is hidden in each veiled hint,
as though Nekrasov's hammer
were smashing in nails in my walls.

Come on now, it's time for you to put your head on the block,
you're seventy years old,
you slovenly old man,
it's time for you to put your boots on.

It's not the ancient spring of Hippocrene,
which will burst through the cardboard walls,
but the gush of age-old terror
which will flood this evil Moscow home.

November 1933 Moscow - Furmanov backstreet

Translated from the Russian by Richard and Elizabeth McKane.

Osip Mandelstam

341

Mounds of human heads are wandering into the distance.
I dwindle among them. Nobody sees me. But in books
much loved, and in children's games I shall rise
from the dead to say the sun is shining.

[1936-7?]

385

Just for its potters the dark blue island,
Crete, the lighthearted, is great. When the earth they baked
rings you can hear their genius.
Do you hear fins of dolphins beating deep in the earth?

Speak of this sea and it will rise
in the clay, to smile in its oven.
And the frigid power of the vessel
became half sea, half eye.

Blue island, give me back what is mine.
Flying Crete, give back my work to me.
Fill the baked vessel
from the breasts of the flowing goddess.

This was, and was sung, and turned blue
in days before Odysseus,
before food and drink
were called 'my', 'mine'.

Grow strong again and shine
o star of ox-eyed heaven,
and you, flying-fish of chance,
and you, o water saying yes.

Voronezh. March [1937]

Translated from the Russian by Clarence Brown and W.S. Merwin

Marina Tsvetayeva

From Poems To Czechoslovakia

8

What tears in eyes now
weeping with anger and love
Czechoslovakia's tears
Spain in its own blood

and what a black mountain
has blocked the world   from the light.
It's time – It's time – It's time
to give back to God   his ticket.

I refuse to be. In
the madhouse of the inhuman
I refuse   to live
With the wolves of the market place

I refuse   to howl,
Among the sharks of the plain
I refuse to swim   down
where moving backs make a current.

I have no need of holes
for ears, nor prophetic eyes:
to your mad world there is
one answer: to refuse!

1938

Translated from the Russian by Elaine Feinstein

Nikolai Zabolotsky

In A Field Somewhere Near Magadan

In a field somewhere near Magadan,
Danger and disaster threatening,
In exhalations of the freezing mist,
They walked behind the low-slung sledge.
From the iron palate of the soldiers,
From the brigand bands that preyed on them,
Only the aid-post could protect them now,
And details into town to fetch some meal.
Two old men, in pea jackets, they trudged,
Two unfortunates, far from their home,
Remembering their distant village huts
And yearning for them at this far remove.
Far from family, far from their dear ones,
They were burnt out, all passion spent,
And weariness that bent their bodies,
Tonight consumed the very souls of them.
Life, in the forms decreed by nature,
Ran its course above their heads.
But the stars, signifying freedom,
Turned their faces from the ways of men.
The universe's miracle play was staged
In the luminous theatre of the north,
Yet its intense and penetrating flame
No longer reached into the human heart.
Intermittently, the blizzard moaned,
Covering up the frigid stumps,
On which, not looking at each other,
The two old Russians sat and froze to death.
The horses stood, the work was over,
Mortal affairs were done with now...
A sweet drowsiness held them,
And led them, sobbing, to a distant land.
Never again will the guard herd them together,
The camp escort will not overtake them now.
Only the constellations of Magadan
Will sparkle, rising overhead.

1956 *(1947/8, according to Struve and Filippov)*

Translated from the Russian by Daniel Weissbort

Nikolai Zabolotsky

A Woodland Lake*

Again the flash of that crystal cup
Dream-shackled, caught my eye in the dark.

Through the battling of wolves and contention of trees,
Where insects suckle the sap of plants,
Where stalks run riot and flowers moan,
Where predatory nature rules its creatures,
I broke through to you and on the threshold
Fell silent, parting the dry undergrowth.

Water lily-garlanded, garbed in sedge,
In a brittle chaplet of vegetal flutes,
Lies this undefiled patch of liquid,
An asylum for fish, for ducks a refuge.
And yet how still, how solemn it is!
And how has such grandeur possessed these brakes?
Why don't the bird hordes rant and rave,
But slumber instead, lulled by sweet dreams?
A solitary sandpiper regrets his lot,
His foolish notes fluted abroad.

And the lake in the smouldering fires of evening,
Deep buried, lies unstirring in its shine,
While the pines stand tall like tapers about it,
Closing up ranks from end to end.
The bottomless cup of crystalline water
Shone there, lost in contemplation,
As a sick man's eye, with infinite longing,
At the first glimmer of the evening star,
No longer aware of the ailing body,
Burns, drawn now by the night time sky.

And the troupes of cattle and wild creatures
Thrusting their horned heads between the firs,
Leaned down towards their font, truth's source,
To drink deep of its life-giving waters.

*This is one of the very few poems by Zabolotsky known to have been written in prison camp
1938

Translated from the Russsian by Daniel Weissbort

NIZAMETDIN AKHMETOV

My miracle blue

My miracle blue, my blue pain!
Girl of my dreams, what is your name?
I'm dreaming swan dreams again,
I cannot still the swan's song in my soul.

There's blue sky beyond black clouds,
there powerful blue birds soar,
the blue-braided stray wind
hurls blue stars at the window.

Dried out and enfeebled by blueness
blue-blue lips stir,
the blue river courses of veins are knotted,
blue lightning has seared the eyelids.

Blue girl – stern and proud –
walks forlornly round the blue town,
calls my blue shade ...
They're waiting, waiting for me in the blue land.

Translated from the Russian by Richard McKane and Helen Szamuely

Nizametdin Akhmetov

Back beyond the burnt out, disfigured day

Back beyond the burnt out, disfigured day
I don't remember myself as young.
Unpardoned by yesterday
I look my shadow in the eyes.

I glide beyond the echo of past words
into myself and deeper, as a ghost.
I follow with chill surprise
the shade of dreams I dreamed.

I go to myself as though to a friend,
a dagger behind my back.
And I have no strength, no anger
to come together with my own self.

1976

Translated by Richard McKane and Helen Szamuely

ANONYMOUS

The Arsenal Prison Psychiatric Hospital Poems

Shake the purse over an empty hand,
knock with a dryish stick on the church porch,
think a bit why you came and at whom
the devil of a star in the sky shine irrelevantly.
Avoid the sancuary of pitiful liars,
lose on the roads the remnant of doubt,
ask about holiness of deaf sages,
give them a stone instead of small change,
burn the milk then after blow on the water,
and beat the innocent bushes like a crow,
lest you smash your face in the mud
tie your head to the bars of the window.

      *   *   *

An unknown track flares
on the wiped-out line on the horizon,
(someone walked over the earth in the rain
and is plunging his way into the sky.)

The horizon
is the frontier of two worlds,
it's difficult to cross it today,
and tomorrow it will be absolutely impossible.

So one has to gather all one's strength
on the frontier of tomorrow and today,
and to go away leaving between them
all that these two countries,
today – the present,
and today – the tomorrow of the past,
fettered you,
throughout the many ages.

      *   *   *

They came in
in crimson and black clothes like ghosts,
we are the servants of your memory,
they said.

We've come to wall up
its loop-holes
Get ready!
Metal flowed in their hands,
the torches burned.
The inquisition was once rich
with such servants.
Get ready.
They said threateningly,
we will exterminate your memory.
You will be stern and angry.
Farewell.
They will burn now on the bonfires
with sentimental shadows.
. . .

I have ceased to be
what I once was,
only that which cannot be ash
I let into my memory.

     *   *   *

A candle on the table,
on the floor a short fur coat.
Snowstorm outside the window,
revolver at the temples.
Emptiness in the eyes,
hopeless, wild,
and the heartbeats
fall off slowly.
Impossible to find
any other decision.
Reason crawled out
like a night snake.
A candle on the table,
and a mass of papers,
and the shot dies down
by the deafened doors.

The candle will burn down on the table,
the papers will flare down under it,
and the cabin will blaze from the candle,
for the universal peace of a man.

Translated from the Russian by Richard McKane

Natalya Gorbanevskaya

Memory of Pyarvalka

On the dark saucer of the bay
the little light-house barely gleams,
and I, a solitary walker,
am sleeping on the shore.
Dawn's not yet alit
upon my frozen cheeks,
my fate's yet silent ...
The gravel will still crunch
like nut-shells underneath me,
freedom and peace have still not played
their valedictory marches,
and the waves cling sleepily to the sand,
as does my cheek to this knapsack,
on the dimmed shores of the bay.

March 1970
Serbsky Institute

And tomorrow you'll not find even a trace

And tomorrow you'll not find even a trace
of that shadow that slides along the walls behind me.
I smile, a bitter tear
freezes to my pupil, like a piece of ice.

As the doll's house mica
affords no sight within,
so nothing can be read from a face
in which the previous day's already done,

yet a new one won't catch fire,
and the tear's track can't be seen or heard,
and it's only a blizzard shakes the door,
through which, in a while, we'll all be leaving.

January 1971
Butyrsky Prison, the hospital,
on the eve of the departure for Kazan

Translated from the Russian by Daniel Weissbort

Bulat Okudzhava

Letter To My Mom

You're sitting on your wooden planks in the middle of Moscow.
Your head's spinning from blind anguish.
On the window is a muzzle, freedom's the other side of the wall,
the thread between you and me is broken.
Behind the iron door struts a soldier...
Forgive him, mom, he's not to blame,
he doesn't take any sin onto his soul,
he's not doing it for himself, after all, he's doing it for the whole people.

The youthful investigator waves his fist.
It's so normal for him to call you an enemy.
He's glad to sweat at his work...
Or should he too be sitting in a cell?
In his pathetic head are three-storey curses...
Forgive him, mom, he's not to blame,
he doesn't take any sin onto his soul,
he's not doing it for himself, after all, he's doing it for the whole people.

A bit further than Krasnoyarsk is your logging camp.
The guard has never been at the front.
He'll [hit] you with his rifle butt, give you a kick,
so you'll never think anymore about anyone.
His fur coat's hot, but his glance is cold...
Forgive him, mom, he's not to blame,
he doesn't take any sin onto his soul,
he's not doing it for himself, after all, he's doing it for the whole people.

The leader's hidden himself in the tower by the Moscow River.
From fear he has paralysis of one arm.
He doesn't trust anyone anymore,
as if he'd built a prison for himself.
Everything's in his power, but he's still not happy...
Forgive him, mom, he's not to blame,
he doesn't take any sin onto his soul,
he's not doing it for himself, after all, he's doing it for the whole people.

Translated from the Russian by Gerald S. Smith

IRINA RATUSHINSKAYA

I will live and survive

I will live and survive and be asked:
How they slammed my head against a trestle,
How I had to freeze at nights,
How my hair started to turn grey...
But I'll smile. And will crack some joke
And brush away the encroaching shadow.
And I will render homage to the dry September
That became my second birth.
And I'll be asked: 'Doesn't it hurt you to remember?'
Not being deceived by my outward flippancy.
But the former names will detonate my memory –
Magnificent as old cannon.
And I will tell of the best people in all the earth,
The most tender, but also the most invincible,
How they said farewell, how they went to be tortured,
How they waited for letters from their loved ones.
And I'll be asked: what helped us to live
When there were neither letters nor any news – only walls,
And the cold of the cell, and the blather of official lies,
And the sickening promises made in exchange for betrayal.
And I will tell of the first beauty
I saw in captivity.
A frost-covered window! No spyholes, nor walls,
Nor cell-bars, nor the long-endured pain –
Only a blue radiance on a tiny pane of glass,
A cast pattern – none more beautiful could be dreamt!
The more clearly you looked, the more powerfully blossomed
Those brigand forests, campfires and birds!
And how many times there was bitter cold weather
And how many windows sparkled after that one –
But never was it repeated,
That upheaval of rainbow ice!
And anyway, what good would it be to me now,
And what would be the pretext for that festival?
Such a gift can only be received once,
And perhaps is only needed once.

Labour camp hospital, 30 November 1983

Translated from the Russian by David McDuff

VLADIMIR VYSOTSKY

Throw Meat To The Dogs

Throw meat to the dogs and perhaps they'll fight.
Give juice to the drunks and perhaps they'll outdrink themselves.
Lest the crows grow fat put up more scarecrows.
To fall in love find a cosy corner.
Throw seeds in the earth and perhaps the corn will sprout.
OK, I'll be obedient, but give me my freedom.

They gave tattered meat to the dogs and they did not fight.
They gave vodka to the drunks and they refused it.
People scare the crows and the carrion crows have no fear.
Couples get together when they should be parting.
They watered the land and lo there were no ears of corn.
Yesterday they gave me my freedom. What will I do with it?

Translated from the Russian by Richard McKane

TITSIAN TABIDZE

Poem-Landslide

I don't write poems ... it's me they write,
My life and the poem's unfold alike.
I call a poem a torrent, a landslide
That sweeps you off and buries you alive.

April was the month that I was born in,
Apple-trees opened their blossom to the skies.
Whiteness rains on me, and in a torrent
The rain, as tears, is gushing from my eyes.

That's how I know that when I come to die
The poem I speak, however, will remain,
Strike a poet's heart and thus buy
Intercession – I can't complain.

'A boy grew up', they'll say, I think,
'By a stream in Orpiri, in poverty.
Poems were his food and drink,
He wouldn't move except for poetry.

And he was tortured to the day he died
By Georgian sun and Georgian earth.
Happiness was a thing he was denied,
Happiness he surrendered to his verse.'

I don't write poems ... it's me they write,
My life and the poem's unfold alike.
I call a poem a torrent, a landslide
That sweeps you off and buries you alive.

Translated from the Georgian by Donald Rayfield

VASYL STUS

From Elegies

I.

In Memory of Alla Horska

[Alla Horska was a Ukrainian artist, murdered, quite possibly by the K.G.B., in December, 1970. Sprigs of a snowball tree, a folklore symbol of Ukraine, were distributed at her funeral, where this poem was first read.]

FLAME fire, soul, flame fire instead of wails.
When a black cloud shrouds our sun,
Seek the snowball's scarlet shadow,
Seek its shadow in black-watered vales.
For we are few, a tiny handful,
Fit for hopes and sighing prayers,
All doomed to an untimely dying
In crimson blood as sharp as any gall.
It stings within our veins forever.
In a white whirlwind of lamenting
Clusters of pain twist and fall in the abyss
And in undying woe tumble all together.

IV.

Sleepless Night

I GLEAN thoughts like grains
From the stubble, sorting ears.
Tears are pricking. Pricking tears
Are like awns in the eye.
The drunkard night tramps
Round the room, bustles by the walls.
Silently, silently. A house-gnome
Would silently walk so.
Planes rumble outside
Like witches to their sabbath.
Over the rooftops,
Over the hushed rooftops,
Over the lull of Kiev – on they roar.
As an exile. Lord, yes. The bed now.

Bars from the window appear on the quilt.
And my pillow now is all rumpled,
And all rumpled now is my head.
What are you catching, you mad
Television aerials like burned-out survivors?
What are you catching, you blackened
Chimney stacks with your sunken mouths?
Is it air that you need? Or smoke?
Weary wits burning alcohol-clear?
A second night has passed, a second sleepless night.
Street lamps turn yellow outside.

V.

SUMMON the lion within you and fathom
The endless walls within the endless rage
When ice-clad cries roar from corner to corner.
Summon the lion within you and bellow.
Let the black clawing roars surround
This universal enclosure, leading your mind
Into a fairy glade where memories prickle like awns,
Where the years are burnt stubble
And where your woes, insatiable hyenas,
Sharpen their fangs and claws for you.
Summon the lion within you and rage
Among the bolts, bars, and locks:
The world is flowering with stubble
And barbed wire.

VI.

HIDE within the copper mountain,
Conceal the arrogant blue.
A shadow trumpets above me,
And a shadow fills in every step.
Hide within the horizon's oboes
And whisper: I am still alive.
A thunder of resurrection on the mountain
Is being announced for me.
Smash your fists against despair,
Hiding within the copper mountain.

VII.

To my Son

NOW you are beyond my memory, in the darkness
Of the loss to which the heart has grown accustomed.
You shine like a star from within
The heights above the sky. You're
Still only five years old, clinging
To your years like a seed to its shell.
My pain that has burned down to ashes!
How unbearable it would be to give birth to you again
And to see you once more as an infant.

Translated from the Ukrainian by Marco Carynnyk

GENNADY AYGI

Song From The Days Of Your Forefathers
(variation on the theme of a Chuvash folk-song)

> *...to drink not from a glass, but from a clear spring.*
> *(Bela Bartok, Cantata Profana)*

I wandered through the field and there was
not a single haycock in it

I went into the village
and there I saw
not a soul

and the girls were sitting
behind washed panes of narrow windows
and knotting the lace
full of eyes

I looked in the window and I saw
they were betrothing my beloved
in a white dress they decked her
placed a beaker in her hand
as she stood before the table

– I wept and I rocked
outside your window
and you were quiet –

like a candle on the sill
of a lofty church

'I see' I said silently
I said silently 'farewell'

having no family I understood – 'people'
long afterwards
'there was something' I knew

and I kept nothing in my head
weeping with my cheeks
in my hands

1957-1959

Translated from the Russian by Peter France

MITTA VASLEYE

Message To Friends

Do not forget those exiled to the depths.
Each of them has encountered his own fate.
To all of you, salaam! Your distant friend
Keeps up his spirit for the longed-for day.

Some time - by chance perhaps - that day will come,
And I shall burn with the same fire again,
No less than young folk at the *agadui*,
Or a master of the wedding with his guests.

I shall return meekly and terribly,
When my land begins once more its weddings.
I have composed my songs of inspiration,
Not to disgrace the wedding of my homeland.

Yes, the master of the wedding will return,
At midnight or by day - do not forget . . .
To all of you, salaam! Your distant friend
Will take into his house the festival! . . .

(end of the 1940s)

Translated from the Russian by Peter France
(from Gennady Aygi's Russian translation of the Chuvash original)

Middle
East

Gülten Akın

The Prison Yard

The yard incomplete
Was perfected by a scream,
Long icicles
Which froze.

The scream froze
Sketching blue-black pictures above us.
– Where did you fetch that scream from, mother?
The guard thought, from the sirens,
The seabirds perhaps,
But where is the sea? The cold sky up there
Without blue, that must be the sea.
Below us,
Below us, beside us, around us,
The prison yard.

The yard where we met and dispersed
Once every seven days
Had become our living part.

The yard,
The huts and barbed wire,
Where the pink-faced scowling guard
On the other six days assembled,
Silence in the grey jail,
Like the silence before an earthquake,
Imperfect without that scream
Which rose to complete
The pointing guns,
The mechanized sounds.
A black presence moved through the yard,
A wreath woven from curses.
It stood before each mother.
It swelled and grew
To the size of a mountain
Until there was no more room
In that prison yard
For us – the mothers.

Translated from the Turkish by Ruth Christie

Nazim Hikmet

Angina Pectoris

If half my heart is here, doctor,
    the other half is in China
with the army flowing
    toward the Yellow River.
And every morning, doctor,
every morning at sunrise my heart
    is shot in Greece.
And every night, doctor,
when the prisoners are asleep and the infirmary is deserted,
my heart stops at a run-down house
                        in Istanbul.
And then after ten years
all I have to offer my poor people
is this apple in my hand, doctor,
one red apple:
                my heart.
And that, doctor, that is the reason
for this angina pectoris –
not nicotine, prison, or arteriosclerosis.
I look at the night through the bars,
and despite the weight on my chest
my heart still beats with the most distant stars.

April 1948

Translated from the Turkish by Randy Blasing and Mutlu Konuk

NAZIM HIKMET

Sunday

It's Sunday,
today for the first time they let me out into the sun
                and for the first time in my life
I was shocked at how far the sky was from me
                        and how vast,
                        how blue,
                        and I stood stock still.
Then I sat on the ground my good friend,
and leaned my back against the wall.

At this moment, no daydreaming,
no freedom, no wife,
just the earth, myself and the sun,
                        and happiness.

Translated from the Turkish by Richard McKane

NAZIM HIKMET

From Poems To Piraye

written between 9-10 at night in prison

How good it is to remember you,
in the midst of news of death and victory,
in prison
and in my fortieth year.
How good it is to remember you,
your hand forgotten on the blue cloth,
the solemn softness of your hair,
the good Istanbul earth.

The happiness of loving you is like being reborn.
The smell of geranium leaf lingering on your fingertips,
a sunny calmness
and the invitation of a body,
a deep,
warm darkness shredded with bright red stripes.

How good it is to remember you,
to write about you,
to lie back in prison and think of you,
the words you said in such and such a place,
on such and such a day,
not the words so much as their world of expression.

How good it is to remember you.
I'm going to carve something out of wood for you again,
a little drawer, or a ring,
and I shall weave three metres of fine silk.
And jumping up from my bed
I'll cling to the bars of my window
and shout out what I've written to you
to the milk-white blueness of freedom.
How good it is to remember you,
in the midst of death and victory,
in prison
and in my fortieth year.

21st September 1945

Our son is sick.
His father's in prison.
Your head is heavy in your tired hands.
Our fate mirrors the world's.
Man will bring to man better days.
Our son will get well.
His father will come out of prison.
The depths of your eyes will smile.
Our fate mirrors the world's.

23rd September 1945

What is she doing now, at this moment, right now?
Is she at home, or out working,
resting, or on her feet?
She might be lifting her arm,
O, my rose, that movement of your white, firm wrist
strips you so naked...

What is she doing now, at this moment, right now?
Perhaps she's stroking a kitten on her lap,
perhaps she's walking, about to take a step:
those darling, dear ballerina feet
that always bring joy to me on my black days...

What is she thinking about, could it be about me?
Or perhaps about the potatoes taking so long to cook,
or why most of humanity is so bad?
What is she thinking about now, at this moment, right now?

26th September 1945

They made prisoners of us, and threw us into jail:
me inside the walls,
you outside the walls.
Ours is small business;
but the worst thing is,
consciously or unconsciously
to have one's soul a prisoner.
Most people are in this situation,
honourable, hard-working people,
worthy of being loved as I love you...

Translated from the Turkish by Richard McKane

Nazim Hikmet

Advice For Someone Going Into Prison

If instead of getting the rope
you're thrown inside
for not cutting off hope
from your world, your country, your people;
if you do a ten or fifteen year stretch,
aside from the time you have left
don't say:
'Better to have swung at the end of a rope like a flag.'

You must insist on living.
There may not be happiness
but it is your binding duty
to resist the enemy,
and live one extra day.

Inside, one part of you may live completely alone
like a stone at the bottom of the well.
But the other part of you
must involve yourself
in the whirl of the world,
that you will shudder on the inside
when outside a leaf trembles on the ground forty days away.

Waiting for a letter inside,
singing melancholic songs,
staying awake all night, eyes glued on the ceiling,
is sweet but dangerous.

Look at your face from shave to shave,
forget how old you are,
protect yourself from lice, and from spring evenings,
and eat your bread to the very last crumb
and don't ever forget the freedom of laughter.

Who knows,
if the woman you love no longer loves you,
it's no small thing,
it's like the breaking of a sappy green twig
to the man inside.
Inside it's bad to think of roses and gardens.

It's good to think of mountains and the seas.

Read and write as much as humanly possible,
and I recommend you do weaving
and silver mirrors.

What I'm saying is that inside, ten years, or fifteen years
or even more can be got through,
they really can:
enough that you never let the precious stone
under your left breast grow dull.

1949

Translated from the Turkish by Richard McKane

NAZIM HIKMET

On Living

I

Living is no laughing matter:
    you must live with great seriousness
        like a squirrel, for example –
  I mean without looking for something beyond and above living,
        I mean living must be your whole occupation.
Living is no laughing matter:
    you must take it seriously,
    so much so and to such a degree
  that, for example, your hands tied behind your back,
                      your back to the wall,
  or else in a laboratory
        in your white coat and safety glasses,
      you can die for people –
  even for people whose faces you've never seen,
  even though you know living
        is the most real, the most beautiful thing.
I mean, you must take living so seriously
    that even at seventy, for example, you'll plant olive trees –
  and not for your children, either,
  but because although you fear death you don't believe it,
  because living, I mean, weighs heavier.

II

Let's say we're seriously ill, need surgery -
which is to say we might not get up
               from the white table.
Even though it's impossible not to feel sad
          about going a little too soon,
we'll still laugh at the jokes being told,
we'll look out the window to see if it's raining,
or still wait anxiously
          for the latest newscast...
Let's say we're at the front –

for something worth fighting for, say.
There, in the first offensive, on that very day,
    we might fall on our face, dead.
We'll know this with a curious anger,
    but we'll still worry ourselves to death
    about the outcome of the war, which could last years.
Let's say we're in prison
and close to fifty,
and we have eighteen more years, say,
    before the iron doors will open.
We'll still live with the outside,
with its people and animals, struggle and wind –
    I mean with the outside beyond the walls.
I mean, however and wherever we are,
    we must live as if we will never die.

III

This earth will grow cold,
a star among stars
    and one of the smallest,
a gilded mote on blue velvet –
    I mean *this*, our great earth.
This earth will grow cold one day,
not like a block of ice
or a dead cloud even
but like an empty walnut it will roll along
    in pitch-black space ...
You must grieve for this right now
– you have to feel this sorrow now –
for the world must be loved this much
    if you're going to say "I lived" ...

Translated from the Turkish by Randy Blasing and Mutlu Konuk

OKTAY RIFAT

The Embrace

Warm me this night,
O my trust in freedom
wrap me warm
against my mattress thin and blanket torn.
Out there is unimaginable cold and wind,
outside – oppression,
torture,
out there – death.
O my trust in freedom
enter deep,
warm me through this night.
On my palm a place is ready
for your hands,
on my thighs a place
to lean your knees.
Enclose me,
sheathe me,
wrap me warm,
O my trust in freedom
wrap me warm this night.

Translated from the Turkish by Ruth Christie

CAN YÜCEL

The Latest Situation In Chile

People got so used to staying indoors
that curfews were declared illegal.

Poem 25

We can show you two kinds of people
who've learned a thing or two about political finesse:
politicians and convicts.
The reason is there for all to see:
for politicians, politics is the art of staying
out of jail,
for convicts it is the prospect of freedom.

Translated from the Turkish by Feyyaz Kayacan Fergar

CAN YÜCEL

Arithmetic

One Turk is worth the whole world, is a saying of Ataturk.
Leaving aside the distant and recent past,
but considering the events lately
in Sebinkarahisar and Gaziantep:
that is, if what the papers say is true –
some Turks have been tortured,
for whatever reason,
they were hanged from the ceiling by their feet,
were subjected to electric shocks here and there etc.
So I repeat, that is, if the news is true,
and if as a nation we take to heart this statement
that one Turk is worth the whole world:
we – I mean some of us
and we can't tell how many –
by torturing some of us
have committed a crime against humanity, against so many worlds –
nobody knows how many –
and against so many worlds beyond this life.

Translated from the Turkish by Esra Nilgun Mirze and Richard McKane

MAHMOUD DARWISH

Victim Number 48

He was lying dead on a stone.
They found in his chest the moon and a rose lantern,
They found in his pocket a few coins,
A box of matches and a travel permit.
    He had tattoos on his arms.

His mother kissed him
And cried for a year.
Boxthorn tangled in his eyes.
    And it was dark.

His brother grew up
And went to town looking for work.
He was put in prison
Because he had no travel permit;
He was carrying a dustbin
    And boxes down the street.

Children of my country,
    That's how the moon died.

Translated from the Arabic by Abdullah al-Udhari

Mahmoud Darwish

Earth Poem

A dull evening in a run-down village
Eyes half asleep
I recall thirty years
And five wars
I swear the future keeps
My ear of corn
And the singer croons
About a fire and some strangers
And the evening is just another evening
And the singer croons

And they asked him:
Why do you sing?
And he answered:
I sing because I sing
....

And they searched his chest
But could only find his heart
And they searched his heart
But could only find his people
And they searched his voice
But could only find his grief
And they searched his grief
But could only find his prison
And they searched his prison
But could only see themselves in chains

Translated from the Arabic by Abdullah al-Udhari

MAHMOUD DARWISH

A Gentle Rain in a Distant Autumn

A gentle rain in a distant autumn
And the birds are blue, are blue,
And the earth is a feast.
Don't say I wish I was a cloud over an airport.
All I want
From my country which fell out of the window of a train
Is my mother's handkerchief
And reasons for a new death.

A gentle rain in a strange autumn
And the windows are white, are white
And the sun is a citrus grove at dusk,
And I, a stolen orange.
Why are you running away from my body
When all I want
From the country of daggers and nightingales
Is my mother's handkerchief
And reasons for a new death.

A gentle rain in a sad autumn
And the promises are green, are green,
And the sun is of mud.
Don't say: we saw you in the killing of jasmine.
Ah, seller of aspirin and death,
My face was like the evening
My death a foetus.
All I want
From my country that's forgotten the speech of the distant ones
Is my mother's handkerchief
And reasons for a new death.

A gentle rain in a distant autumn
And the birds are blue, are blue,
And the earth is a feast.
The birds have flown to a time which will not return.
You'd like to know my country?
And what's between us?
My country is the joy of being in chains,

A kiss sent in the post.
All I want
From the country which slaughtered me
Is my mother's handkerchief
And reasons for a new death.

Translated from the Arabic by Abdullah al-Udhari

Samih Al-Qasim

The Clock on the Wall

My city collapsed
The clock was still on the wall
Our neighbourhood collapsed
The clock was still on the wall
The street collapsed
The clock was still on the wall
The square collapsed
The clock was still on the wall
My house collapsed
The clock was still on the wall
The wall collapsed
The clock
Ticked on

End Of A Discussion With A Jailer

From the window of my small cell
I can see trees smiling at me,
Roofs filled with my people,
Windows weeping and praying for me.
From the window of my small cell
I can see your large cell.

Translated from the Arabic by Abdullah al-Udhari

ADONIS

From The Desert

The Diary of Beirut under Siege, 1982

I

3
I said: This street leads to our house. He said: No.
>   You won't pass. And pointed his bullets at me.

Fine, in every street
>   I have homes and friends.

6
They found people in sacks:
>   One without a head
>   One without a tongue or hands
>   One strangled
>   The rest without shape or names.
Have you gone mad? Please,
>   Don't write about these things.

10
From the palm wine to the calmness of the desert . . . etc.
From the morning that smuggles its stomach and sleeps on the corpses of the
>   refugees . . . etc.
From the streets, army vehicles, concentration of troops . . . etc.
From the shadows, men, women . . . etc.
From the bombs stuffed with the prayers of Muslims and infidels . . . etc.
From the flesh of iron that bleeds and sweats pus . . . etc.
From the fields that long for the wheat, the green and the workers . . . etc.
From the castles walling our bodies and bombarding us with darkness . . . etc.
From the myths of the dead which speak of life, express life . . . etc.
From the speech which is the slaughter, the slaughtered and the slaughterers
>   . . . etc.
From the dark dark dark
I breathe, feel my body, search for you and him, myself and others,
And hang my death
Between my face and these bleeding words . . . etc.

16
Bourje Square - (inscriptions whispering their secrets
                        to broken bridges . . .)
Bourje Square - (memory looking for itself
                        in fire and dust . . .)
Bourje Square - (an open desert
                        swept and dragged by the winds . . .)
Bourje Square - (witchcraft
                            to see corpses moving/their limbs
                            in a backstreet/their ghosts
                            in a backstreet/you hear them sighing . . .)
Bourje Square - (west and east
                        gallows standing,
                        martyrs and guardians . . .)
Bourje Square - (a trail
                            of caravans: myrrh
                                        frankincense and musk
                            and spices opening the festival . . .)
Bourje Square - (a trail
                            of caravans: thunder
                                        and explosion and lightning
                            and hurricanes opening the festival . . .)
Bourje Square - (I have called this era
                        by the name of this place)

                        II

I
My era tells me bluntly:
You do not belong.
I answer bluntly:
I do not belong,
I try to understand you.
Now I am a shadow
Lost in the desert
And shelter in the tent of a skull.

6
He shuts the door
Not to trap his joy
. . . But to free his grief.

12
He wrote a poem
        (how can I convince him my future is a desert?)
He wrote a poem
        (who will shake the stoneness of words off me?)
He wrote a poem
        (you don't belong if you don't kill a brother)
He wrote a poem
        (how can we understand this fugitive language caught
        between the question and the poem?)
He wrote a poem
        (can the refugee dawn embrace its sun?)
He wrote a poem
        (there's confusion between the sun's face and the sky)
He wrote a poem (. . ./let him die . . .)

20
You do not die because you are created
        Or because you have a body
You die because you are the face of the future.

30
A creator devoured by his creatures, a country
        Hiding in the blood running from his remains.
This is the beginning of a new era.

31
Whenever I say: my country is within reach
        And bears fruit in a reachable language
Another language kicks me
To another language.

33
All the certainty I have lived slips away
All the torches of my desire slip away
All that was between the faces that lit my exile and me slips away
I have to start from the beginning
To teach my limbs to reach the future,
To talk, to climb, to descend from the beginning
In the sky of beginnings, in the abyss of the alphabet.

34
They are falling, the land is a thread of smoke
               Time a train
               Travelling along a track of smoke . . .
My obsession is here now, loss.
My concern is the end
               Is not over
They are falling, I am not looking for a new beginning.

A Mirror For The Twentieth Century

A coffin bearing the face of a boy
A book
Written on the belly of a crow
A wild beast hidden in a flower

A rock
   Breathing with the lungs of a lunatic:

     This is it
     This is the Twentieth Century.

Translated from the Arabic by Abdullah al-Udhari

Ahmed Fouad Negm

Prisoner's File

Name	Sabr*
Charge	That I am Egyptian
Age	The most modern age; (though grey hair in braids flows from my head down to my waist).
Profession	Heir, of my ancestors and of time, to the creation of civilisation and life-force and peace
Skin	Wheat-coloured
Figure	As slim as a lance
Hair	Rougher than dried clover
Colour of eyes	Jet black
Nose	Aquiline like a horse's
Mouth	Firmly in place (when I attempted to budge it, some mischief happened)
Place of birth	In any dark room under the sky, on the soil of Egypt. From any house in the middle of palm trees, where the Nile flows – as long as it is not a palace.
Verdict	For seven thousand years I have been a prisoner asleep, grinding stones with my molars, out of frustration, spending the nights in grief.
The question of release	Someone asked me:

"Why is your imprisonment so long?'
"Because I am a peaceful and a humorous man.
I did not break the law,
because I am afraid of it;
the law holds a sword in its hands.

Anytime you want –
ask the informers about me
and you will hear and understand
my story from A to Z.

My name is Sabr,
Ayyub,** patient with catastrophes,
like a donkey,
I carry my share of the burden
and wait.
I drown in rivers of sweat
all day long.
At night I gather together my troubles
and upon them I lie,
do you know why?"

* Sabr is a common Arabic name which means "patience."
** Ayyub - a personality in Arab folk literature known for his unending patience.

Translated from the Arabic by Janet Stevens and Moussa Saker

SA'DI YUSUF

Hamra Night

A candle in a long street
A candle in the sleep of houses
A candle for frightened shops
A candle for bakeries
A candle for a journalist trembling in an empty office
A candle for a fighter
A candle for a woman doctor watching over patients
A candle for the wounded
A candle for plain talk
A candle for the stairs
A candle for a hotel packed with refugees
A candle for a singer
A candle for broadcasters in their hideouts
A candle for a bottle of water
A candle for the air
A candle for two lovers in a naked flat
A candle for the falling sky
A candle for the beginning
A candle for the ending
A candle for the last communiqué
A candle for conscience
A candle in my hands.

Hamra: a fashionable district in Beirut.

Translated from the Arabic by Abdullah al-Udhari

Reza Baraheni

The Doves

outside doves perch everywhere
it is clear from
their cooings of love and delight
it is clear from
the whirr of their wings
wings which seem to fan me in my prisoner's sleep
it is clear outside
doves perch everywhere

the night is like a day on the other side of the bars
on this side the day is like the night

Translated from the Persian by the author

Reza Baraheni

Barbecue

– would the man whose buttocks are roasted like to sit down?

– no, never! I would rather die than sit down!

he sleeps on his heart and on his knees
he arches his back
and purrs with pain
the puss and blood stick his ass to his shorts and to his pants

– doesn't the man whose back is burnt want to undress?

– no, never! I'd rather die than undress! They undressed
   me once! Isn't that enough? In a quarter of an hour you
   could roast a cow on that bed!
   I burn, burn, burn, burn forever!

I lift him under his knees
I lift him on my back
from my back his hands grip my arms
I shout behind the door
    Guard! Seventeen! Toilet!
       Guard! Guard!
slowly the cool guard comes from right or from left
with cold theatrics he throws the door open
the smell of burning nauseates him
my load is heavy but I have to run to run
crying and groaning behind my back he pulls down his pants
    pulls down his shorts
crying groaning moaning he shits as he stands

he'd rather die than sit
    or wipe himself
we return the way we came
the reek of roasting fills his mind
he's disgusted by meat
he says it's as if I was roasted
    barbecued
when I see cooked meat
I say that's me
    roasted
       barbecued

Translated from the Persian by the author

REZA BARAHENI

Hosseinzadeh,
The Head Executioner

Azudi lights his cigarette
– say *Doctor* Azudi!
 and *Doctor* Hosseinzadeh! –
he's short, with a bald head, and eyes uneasy
as the asshole of a nervous rooster
he is a man of great renown:
he always stubs his cigarette on the back of a human hand
he never smokes more than forty a day
and the first caress is always
the privilege of this *Pahlavi* slut
and the last caress too
between the two cuffs
Azudi and Rassuli and Shadi and Manuchehri
Azudi and Parvizkhan and Rezavan and Hosseini nurse
 the patient
one extracts his nails
another his teeth
a third scours the skin
a fourth provides the shock treatment
a fifth the reflagellation
and the sixth prepares the ailing for the *coup de grace*
there's a short man whose name is Ardalan
 – say *Doctor* Ardalan! –
he fucks the afflicted
man and woman are the same to him
he holds a Ph.D. in rapacity

(and you, prisoner! you try all this time to forget
the name of the half-blind man who printed that
article of yours. He has a wife, three children, a
father and a mother, and he provides for them all)

and then Hosseinzadeh
 – say *Doctor* Hosseinzadeh! –
administers the final cuff
the final verdict to shoot you
comes between the two caresses

Translated from the Persian by the author

Reza Baraheni

What Is Poetry?

poetry
is a shark's fin cutting a prisoner's throat
    delicately and precisely

poetry
is the sharp teeth of a rabid wolf on the shoulders
    of a wounded doe

poetry
is the exact meaning of the earth's intestines
    when broken into the small syllables of prison cells

poetry
is a cliff where executioners hurl poets into canyons below

poetry
is not a cure but the pain of a man treading the air
between an army helicopter and the waters of Hoz-e Sultan
    at 200 miles per hour

poetry
is the vertical descent of a satellite of meat
    to the salt bogs of Hoz-e Sultan

poetry
is a swamp brimming over with the corpses of epic poets

poetry
is a thousand poets shot at noon by the gate of Allah Akbar
    and the Mossalah of Shiraz

poetry
is the poet's fall from Tabriz Arc

poetry
is the immense pressure of four hands on the back of
the poet's neck when his mouth and belly are filled
    with water and the newspaper calls it suicide

poetry
is the blindfold used by prison guards to cover the
    truth of your eyes like a metaphor

poetry
is the handcuffs which do not bind your hands
    but seal your lips

poetry
is the needle used to sew up Farrokhi's lips

poetry
is the full height of Sur-e Esrafil on the gallows
    and the rags of Mirza Reza-ye Kermani on history's
        tall form

here in prison
poetry
is this   nothing else   nothing else

Translated from the Persian by the author

Reza Baraheni

F.M.'s Autobiography

sir
it's not easy for me to talk to you
here in prison there's a rumour that you're
a poet   I never wrote a word of poetry in
my life   I never even read a word of poetry
but I can tell you about the life of
a labourer in which there's no poetry
if the pain in your feet permits   if you can
forget the questions you will have to answer
in an hour   if you don't fear that your brother
has been taken away   or that your mother has had
a stroke   if you can believe that your daughter
has not been seized   listen to the words of this humble
prisoner: I am nineteen years old   when I was
three my mother beat me   at six it was my father who
whipped me   I started work when I was five
when I was eight the landlord's
sixteen year old son tried to rape me   he did not
succeed   because after all everything has its
limit   the mulberry cannot carry the fruit
of the melon   and the ant is not made to carry
a tree   the prick of a thick-necked rich youth
who eats butter honey meat chicken and turkey
cannot dig into the ass of a working boy
who shits none of these things   but when I was
twelve the landlord succeeded in taking the
revenge of the rich bastard   my father hanged himself
he'd wanted to kill himself for years   now he
used my disgrace for his excuse   at fourteen
I threw up the bricks of the master's house alone   at fifteen
I was pushed from a rug factory to a sock factory to
a textile factory   at sixteen the leaden air of the
printing house set in my chest   I'm a typesetter
now   for three years I had typeset *Long Live the Shah*
six days ago I decided to typeset *Long Live Liberty*
they got me five days ago   they've been pulling my
nails ever since   I've forty nails   twenty of them
belong to my hands and feet   and twenty
more belong to my hands and feet in my mind
Ardalan raped me three days ago   they haven't

raped you, have they?   that's not important
Ardalan is like a copulating dog   the bite of
his teeth is still in my shoulders   there were
of course lashes slaps kicks and obscenities too
you're a poet and they say poets know
many things   tell me what I should do next
what they will do next   pardon me for this headache
I've given you   well   what can we do after all
it's a labourer's life

someone should tell us what to do

Translated from the Persian by the author

Parviz Khazrai

The Art Of Miracle

In the country where the sobs of those shut away
Drown
As a stone sinks in a pond
In the piling up of caked blood and sludge,
In the crypt where songs
Moan or cries of anger
Form the coffin of singers,
Of all the horizons I call up
The terror-stricken looks of those who love
I make their pale lights pass each other
And in the heart of black dungeons
I revive
The morning star.

In the country where each dawn
The hands of machine guns shoot down
The green hands of so many fresh gardens,
In the country where no path grows,
                              except in the imagination,
I start out again on secret paths
The plants of source and light,
And I graft the sounds upon subterranean waters
And look on the sun from another orbit.

Yes!
I, in hitting the silex of night
On the broken heart of love
I make sparks fly.

Yes!
I am learning
                The art of the garden,
I am learning
                The art of miracle.

Translated from the Persian by Joan MacDougall and the author

Sherko Bekas

from Small Mirrors

I

Land

When I touched the bough of a tree
it trembled in pain

When I held out my hand to the branch
the trunk started to weep
when I embraced the trunk
the soil under my feet shuddered
the rocks groaned

this time when I bent down and collected
a handful of earth
all Kurdistan screamed.

1985

V

The Gun

To make the mountain happy
the trees asked the wind
to play music with them like flutes

To alleviate the garden of tedium
the bird asked the river
to let its waves hold hands and dance

And in order to set the poetry free
the land asked the peshmergas guns
to set fire to this dark night
and die in the arms of the sun.

XI

In My Country

In my country
newspapers are born dumb
radios are born deaf
televisions are born blind

and those in my country
who want these to be born healthy and free

They make them dumb and kill them
they make them deaf and kill them
they make them blind and kill them

this is what happens
in my country

XVII

The Seeds

We were millions
we were old trees
newly growing plants
and seeds.

From the helmet of Ankara
they came at dawn
they uprooted us
they took us away
far away.

On the way the heads of
many old trees drooped
many new plants died in the cold
many seeds were trampled under foot
lost and forgotten

We grew thin like the summer river
we diminished like flocks of birds
towards the time of autumn
we diminished to mere thousands

We had seeds
carried back by the wind
they reached the thirsty mountains again
they hid inside rock clefts
the first rain
the second rain
the third rain
they grew again
Now again we are a forest
we are millions
we are seeds

plants
and old trees
the old helmet died!
And now you the new helmet
why have you put the head of the spear
under your chin?
Can you finish us off?

But I know
and you know
as long as there is a seed
for the rain and the wind
this forest will never end?

20 September 1987 Stockholm

Translated from Sorani Kurdish by Kamal Mirawdeli

Maghreb

Leila Djabali

For My Torturer, Lieutenant D...

You slapped me –
    no one had ever slapped me –
electric shock
and then your fist
and your filthy language
I bled too much to be able to blush
All night long
a locomotive in my belly
rainbows before my eyes
It was as if I were eating my mouth
drowning my eyes
I had hands all over me
and felt like smiling.

Then one morning a different soldier came
You were as alike as two drops of blood.
Your wife, Lieutenant –
Did she stir the sugar in your coffee?
Did your mother dare to tell you you looked well?
Did you run your fingers through your kids' hair?

Translated from the French by Anita Barrows

Tahar Djaout

March 15, 1962

how to curb their rage to dissolve the stars
and to birth eternal night
I challenge their iron
and the enraged ire with which they multiply the chains

in the blue smile
of the Admiralty open on the promises
today in long swallows I gulp
– sun thundering over Algiers –
the joys of a feasting
where resurrected dawns gambol
and yet I think on the holocausts
unleashed to make dawn break
I think of Feraoun
– smile frozen in the sun's circumcision

they are afraid of the truth
they are afraid of the straight pen
they are afraid of truly human humans
and you, Mouloud, you insisted and spoke
about wheat fields for the sons of the poor
and spoke of pulverizing all the barbed wire
that lacerated our horizons

they speak of you and say that you were too good
that you felt revolted
hearing shells greet each dawn
that you believed human beings to be born so as to be brothers
and though challenging all the orgies of horror
you were incapable of hatred

one day, Mouloud, goodness finally triumphed
and we could wear the sun's trident
and we could honor the memory of the dead
because
     with
         your hands, those gleaners of dawn's mysteries,
and your dreamy inveterate poet's face,
you have known how to fulfill our truths
written in sun scraps
on the breasts of all those who revolt

Translated from the French by Pierre Joris

ABDELLATIF LAÂBI

Hunger Strike

So let's talk about this hunger strike
it's a form of struggle
that those in my position
have used throughout the long history
of mutilation
Very true, it's only passive
but when you only have your naked stomach
with which to take on
the whole arsenal of despotism
you use your only weapon
this irrepressible spirit within yourself
you use it to the point of exhaustion
even risk its extinction
to protect your dignity

the sun is tasteless
when you're hungry
and the sleepless nights are icy
you think of so many things
both serious and funny
I swear that when I was really ill
I was tormented by the idea of real food
I used to imagine delicious meals
all my gastronomic inheritance passed
before my eyes
but alright, I'm not ashamed of these thoughts
for what's crucial
is this trial
this voyage into the unknown
is the feeling of great power at the heart of
the greatest weakness
the superiority of he who resists
when confronted with he who oppresses
Yes, life itself is a formidable weapon
which will always amaze
the armed corpses
What's crucial
is to always share the suffering
of those tortured by hunger
that is this rotten, bloody taste in the mouth

these rolling cold eyes in the foggy day
these guts which twist and snake
with the despair of emptiness
What's crucial
is once again the brotherhood of suffering
profound ideas arise in the night
become real
they are not mine or his or his

but they belong
to all those deprived of the sun
What's crucial
is once again the brotherhood of suffering
for our hunger
is not for wealth
it's not the greed of the monster
on his knees
before the golden calf of debauchery
our hunger is for a new world
inhabited by new men
of a sun shared
limitlessly
of an incurable peace
which can only hurt the division makers
Also
in these days of abstinence
it was a source of pride to me
to be hungry
and so to disturb a little
the shameful peace
of those who starve our people.

Translated from the French by Jacqueline Kaye

Africa

BREYTEN BREYTENBACH

Letter To Butcher From Abroad

for Balthazar

the prisoner says
now I'm not sure
that sweet Jesus roared
but a first fly is dancing
droning against the panes
a blossom tossed against the sky
the walls are glistening with blood
my heart hangs motionless
for fear this ecstasy might ebb
I must preserve all these minute amazements
food for the journey of the dull grey man
already lurking a companion of the body

the prisoner states
Li Chang-Yin warned against holes for rain –
'Let your heart never unfold with the flowers of spring
An inch of love is an inch of ashes'
I hope you will identify my grey bones
in the extinquished fire of the earth

as for me I shall set out on a journey
I shall lie on the upper deck of my body
feeling the tremors of the boat in my flesh
the ropes dozing prepared in the shadows
the mast shall point directions in the blue
the sea shall stir the sea shall smell
the sea shall be teeming with dolphins
gulls shall swarm above the heart
and in spite of all it will be silenced to a state of light
with the sound of a tongue the sun
shall rape each fibre grain and cell
but as for me I shall set out on a journey

the prisoner confesses
when your dreams are finally crushed
and far from friends you await the dark
like the pine-tree yearning for a blaze of sails

its lament shuddering a white wind in the wood
to crouch on Monday mornings crippled like a crow
at the lips of the ocean
then you are prepared
trembling in the soil
to feed the worms
and make confessions deep down in the earth

I can testify
I can describe the colours from within
the walls are black the snot is golden
the blood and pus are ice and berry-juice
the bird is pecking outside on the fortress walls

I'm standing on bricks before my neighbours
I am statue of liberty and liberation
trying to scream light in the dusk
with electrodes tied to my testicles
I'm writing slogans in crimson urine
across my skin across the floor
I'm keeping watch
smothered by the ropes of my entrails
slipping on a bar of soap I break my bones
I kill myself with the evening paper
and tumble from the tenth sphere of heaven
in search of redemption in a street surrounded by people

and you, butcher
you burdened with the security of the state
what are your thoughts when night begins to bare her bones
when the first babbling scream is forced
from the prisoner
like the sound of birth
and the fluids of parturition?
do you then feel humble before this bleeding thing
with its almost human shuddering shocks
and its broken breath of dying
in your hands?
does your heart tauten in your throat
when you touch the extinguished limbs
with the very hands that caress the secrets of your wife?

tell me, butcher
so that the obstetrics you're forced to perform
in the name of my survival

may be revealed to me
in my own tongue

the prisoner said
I do not want to die inside
I want to be hanged outside in the desert
with my heart turned towards the cold of dawn
where like flies the mountains feed on the horizons
where the sand is burning in a myriad of silver tongues
where the moon rotten like a shipwreck
sinks through the blue smoke

now tell me, butcher
before this thing becomes a curse
before only through the mouths
of graves
you can still plead before the risen prisoners of Africa

Translated from the Afrikaans by André P. Brink

Dennis Brutus

Hanged

In Memoriam: Solomon Mahlangu Hanged
by the Apartheid Government, Pretoria
Dawn, April 6, 1979

I

Singing
he went to war
and singing
he went to his death

II

There was sunlit
Goch Street
and the clear
pale blue sunlight
of the Highveld

and the sunlit bustle
of Edgar's Store
and the goodly things
money might buy
for the rich and white

and the overalled workers
delivery "boys"
messenger "boys"
sitting on curbs
with nowhere to rest

and the sharp crack
of gunfire
and screams of pain
and barked commands
the thud of falling bodies

Afterwards
there was the long grey corridor
the rattling salute on metal bars
the stark shape of the gallows
the defiant shouts of "Amandla"

Singing he went to war
and singing he went to his death

III

One simply poses
one's life
against another's
one's death
against another's death:

but the sides are different:
ours is life
joyous life
a free life, for the free
and theirs
is the monstrous life of a monstrous thing
who lives on the death of others
on our deaths

IV

The body buried secretly
in Mamelodi
and friends excluded
thousands of mourners barred

At the cemetery
in Mamelodi
Mahlangu's mother
and thousands of friends
wait

The thousands waiting
weeping, angry
are told to disperse

The police announce
"The corpse you are waiting for
will not be delivered."

In the centre of Mamelodi
the police
swinging heavy rubber clubs
disperse 200 students
gathered to protest

Mahlangu knew
he might have to die:
he gave his life
for liberty.

V

(Eschel Rhoodie's father
was a hangman

the South African Secret Police
prowl the U.S. Campuses

their agents
function as academics

they hire mercenaries
as their hitmen

– Mr. and Mrs. Smit lie bullet-riddled
beside their family hearth –

their ruthless desperation
has no limit on criminality

theirs
and their corporate bosses)

VI

In the dimly-lit
mostly empty auditorium

the curious nervous
attentive crowd

the careful welcomes
focus mainly on me

there are complaints
of college harassment

the Dean of Spies
is falsely cordial

I pour scorn on stooge Mobutu
challenge Uncle Tom Sullivan

I evoke Mandela, Biko
Sharpeville and Soweto

a shooting in Johannesburg
stone-breaking on Robben island

Solomon
Mahlangu

His gallant life
His gallant death

VII

Blue spruce
White pine
Yellow poplars

a weak dawn
seeps red
over the Appalachian foothills

here
blacks and slaves were brought
as strikebreakers

now
the subdued miners
can oppress minorities

ahead
red-raw lumber
scattered on the road

and overturned trailer
wheels in the air
like a docile beagle's paws

a driver
his head severed;
a death in the dawn

VIII

On the road
to the airport
I search the news
till I find the dread item;
He was hanged at dawn

IX

All night
his name
his face
his body
his fate
the cell
the gallows
pressed on my awareness
like a nail
hammered in my brain

Solomon
Mahlangu
till dawn
till the time
till the news
the newspaper report

he had been hanged

then the nail
was pulled from my brain
and the drip
of tears inside my skull
began

X

Singing
he went
to war
and singing
he went
to his death

Frank Mkalawile Chipasula

A Hanging

Zomba Central Prison

His pendulous body tolled
its own death knell from the rope
yet refused obstinately
to die, clinging desperately
to the last thread
of his condemned life.

That morning oh!
his body sang until it could not
stand its own song;
like a guitar it hummed
and they could not but listen, stunned.
Every part of his body
opened its mouth and sang
death songs, Orphic heart songs,
shrill and sweet pent-up
songs of freedom or sad and solemn
as the national anthem.

The heartstrings raised their harp
in a flood of insistent rhythm
and a slow drumming dance:
All his blood stood up and sang,
twisting towards the throat.
All the silent mouths raised their voices
and cried out their chorus.
No one could gag or stop the prison
walls from singing;
No one could muzzle or shield the ringing
echoes of Zomba mountain.
And the whispering pines on Queen's Point,
witnesses to the sordid deed,
raised their frosty mourning.

His heart was a cube of golden light,
a nest of incense where weaver-
birds had made their welcome permanent,

weaving a wall of thin silken tears
that sang with the lips of broken earth,
rolled waves, resistant and durable wind.
From every pore on his body a river of song
or wail sprang and poured out.
His feet opened out like dark petals and chirped;
his fingers bloomed and plucked his heartstrings.
The song twined into the *makako* and jammed it;
the looped noose would not close, numbed.

Being political, he was not entitled
to the miraculous luck of criminals.
So they called in the prison doctor
to administer the *coup de grâce*.
He stabbed the chest with a thick
syringe and pumped the poison
into the heart with orgasmic release.

The heart made a sudden excited leap,
missed only one deceptive beat
and resumed its journey as usual.
Slowly he turned into a deep emerald green
and covered the whole country.

Like a stone he would not die.
They summoned a hard-core life prisoner,
placed a rock hammer in his hand
and ordered him to locate the victim's heart.
He bashed in the chest completely
and left a wide yawning gap. Not murder
technically, only routine execution.

Then a waterfall of blood! There was no one
that the blood did not touch and baptize.
Pilate searched vainly for water
to cleanse his hands of the *business*.
The song gushed out in a steady jet.
The body tolled its final knell
and then momentarily froze, then in a futile
move to cross the dark river before him,
he spread out his legs and kicked
and tried to rip the darkness that cloaked him.

Then...ah, this is *it* .
The final parting moment, the end, the last

wisp of breath escaping from his gaping mouth
again with the song rising like smoke.
He wanted the last swing, the final
expression of his freedom, arrested and preserved

before the sandbags dragged his compressed body
into the dark hole, into total oblivion.

JOSÉ CRAVEIRINHA

Cell 1

Here I am neurasthenic
like a dog
gone mad licking salty
scabs of old wounds.

With what words
and with what face
am I going to tell
my orphaned children to forget their father?

Translated from the Portuguese by Don Burness

José Craveirinha

Black Protest

I am coal!
And you uproot me brutally from the earth
And make me your mine
Boss!

I am coal!
And you set me on fire, boss
To serve you eternally as a source of energy
But not eternally
Boss!

I am coal!
And yes, it is my nature to become heat
And burn everything with the force of my combustion.

I am coal!
I must burn your world of exploitation
Burn until I become cinders of malediction
Burn with live heat like tar, my Brother
Until I am no longer your mine
Boss!

I am coal!
It is my nature to become heat
And burn everything with the fire from my combustion.

Yes!
I will be your coal
Boss!

Translated from the Portuguese by Don Burness

ANTÓNIO JACINTO

Monte Gracioso

Beyond the gratings
     The barbed wire
     The trench
Beyond the turrets
The soldiers, the sentry boxes, the sentries
     Gracioso

Called the
     "dry, fierce, sterile mountain" by Camôes
     Gracioso
The breadth of the sparrow hawks and xinxerotes
And the unconquerable imagination of the poet

Between earth and sky
Atop the pinnacle of the mountain
You Poetry, with a halo of clouds
Swept by winds from the Sahara
You Poetry
With a nod just for me.

1966

Translated from the Portuguese by Don Burness

JACK MAPANJE

Scrubbing The Furious Walls Of Mikuyu

Is this where they dump those rebels,
these haggard cells stinking of bucket
shit and vomit and the acrid urine of
yesteryears? Who would have thought I
would be gazing at these dusty, cobweb
ceilings of Mikuyu Prison, scrubbing
briny walls and riddling out impetuous
scratches of another dung-beetle locked
up before me here? Violent human palms
wounded these blood-bloated mosquitoes
and bugs (to survive), leaving these vicious
red marks. Monstrous flying cockroaches
crashed here. Up there the cobwebs trapped
dead bumblebees. Where did black wasps
get clay to build nests in this corner?

But here, scratches, insolent scratches!
I have marvelled at the rock paintings
of Mphunzi Hills once but these grooves
and notches on the walls of Mikuyu Prison,
how furious, what barbarous squiggles!
How long did this anger languish without
charge without trial without visit here and
what justice committed? This is the moment
we dreaded; when we'd all descend into
the pit, alone; without a wife or a child
without mother; without paper or pencil
without a story (just three Bibles for
ninety men) without charge without trial.
This is the moment I never needed to see.

Shall I scrub these brave squiggles out
of human memory then or should I perhaps
superimpose my own, less caustic; dare I
overwrite this precious scrawl? Who'd
have known I'd find another prey without
charge without trial (without bitterness)
in these otherwise blank walls of Mikuyu
Prison? No, I will throw my water and mop
elsewhere. We have liquidated too many
brave names out of the nation's memory;
I will not rub out another nor inscribe
my own, more ignoble, to consummate this
moment of truth I have always feared!

JACK MAPANJE

To The Unknown Dutch Postcard Sender (1988)

I

Your *Groeten uit Holland* postcard, with
Five pictures, dear unknown fighter for
My freedom, should not have arrived here
Really; first, your shameless address:
There are too many villages 'NEAR ZOMBA,
MALAWI', for anything to even stray into
Mikuyu Prison; then, I hear, with those
Bags upon bags of protest letters, papers,
Books, literary magazines, postcards,
Telexes, faxes and what not, received at
Central Sorting Office Limbe Post Office
Everyday, later dispatched to my Headmaster
And his henchpersons and the Special
Branch and their informers to burn, file
Or merely sneer at and drop in dustbins;
Your postcard had no business reaching
Mikuyu Prison. And how did you guess I
Would eventually sign my Detention Order
(No. 264), October 21, and I desperately
Desired some other solidarity signature
To stand by (to give me courage and cheer)
However Dutch, however enigmatic, stamped
Roosendaal, posted Den Haag 23 Oktober
1988, to buttress this shattered spirit
And these mottled bare feet squelching
On this sodden life-sucking rough cement
Of Mikuyu Prison ground? But many thanks,
Many thanks on behalf of these D4s too!

II

You send me those Dutch tourist colours
I'd probably have spurned outside; but
In these soggy red-brick and cracking
Cement walls, a sun-burned Dutch *clogger*

In black cap, blue shirt, orange apron,
Chocolate trousers and brown wooden shoes
Selling white, red, and yellow clogs,
Beside a basketful of more white clogs
Is spectacle too tantalizing for these
Badly holed Levi's shoes and blistered
Feet! You offer me Dutch menfolk in
White trousers and white shirts and red,
Blue, and yellow hats declaring heaps
On heaps of Edam cheeses on oval-shaped
Pine trays buoyantly shaming our ghoulish
Goulash of gangrenous cow bones mashed
In rabid weevil-ridden red kidney beans!
You proffer Dutch bell-shaped houses beside
Fruit trees, a family strolling along
The avenue; this concrete church with
Arches and Corinthian columns probably
Beat the bombs; a Dutch mother and daughter
In white folk-hats and black and white
Pretty frocks sitting on trimmed green
Lawn, offer each other red tulips beside
A colony of yellow tulips; and I present
You these malaria infested and graffiti
Bespattered walls, without doctors, priests
And twelve months of barred visits from
Wife, daughters, son, relatives, friends!

III

But however these colours slipped through
The sorters, your *Groeten uit Holland*,
My dear, has sent waves of hope and reason
To hang-on to the fetid walls of these
Cold cells; today the midnight centipedes
Shriller than howling hyenas will dissolve;
We will not feel those rats nibbling at
The rotting corns of our toes; and that
Midnight piss from those blotched lizards
Won't stink; and if that scorpion stings
Again tonight, the stampede in D4 will jump
In jubilation of our *Groeten uit Holland*.

Agostinho Neto

In Exhaustion He Thus Clamoured

I will say nothing
I never did anything against your country
but you stabbed ours
I never conspired never spoke with friends
or with the stars or the gods
never dreamed
I sleep like a stone flung in a well
and am stupid as vengeful butchery
I have never thought I am innocent
I will say nothing I know nothing
even if you beat me
I will say nothing
even if you offer me riches
I will say nothing
even if the *palmatória* crushes my fingers
I will say nothing
even if you offer me freedom
I will say nothing even if you shake my hand
I will say nothing even if threatened with death

Ah!
death
Someone died in my home
In my home was a small daughter
a shining star in the sky of my poverty
she died
I see the white garland of her innocence
trailing in waters over her body
black Ophelia in this putrid river of slavery
She died and who will hold her funeral?
who nail down her coffin?
who will dig her grave
who throw earth over her eternal bed?
Enclosed between four walls
without light
without seeing even the dead face of my daughter
I suffer the anguish of darkness

Burn me rather
take me to the lime kiln

incinerate my viscera and brain
and these hands that can do nothing
against the walls
against this metal door
against these armed men filled with fear
against torture

Roast me in the lime kiln
to end this torture of sleepless nights
to the lime kiln

On this infernal dawn
to the lime kiln
to the lime kiln

Who will bury my daughter?
The witchdoctors?
I already hear them dancing in the night
I see earth worms shining with funereal fat
carrying torches of fire to consume her

To the lime kiln
to end this torture
my daughter was burned in the lime kiln
suffering has ended for me
what will my brothers my friends say
those who hear my cries in this tomb
what will you say of a father who lets them burn
his daughter in a lime kiln?
Fling me into the flames
with the daughter of my love
my little star
to the lime kiln
to embrace my daughter
to the lime kiln
I will say nothing
I want no injections or sedatives
Ah! what a dream
To the lime kiln
To the lime kiln...

PIDE prison in Luanda, June 1960

Translated from the Portuguese by Marga Holness

SIPHO SEPAMLA

Tell Me News

Tell me of a brother
who hanged himself in prison
with a blanket
was he punch-drunk

Tell me of a brother
who flung himself to death
from the ninth floor of a building
did his grip fumble with the loneliness up there

Tell me of a hooded man
who picked out others of his blood on parade
was his skin beginning
to turn with solitude

Oh, tell me of a sister
who returned home pregnant
from a prison cell
has she been charged under the Immorality Act

Tell me of a brother
who hanged himself in jail
with a piece of his torn pair of jeans
was he hiding a pair of scissors in the cell

Tell me, tell me, sir
has the gruesome sight
of a mangled corpse
not begun to sit on your conscience

Noémia De Sousa

The Poem Of João

João was young like us
João had wide-awake eyes
and alert ears
hands reaching forwards
a mind cast for tomorrow
a mouth to cry an eternal "no"
João was young like us.

João enjoyed art and literature
enjoyed poetry and Jorge Amado
enjoyed books of meat and soul
which breathe life, struggle, sweat and hope
João dreamt of Zambezi's flowing books spreading culture
for mankind, for the young, our brothers
João fought that books might be for all
João loved literature
Joã was young like us.

João was the father, the mother, the brother of multitudes
João was the blood and the sweat of multitudes
and suffered and was happy like the multitudes
He smiled that same tired smile of shopgirls leaving work
He suffered with the passivity of the peasant women
he felt the sun piercing like a thorn in the Arab's midday
he bargained on bazaar benches with the Chinese
he sold tired green vegetables with the Asian traders
he howled spirituals from Harlem with Marian Anderson
he swayed to the Chope* marimbas on a Sunday
he cried out with the rebels their cry of blood
he was happy in the caress of the manioc-white moon
he sang with the *shibalos* their songs of homesick longing
and he hoped with the same intensity of all
for dazzling dawns with open mouths
to sing
Jaão was the blood and sweat of multitudes
João was young like us.

João and Mozambique were intermingled
João would not have been João without Mozambique
João was like a palm tree, a coconut palm

a piece of rock, a Lake Niassa, a mountain
an Incomati, a forest, a maçala tree
a beach, a Maputo, an Indian Ocean
João was an integral and deep-rooted part of Mozambique
João was young like us.

João longed to live and longed to conquer life
that is why he loathed prisons, cages, bars
and loathed the men who make them.
For João was free.
João was an eagle born to fly
João loathed prisons and the men who make them
João was young like us.

And because João was young like us
and had wide-awake eyes
and enjoyed art and poetry and Jorge Amado
and was the blood and sweat of multitudes
and was intermingled with Mozambique
and was an eagle born to fly
and hated prisons and the men who make them
Ah, because of all this we have lost João
We have lost João.

Ah, this is why we have lost João
why we weep night and day for João
for João whom they have stolen from us.

And we ask
But why have they taken João,
João who was young and ardent like us
João who thirsted for life
João who was brother to us all
why have they stolen from us João
who spoke of hope and dawning days
João whose glance was like a brother's hug
João who always had somewhere for one of us to stay

João who was our mother and our father
João who could have been our saviour
João whom we loved and love
João who belongs so surely to us
oh, why have they stolen João from us?
And no one answers
indifferent, no one answers.

But we know
why they took João from us
João, so truly our brother.

But what does it matter?
They think they have stolen him but João is here with us
is here in others who will come
in others who have come.
For João is not alone
João is a multitude
João is the blood and the sweat of multitudes
and João, in being João, is also Joaquim, José
Abdullah, Fang, Mussumbuluco, is Mascarenhas
Omar, Yutang, Fabiao
João is the multitude, the blood and sweat of multitudes.

And who will take José, Joaquim, Abdullah
Fang, Mussumbuluco, Mascarenhas, Omar, Fabiao?
Who?
Who will take us all and lock us in a cage?
Ah, they have stolen João from us
But João is us all
Because of this João hasn't left us
and João "was" not, he "is" and "will be"
For João is us all, we are a multitude
and the multitude
who can take the multitude and lock it in a cage?

* The Chope are a people of Inhambane Province and other parts of southern Mozambique who are master musicians and have been recruited to work in the South African mines.

Translated from the Portuguese by Margaret Dickinson

Kofi Awoonor

On Being Told Of Torture

For each hair on man, there is
a ledger in which the account
        will be written.
Time is not measured by the hourglass
but by the rivulets of blood
            shed
        and will be shed
Even though our bones crunch
our spirits will not break
        until we make a
                reckoning in the red bright book
                    of history.

He said he saw him lying
on the floor in his own blood
            unconscious
        delirium was his refuge
        from pain. In that state,
        my mother will bear arms
        and urge me to topple a govt.
        But, no matter what,
        there is still a tree blossoming
        now this New Year,
        there is goodwill on earth
            children still laugh
                lovers hold hands in dark corners,
            and the moon is new on all of us.

Weep not now my love
for as all die, so shall we
but it is not dying that should pain us.
It is the waiting, the
                intermission when we cannot act,
        when our will is shackled by tyranny.

That hurts.
Yet somehow, I know
the miracle of the world
will be wrought again.
        the space will be filled
        in spite of the hurt
        by the immensity of love
        that will defy dying
            and Death
                Good night, my love.

KOFI AWOONOR

From The Wayfarer Comes Home
(A poem in five movements)

For Naana in remembrance of her
      devotion and love
For Joseph Bruchac and my comrades in America
      whose concern I'll always cherish

I. The Promise

Even here in my cell
in the house of Ussher
I hear the guns.
They are killing the children of Soweto
      Even now
            as the southern winter ends
            and the first heat of Africa
            steadies itself for a journey,
            the children of Africa die.
It is not only the guns
Of Vorster you hear.
Listen again, carefully.
Then I heard a wren
in the morning of the alley sun
      Sing.
It is a long time since
I heard a bird cry.

So I came into the city alone
having walked the listening shore
where the salmon and the turtle store
their love among the water willows.
Of a sinning time I've already confessed
      abundantly. I rest now in my days of quietude.

What animals eat here
on this disastrous shore?
What says this black storm
in the fathomable wave of my river?
I love I love I love,
not the wispy geranium or the lily
but the curvature of your arms

the fragrance of your armpit after the rain
where the seed our son hides
waiting to be born.
I too have come home to be born
in the wake of the seed.
In the single way journey upon the sea.
My companions the flying fish
     heading towards the coast to Senegal.
  · We rode, we rode
     taking the waves
     as we traced the Middle Passage backwards
     in the smell of vomit
     our light bent for home
     grey in the August moon.
I sang on the sea of my love,
of you, home and invisible woman
whom I've known since conception
though you were lost once
among the high grass of infancy.
I searched for you in foreign lands
in the faces of strangers in the cities of Europe
on the subways of Manhattan
in the dripping trams of Chicago.
I searched for you among the picnic crowds
in Santa Barbara and Babylon
and once I thought I saw you
on the horizon in Texas or Louisiana
between Corpus Christi and Baton Rouge,
another time on the crowded train
between Tokyo and Hiroshima.

But you were another spirit
of another time and place.
You were the tired salmon
after the torrent time of the river
     But like the spirit
       and the fish
You swam on upon your journey.
You remain the visible flame of youth
the interstice between birth and dying,
the heady era of stolen drinks and kisses.

Will it be enough now
that I sing you, my love
in the slave fort of Ussher

the sun bleary eyed this September morning
annoyed dopey sulking
      in a corner of history's last day?
Will it be enough
that I cry for you my love
of nights in solitary
in my vast cell
listening to the prison cats in heat?

Oh how needless are all our days
and hours spent cutting our nails
spent dreaming of victory.
How futile the child's request in the night
when he knows
he seeks the impossible

So we share companionship
      with evil animals
           our fellow travellers in a leaky canoe.

I was once king of the moutain
I mean the range that stretches across Togo.
I was the lion that roamed the violent shores.
The Volta was a river of passion then
And in the valley Datsutagba
history was made by ancestral spears.
I was once the ferryman of the river.
      But now I weep now
      in a slave cell
      remembering only the whisper of your face
      the abundance and multitude of your promise

      Is it enough
that the children of the mountain
      and the salt waters
      die in the storm in a leaky canoe?
It is enough
      the valley's lost its shimmer
      on this sultry September day?

Ussher Fort Prison, 17-22 September 1976

WOLE SOYINKA

To The Madmen Over The Wall

Howl, howl
Your fill and overripeness of the heart,
I may not come with you
Companions of the broken buoy
I may not seek
The harbour of your drifting shore.

Your wise withdrawal
Who can blame? Crouched
Upon your ledge of space, do you witness
Ashes of reality drift strangely past?
I fear
Your minds have dared the infinite
And journeyed back
To speak in foreign tongues.

Though walls
May rupture tired seams
Of the magic cloak we share, yet
Closer I may not come
But though I set my ears against
The tune of setting forth, yet, howl
Upon the hour of sleep, tell these walls
The human heart may hold
Only so much despair.

WOLE SOYINKA

Your Logic Frightens Me, Mandela

Your logic frightens me, Mandela
Your logic frightens me. Those years
Of dreams, of time accelerated in
Visionary hopes, of savoring the task anew,
The call, the tempo primed
To burst in supernovae round a "brave new world"!
Then stillness. Silence. The world closes round
Your sole reality; the rest is . . . dreams?

Your logic frightens me.
How coldly you disdain legerdemains!
"Open Sesame" and – two decades' rust on hinges
Peels at the touch of a conjurer's wand?
White magic, ivory-topped black magic wand,
One moment wand, one moment riot club
Electric cattle prod and whip or *sjambok*
Tearing flesh and spilling blood and brain?

This bag of tricks, whose silk streamers
Turn knotted cords to crush dark temples?
A rabbit punch sneaked beneath the rabbit?
Doves metamorphosed in milk-white talons?
Not for you the olive branch that sprouts
Gun muzzles, barbed-wire garlands, tangled thorns
To wreathe the brows of black, unwilling Christs.

Your patience grows inhuman, Mandela.
Do you grow food? Do you make friends
Of mice and lizards? Measure the growth of grass
For time's unhurried pace?
Are you now the crossword puzzle expert?
Chess? Ah, no! Subversion lurks among
Chess pieces. Structured clash of black and white,
Equal ranged and paced? An equal board? No!
Not on Robben Island. Checkers? Bad to worse.
That game has no respect for class or king-serf
Ordered universe. So, scrabble?

Monopoly? Now, that . . . ! You know
The game's modalities, so do they.

Come collection time, the cards read "White Only"
In the Community Chest. Like a gambler's coin
Both sides heads or tails, the "Chance" cards read:
Go to jail. Go straight to jail. Do not pass "GO".
Do not collect a hundredth rand. Fishes feast,
I think, on those who sought to by-pass "GO"
On Robben Island.

Your logic frightens me, Mandela, your logic
Humbles me. Do you tame geckos?
Do grasshoppers break your silences?
Bats' radar pips pinpoint your statuesque
Gaze transcending distances at will?
Do moths break wing
Against a light bulb's fitful glow
That brings no searing illumination?
Your sight shifts from moth to bulb,
Rests on its pulse-glow fluctuations –
Are kin feelings roused by a broken arc
Of tungsten trapped in vacuum?

Your pulse, I know, has slowed with earth's
Phlegmatic turns. I know your blood
Sagely warms and cools with seasons,
Responds to the lightest breeze
Yet scorns to race with winds (or hurricanes)
That threaten change on tortoise pads.

Is our world light-years away, Mandela?
Lost in visions of that dare supreme
Against a dire supremacy of race,
What brings you back to earth? The night guard's
Inhuman tramp? A sodden eye transgressing through
The Judas hole? Tell me Mandela,
That guard, is he *your* prisoner?

Your bounty threatens me, Mandela, that taut
Drumskin of your heart on which our millions
Dance. I fear we latch, fat leeches
On your veins. Our daily imprecisions
Dull keen edges of your will.
Compromises deplete your act's repletion –
Feeding will-voided stomachs of a continent,
What will be left of you, Mandela?

South-East Asia
Pacific Rim
Australia

AI QING

Dayanhe – My Wet-Nurse

Dayanhe, my wet-nurse:
Her name was the name of the village which gave her birth;
She was a child-bride:
My wet-nurse, Dayanhe.

I am the son of a landlord,
But I have been brought up on Dayanhe's milk:
The son of Dayanhe.
Raising me Dayanhe raised her own family;
I am one who was raised on your milk,
Oh Dayanhe, my wet-nurse.

Dayanhe, today, looking at the snow falling makes me think of you:
Your grass-covered, snow-laden grave,
The withered weeds on the tiled eaves of your shut-up house,
Your garden-plot, ten-foot square, and mortgaged,
Your stone seat just outside the gate, overgrown with moss,
Dayanhe, today, looking at the snow falling makes me think of you.

With your great big hands, you cradled me to your breast, soothing me;
After you had stoked the fire in the oven,
After you had brushed off the coal-ashes from your apron,
After you had tasted for yourself whether the rice was cooked,
After you had set the bowl of black soybeans on the black table,
After you had mended your sons' clothes, torn by thorns on the mountain
        ridge,
After you had bandaged the hand of your little son, nicked with a cleaver,
After you had squeezed to death, one by one, the lice on your children's shirts,
After you had collected the first egg of the day,
With your great big hands, you cradled me to your breast, soothing me.

I am the son of a landlord,
After I had taken all the milk you had to offer,
I was taken back to my home by the parents who gave me birth.
Ah, Dayanhe, why are you crying?

I was a newcomer to the parents who gave me birth!
I touched the red-laquered, floral-carved furniture,
I touched the ornate brocade on my parents' bed,
I looked dumbly at the 'Bless This House' sign above the door - which I
        couldn't read,

I touched the buttons of my new clothes, made of silk and mother-of-pearl,
I saw in my mother's arms a sister whom I scarcely knew,
I sat on a laquered stool with a small brazier set underneath,
I ate white rice which had been milled three times.
Still, I was bashful and shy! Because I,
I was a newcomer to the parents who gave me birth.
Dayanhe, in order to survive,
After her milk had run dry,
She began to put those arms, arms that had cradled me, to work,
Smiling, she washed our clothes,
Smiling, she carried the vegetables, and rinsed them in the icy pond by the
     village,
Smiling, she sliced the turnips frozen through and through,
Smiling, she stirred the swill in the pigs' trough,
Smiling she fanned the flames under the stove with the broiling meat,
Smiling, she carried the baling baskets of beans and grain to the open square
     where they baked in the sun,
Dayanhe, in order to survive,
After the milk in her had run dry,
She put those arms, arms that had cradled me, to work.

Dayanhe was so devoted to her foster-child, whom she suckled;
At New Year's, she'd busy herself cutting winter-rice candy for him,
For him, who would steal off to her house by the village,
For him, who would walk up to her and call her 'Mama',
Dayanhe, she would stick his drawing of Guan Yu, the war god, bright green
     and bright red, on the wall by the stove,
Dayanhe, how she would boast and brag to her neighbors about her foster-
     child.
Dayanhe, once she dreamt a dream she could tell no one,
In her dream, she was drinking a wedding toast to her foster-child,
Sitting in a resplendent hall bedecked with silk,
And the beautiful young bride called her affectionately, 'Mother.'
....
Dayanhe, she was so devoted to her foster-child!

Dayanhe, in a dream from which she has not awakened, has died.
When she died, her foster-child was not at her side,
When she died, the husband who often beat her shed tears for her.
Her five sons each cried bitter tears,
When she died feebly, she called out the name of her foster-child,
Dayanhe is dead:
When she died, her foster-child was not at her side.

Dayanhe, she went with tears in her eyes!
Along with forty-nine years, a lifetime of humiliation at the hands of the world,
Along with the innumerable sufferings of a slave,
Along with a two-bit casket and some bundles of rice-straw,
Along with a plot of ground to bury a casket in a few square feet,
Along with a handful of ashes, from paper money burned,
Dayanhe, she went with tears in her eyes.

But these are the things that Dayanhe did not know:
That her drunkard husband is dead,
That her eldest son became a bandit,
That her second died in the smoke of war,
That her third, fourth, her fifth,
Live on vilified by their teachers and their landlords,
And I - I write condemnations of this unjust world.
When I, after drifting about for a long time, went home
On the mountain ridge, in the wilds,
When I saw my brothers, we were closer than we were 6 or 7 years ago,
This, this is what you, Dayanhe, calmly sleeping in repose,
This is what you do not know!

Dayanhe, today, your foster-child is in jail,
Writing a poem of praise, dedicated to you,
Dedicated to your spirit, purple shade under the brown soil,
Dedicated to your outstretched arms that embrace me,
Dedicated to your lips that kissed me,
Dedicated to your face, warm and soft, the color of earth,
Dedicated to your breasts that suckled me,
Dedicated to your sons, my brothers,
Dedicated to all of them on earth,
The wet-nurses like my Dayanhe, and all their sons,
Dedicated to Dayanhe, who loved me as she loved her own sons.

Dayanhe,
I am one who grew up suckling at your breasts,
Your son.
I pay tribute to you,
With all my love.

On a snowy morning,
January 14, 1933

Translated from the Chinese by Eugene Chen Eoyang

BEI DAO

Declaration

for Yu Luoke

Perhaps the final hour is come
I have left no testament
Only a pen for my mother
I am no hero
In an age without heroes
I just want to be a man

The still horizon
Divides the ranks of the living and the dead
I can only choose the sky
I will not kneel on the ground
Allowing the executioners to look tall
The better to obstruct the wind of freedom

From star-like bullet holes shall flow
A blood-red dawn

Translated from the Chinese by Bonnie S. McDougall

BEI DAO

An End Or A Beginning

for Yu Luoke

Here I stand
Replacing another, who has been murdered
So that each time the sun rises
A heavy shadow, like a road
Shall run across the land

A sorrowing mist
Covers the uneven patchwork of roofs
Between one house and another
Chimneys spout ashy crowds
Warmth effuses from gleaming trees
Lingering on the wretched cigarette stubs
Low black clouds arise
From every tired hand

In the name of the sun
Darkness plunders openly
Silence is still the story of the East
People on age-old frescoes
Silently live forever
Silently die and are gone

Ah, my beloved land
Why don't you sing any more
Can it be true that even the ropes of the Yellow River towmen
Like sundered lute-strings
Reverberate no more
True that time, this dark mirror
Has also turned its back on you forever
leaving only stars and drifting clouds behind

I look for you
In every dream
Every foggy night or morning
I look for spring and apple trees
Every wisp of breeze stirred up by honey bees
I look for the seashore's ebb and flow

The seagulls formed from sunlight on the waves
I look for the stories built into the wall
Your forgotten name and mine

If fresh blood could make you fertile
The ripened fruit
On tomorrow's branches
Would bear my colour

I must admit
That I trembled
In the death-white chilly light
Who wants to be a meteorite
Or a martyr's ice-cold statue
Watching the unextinguished fire of youth
Pass into another's hand
Even if doves alight on its shoulder
It can't feel their bodies' warmth and breath
They preen their wings
And quickly fly away

I am a man
I need love
I long to pass each tranquil dusk
Under my love's eyes
Waiting in the cradle's rocking
For the child's first cry
On the grass and fallen leaves
On every sincere gaze
I write poems of life
This universal longing
Has now become the whole cost of being a man

I have lied many times
In my life
But I have always honestly kept to
The promise I made as a child
So that the world which cannot tolerate
A child's heart
Has still not forgiven me

Here I stand
Replacing another, who has been murdered
I have no other choice
And where I fall

Another will stand
A wind rests on my shoulders
Stars glimmer in the wind

Perhaps one day
The sun will become a withered wreath
To hang before
The growing forest of gravestones
Of each unsubmitting fighter
Black crows the night's tatters
Flock thick around

AUTHORS NOTE: The first draft of this poem was written in 1975. Some good friends of mine fought side by side with Yu Luoke, and two of them were thrown into prison where they languished for three years. This poem records our tragic and indignant protest in that tragic and indignant period.

Translated from the Chinese by Bonnie S. McDougall

BEI DAO

A Picture

for Tiantian's fifth birthday

Morning arrives in a sleeveless dress
apples tumble all over the earth
my daughter is drawing a picture
how vast is a five-year-old sky
your name has two windows
one opens towards a sun with no clock-hands
the other opens towards your father
who has become a hedgehog in exile
taking with him a few unintelligible characters
and a bright red apple
he has left your painting
how vast is a five-year-old sky

* Tiantian, the nickname given to the poet's daughter, is written with two characters which look like a pair of windows. The same character also forms a part of the character for the word 'picture'.

Translated from the Chinese by Bonnie S. McDougall and Chen Maipeng

DAI WANGSHU

A Severed Finger

On an old bookshelf heavy with dust
I keep a severed finger in a jar.
Whenever boredom finds me looking out some ancient tome,
A memory's recalled, which fills me with its muted sadness.
It was cut from the hand of a friend who gave his life.
It is pale and wiry like my friend.
I am often preoccupied, recalling those times when
He gave me his finger. They are often clearly before me:

'Keep this laughable, this pitiable, fond remembrance for me, Wangshu;
On the lonely edges of existence, it can only increase my misfortune.'
His speech was deep and gentle, like a sigh,
And his eyes held tears, though they were smiling.

I am uncertain about his 'pitiable and laughable love',
But I do know that he was taken from the home of a worker,
And then it was torture, and then it was a miserable cell,
And then it was execution, and now we all expect to die.

I am uncertain about his 'laughable and pitiable love'.
The last time he spoke of it, we were both drunk,
But I imagine it *was* a pitiable tale – which he kept secret –
Which he believed would be forgotten, along with its severed finger.

This severed finger shows its scars through printer's ink.
They are red, they are a lovely gleaming red.
They glisten and shine on the severed finger
Like his glances in my heart:
   still reproaching the cowardice of others.

This severed finger summons up a gentle but persistent sadness,
But for me it is also my most necessary treasure.
Whenever I come to a time of triviality or despair
I shall say, 'Right now, let's fetch down that glass jar.'

Translated from the Chinese by John Cayley

GU CHENG

A Generation

The pitch black night gave me two deep black eyes
with which to search for light.

Translated from the Chinese by Sam Hamill

An Ending

In the blink of an eye –
the landslide had come to a halt,
a heap of great men's skulls at the river's edge.

A schooner draped in mourning
passed slowly by
unfurling its darkened shroud.

How many graceful verdant trees,
their trunks deformed by pain,
are consoling the brave and strong with their tears.

God buries the broken moon
in heavy mists –
already everything is ended

Translated from the Chinese by John Cayley

LIAO YIWU

From Slaughter

Part IV

Cry Cry Cry Cry Crycrycrycrycrycrycrycry
While you still haven't been surrounded and annihilated, while you still have
    strength left to suck milk, crycrycry
Let your sobs cast you off, fuse into radio, television, radar, give repeated
    testimony of the slaughter
Let your sobs cast you off, fuse into plant life, semi-vegetative life
        and micro-organisms, blossom into flower after flower, year
                after year mourning the dead, mourning yourself
Let your sobs be distorted, twisted, annihilated by the tumult of the sacrosanct
    battle
The butchers come from the east of the city, from the west of the city, from
    the south and north of the city
Metal helmets glint in the light. They're singing . . . . .
The sun rises in the east, the sun rises in the west, the sun rises in the south
    and north
Putrid, sweltering summer, people and ghosts sing . . . . .
Don't go to the east, don't go to the west, don't go to the south and north

We stand in the midst of brilliance, but all people are blind
We stand on a great road, but no one is able to walk
We stand in the midst of a cacophony, but all are mute
We stand in the midst of heat and thirst, but all refuse to drink

People with no understanding of the times, people in the midst of calamity,
    people who plot to shoot down the sun
You can only cry, you're still crying, crycrycrycrycrycrycry!
    CRYCRY! CRY!
You've been smothered to death, baked to death, your whole body is on fire!
    And still you're crying
You get up on stage and act out a farce, you're paraded before crowds in
    streets, and still you're crying
Your eyeballs explode, scald the surrounding crowd, and still you're crying
You post a bounty on yourself, find out yourself, you say you were mistaken,
    this accursed epoch is all wrong! And still you're crying
You are stamped into meat pie, you cry
From meat pie you're stamped into minced meat, you cry
A dog licks up the minced meat, you cry inside a dog's belly!
    CRYCRYCRY!

In this historically unprecedented slaughter only the spawn of dogs can survive

Translated from the Chinese by Michael Day

WEN YIDUO

Quiet Night

This light, and the light-bleached four walls,
The kind table and chair, intimate as friends,
The scent of old books, reaching me in whiffs,
My favourite teacup as serene as a meditating nun,
The baby sucking contentedly at his mother's breast,
A snore reporting the healthy slumber of my big son...
This mysterious quiet night, this calm peace.
In my throat quiver songs of gratitude,
But the songs soon become ugly curses.
Quiet night, I cannot accept your bribe.
Who treasures this walled-in square foot of peace?
My world has a much wider horizon.
As the four walls cannot silence the clamor of war,
How can you stop the violent beat of my heart?
Better that my mouth be filled with mud and sand,
Than to sing the joy and sorrow of one man alone;
Better that moles dig holes in this head of mine,
And vermin feed on my flesh and blood,
Than to live only for a cup of wine and a book of verse,
Or an evening of serenity brought by the ticking clock,
Hearing not the groans and sighs from all my neighbours,
Seeing not the shivering shadows of the widows and orphans,
And the convulsion in battle trenches, and men biting their sickbeds,
And all the tragedies ground out under the millstone of life.
Happiness, I cannot accept your bribe now.
My world is not within this walled-in square foot.
Listen, here goes another cannon-report, another roar of Death.
Quiet night, how can you stop the violent beat of my heart?

1927

Translated from the Chinese by Kai-Yu Hsu

Yang Lian

1989

who says the dead can embrace?
like fine horses   manes silver grey
standing outside the window in the freezing moonlight
the dead are buried in the days of the past
in days not long past   madmen were tied onto beds
rigid as iron nails
pinning down the timbers of darkness
the coffin lid each day closing over like this

who says the dead are dead and gone?   the dead
enclosed in the vagrancy of their final days
are the masters of forever
four portraits of themselves on four walls
butchery yet again   blood
is still the only famous landscape
slept into the tomb they were lucky   but they wake again in
a tomorrow the birds fear even more
this is no doubt a perfectly ordinary year

Translated from the Chinese by Brian Holton

Bo Yang

To My Daughter Jiajia
On The Eve Of My Release

When you were first born
The autumn rain was just falling
I kept a solitary watch in the long hall
Muttering prayers to the gods
The nurse came at last to announce
She said a girl had been born
That girl was you of course
My heart was like a cow's as she licks her new calf
You cried and my heart broke
You laughed and my heart rejoiced
I watched as you slowly grew up
Taking your first wobbly steps
When you first entered the nursery
You wept as soon as we parted
Carrying you I came straight back
And helped you make a pony tail
When you caught the pox you couldn't bear air or light
So we kept your door and window closed day and night
The fever burned your body like a flame
As I held you terror clutched me again and and again
You've hated to eat ever since you were young
As soon as mealtime came so did mischief
Once you sneaked some dog food
And were so sick you almost died
In the hospital you lay in your bed
I kept you company lying on the floor
When you answered the phone at age five
You were already quick with your words
When you were angry you'd shout 'stinking daddy'
And stamp your foot like a thunderclap
When you were six you tested into kindergarten
100 percent your grade was the highest
You would play on the slide over and over
I'd call you a thousand times but you wouldn't leave
Going to class we'd have someone take you
Coming home I would meet you myself
On the way back you clung to my arms
I felt as if I were a swing

You'd climb up onto my shoulders and smell the cigarette smoke
Then climb over and sit on my knee
Whenever you got into trouble you'd look for me
And hug my neck and whisper in my ear
You'd run off to find your friends and wouldn't come back
Frightening me so much I'd roam the streets looking for you
As frantic as a wild man
Sweat drenching my body
On the day that I left home
You were already in the eighth grade
Sitting on the floor watching televison
You even joked with the police
It's been eight years since I left
Each time I remember my heart goes cold
In my dreams I still call you
On waking I get up and sit again
Now that I'm about to return home
You've already grown tall and straight
My home has been broken
My child has survived
You no longer know me
Thinking of you I cry

Translated from the Chinese by Stephen L. Smith and Robert Reynolds

Kim Chi Ha

The Yellow Dust Road

Following the vivid blood, blood on the yellow road,
I am going, Father, where you died.
Now it's pitch dark, only the sun scorches.
Hands are barbed-wired.
The hot sun burns sweat and tears and rice-paddies
Under the bayonets through the summer heat.
I am going, Father, where you died,
Where you died wrapped in a rice-sack
When the trout were jumping along the *Pujuu* brookside,
When the blaze rose from *Opo* Hill every night,
On that day when the sun shone brightly on the yellow land,
The muddy land resilient as the gorse that grows intrepidly green.

Shall we cry out the call of that day?
Shall we sing the song of that day?

In small *Whadang* village embraced among the sparse bamboo-bushes,
Blood surges up in every well, every ten years.
Born in this barren colony,
Slain under the bayonets, my Father,
How could the dew in the bamboo-buds that spring
Forget, ever forget the crystal brightness of May?
It was a long and cruel summer,
When even the children were starving,
That sultry summer of blatant tyranny
That knew not of the Heavens
Or the yellow road, eternally our motherland,
Our hope.

Following the muddy beach where the sun burns the old wooden boats to dust,
Again through the rice paddies
And over the bleached, whitish furrows.
It's been ten years since the call of that day
That thundered against the ever blue and high firmament –
The flesh, the breath, tightened by barbed-wire.
I can hear your voice.

I am going now, Father, where you died
When the trout were jumping along the *Pujuu* brookside,
Where you died
Wrapped in a rice-sack.
Where you died.

Kim Chi Ha's native Cholla-Do province has for centuries been a hotbed of revolutionary fervor. The Yellow Dust Road commemorates a rising of Cholla-Do villagers in protest against the abject circumstances of the early postwar period. Whadang's bamboo bushes were cut and fashioned into staves to be used against the military forces sent to quell the rebellion by the Synghman Rhee government. The fires ignited on Opo Hill signalled the start of the uprising, in which one-third of the village's six hundred farmers were massacred alongside Pujuu Brook.

Translated from the Korean by an international group of Kim Chi Ha's friends and associates and the editorial staff of Autumn Press.

Ko Un

Sunlight

It's absolutely inevitable!
So just take a deep breath
and accept this adversity.
But look!
A distinguished visitor deigns to visit
my tiny north-facing cell.
Not the chief making his rounds, no,
but a ray of sunlight as evening falls,
a gleam no bigger than a screwed-up stamp.
A sweetheart fit to go crazy about.
It settles there on the palm of a hand,
warms the toes of a shyly bared foot.
Then as I kneel and, undevoutly,
offer it a dry, parched face to kiss,
in a moment that scrap of sunlight slips away.
After the guest has departed through the bars,
the room feels several times colder and darker.
This military prison special cell
is a photographer's darkroom.
Without any sunlight I laughed like a fool.
One day it was a coffin holding a corpse.
One day it was altogether the sea.
A wonderful thing!
A few people survive here.

Being alive is a sea
          without a single sail in sight.

Translated from the Korean by Brother Anthony of Taizé and Young-Moo Kim

KO UN

When May Is Gone

What shall we do when May is gone?
What shall we do when May is gone?
One day in May at dark midnight
          martial law dropped down on us;
we were dragged away like so many dogs,
beaten and punched as we went along;
so what shall we do when May is gone?
One day in May we all rose up,
clasping a thousand years' rage in our hands,
          clenching bare fists, we all rose up.
Charging down the green-leafed road,
down Kumnam Street—Liberation Road, our road—
          we all rose up that day;
our hearts were ablaze
as we drove out dark night.
Our cry: Democracy! The Masses! The Nation!
We rose up against our land's division,
imposed betrayal,
against the tanks reinforcing
forty years' brutal martial law.
Sing! Fight! Sadly bury these bodies!
Down the green-leaved road, our road,
soon we were felled, felled by their guns,
spouting blood, we dropped,
          spouting crimson blood.
We were dragged away, fallen corpses
covered in grey dust, covered in ashes,
we were carried away like so many dead dogs,
carried off somewhere in fast army trucks.
Ah, Mangwoldong! Not only there! Not only there!
Still they lie in unknown places,
buried there. Seven hundred? Eight hundred?
          Two thousand of us?
What shall we do when May is gone?
One day in May we fought to the end;
around the Provincial Government Capitol,
down scattered back-alleys we fought on and on,
trampling the stains of our dead comrades' blood.
We fought on, proudly bearing the name of
the Kwangju Struggle Citizens' Army.

Brought low by foreign interests,
brought low by compradors,
brought low by all the dregs of Yushin;
defending our land from further disgrace,
our breasts were pierced and so we died.
What shall we do when May is gone?
As night was falling a high school boy
came tearing his clothes out there in the road
in front of the Capitol,
his shout went echoing down the street:
My sister's been murdered! It's brutal, inhuman!
Give me a gun! I can fight too!
Just then they shot him, that student died there.
A girl's sweet milky breast was sliced like curds,
       and so they sliced
gentle girls, pregnant wives, and they all died.
Down roads, down side-streets, and cul-de-sacs,
men died and were brutally hauled away.
Democracy! The Masses! The Nation!
Down that street, one day in May,
suddenly, alas, the savages drew near:
the 20th Division from Yangpyong,
       special troops,
the 31st Divison,
the 7th airborne, the 3rd, the 11th,
martial law troops came smashing through.
Striking at random with M16 rifles,
smashing down butt-ends,
slashing and slashing with bayonets fixed,
stinking strong of drink;
all who surrendered were shot, as well.
Ah, it was hell; screaming and crying
       surging like waves.
What shall we do when May is gone?
What shall we do when May is gone?
Then over all that whirlpool of terror
spread a tomb-like silence,
covering the dead and the living alike.
What shall we do when May is gone?
We really should have started all over again
       out of death;
those who lived, forgetting to grieve,
should have started again
       out there on the streets of death;
but we have died and have no words,

we're alive and have no words,
we're in prison cooking grit,
with never a glimpse of the sky above,
we're all of us silently gnashing our teeth,
            each heart brimming full
with a thousand years' bitter resentment,
swallowing down this age of shame.
The 5th Republic's army boots go clattering
            down the streets of outrage.
When that May was past, we loaded death
            on our backs,
and one bitter day for the first time went out
to Kumnam Street and Chungjang Street;
we recognized each other and retrieved
            the handshakes they had robbed us of:
You're still alive! You're still alive too!
But then we went quickly to Mangwoldong,
            and there we wept.
Since then we have united every year
            and risen up again.
Several times we have seen how
with two puffs of our hot breath
we could identify
shadowy enemies, our foes on the other side.
In our country's sky
the Stars and Stripes flies high.
Over our country, see, Japanese swarming.
Kwangju today is no longer Kwangju.
Kwangju is not just Kwangju.
It is the nucleus of our country's history.
Since then, every street has risen up.
Every village has gathered murmuring.
With workers' lives turned into lumps of coal,
with beef bought no dearer than a load of shit,
farmers have swallowed pesticide,
too many of them have fallen and died.
Taxi drivers have died in a sea of flame,
families have died by coal-brick fumes.
What shall we do when May is gone?
Students have committed self-immolation,
            a heroic end.
Dozens have volunteered,
and wait to do the same.
What shall we do when May is gone?
Billions of Won spent on tear gas bombs,

apple-shaped bombs, zig-zag bombs,
bombs have hit eyes and put them out,
bombs have hit breasts and put lives out.
You throw just one stone, you're carted off,
beaten with truncheons till you vomit blood.
What shall we do when May is gone?
What shall we do when May is gone?
In factoies, in schools,
the fight for justice goes on unending,
in prison too, till victory comes.
But in the towns of deceit
the flag of America proudly flies.
The Japanese LDP come and go merrily.
They come and go like eunuchs
making visits to parents-in-law.
Even Yushin rubbish makes a return,
intent on grabbing its fair share too.
What shall we do when May is gone?
If we're to smash these foreign powers,
these compradors, this treachery,
if we're to sweep away our land's division,
and this fascist rabble here,
if we're to achieve our autonomy,
our equality, our reunification,
if we're to dance for once our dance
upon old history's dance-floor here,
today we have to let our bodies
grimly rot and die.
Then, buried deep within this history,
dead, we shall fight on.
Feverishly living, we shall fight on.
For see how now we live suffocating.
Ah, May, May!
Glorious fresh green,
dazzling days, ah May!
What shall we do when May is gone?
Days thick with tear gas,
tears pouring down,
hacking coughs,
the cuckoo is calling, in the night,
sadly, the cuckoo is calling.
What shall we do when May is gone?
Alas, dead champions, departed friends!
Our hundred year's battle is still not done!
We shall have to fight on

a hundred years more, old friends!
We shall have to fight on from age to age!
What shall we do when May is gone?
What shall we do when May is gone?
But always we'll unite anew.
Scattered, we'll always gather again.
Blood-seething May!
Month of struggle, tossing body and soul,
May, you are us!
See us advancing united,
through the parting ocean waves!
Though May must go by,
for us May is ever alive.
Yes, we, we are May, we are May!
A great outcry arises from our people's seventy million throats.
The frontline of joy exploding that morning
in this land!
Embrace!
For such is our May! Liberation arising out of death.
May that day quickly come!

Translated from the Korean by Brother Anthony of Taizé and Young-Moo Kim

Yi Yuksa

Deep Purple Grapes

In July in my native land
Purple grapes ripen in the sun.

Village wisdom clusters on the vines
As distant skies enter each berry.

The sea below the sky opens its heart,
A white sail moves toward shore.

The traveler I long for would come then,
Wrapping his wayworn body with a blue robe.

If only I could share these grapes with him
I wouldn't mind if the juice wet my hands.

Child, take out a white linen napkin,
Spread it on our table's silver platter.

Translated from the Korean by Peter H. Lee

Ho Chi Minh

From Prison Diary

Tungzhen

Tungzheng jail can be compared to Pingma:
Each meal a bowl of gruel, the stomach as good as empty.
But water and light we can have aplenty,
And each day for airing the cells are twice opened.

The Stocks

I

Opening a hungry mouth like a wicked monster,
Each night the stocks seize the ankles of the prisoner.
Their jaws grip the right leg of the wretch;
Only the left is free to bend and stretch.

II

There happen in this world things even stranger:
People jostle to get their feet in first.
For once locked in there's some hope of peaceful slumber;
Otherwise, where to lie tranquil on this crowded ground?

Transferred To Tianbao On "Double Ten" Day

Every house is decked with lanterns and flowers:
It's national day, the whole country is filled with delight.
But this is the moment I am put in chains for transfer:
Contrary winds continue to hamper the eagle's flight.

Tenth of October, the Chinese National Day under the Kuomintang regime.

Overnight Stop At Lungquan

All day my two horses* have trotted, tireless.
When night comes I'm served with five spice chicken.**
Bed-bugs and cold draughts attack, merciless.
How welcome, the dawn song of the golden oriole!

*Jokingly, the two legs
**To cook this dish, the legs of the chicken are tied crosswise. A jocular description of the way the prisoner's limbs are bound at night.

Scabies

Blotched red and blue as though dressed in brocade;
Scratching all day you'd think we were playing the guitar.
As honoured guests, we make a parade of our rich attire.
Strange virtuosos, sharing an itch for music we surely are!

Good-bye To A Tooth

You were, my friend, hard and unyielding;
Not like the tongue, soft and sinuous.
The bitter and the sweet we have shared till now,
But this day each of us must go his way.

Cold Night

In the cold autumn night, with neither quilt nor mattress
I curl myself up for warmth but cannot close my eyes.
Moonlight on the banana-palms adds to the chill.
I look through the bars: the Little Bear has lain down in the skies.

Note: Ho Chi Minh originally wrote these quatrains in Chinese

Translated from the Vietnamese by Dang The Binh

NGUYEN CHI THIEN

I Kept Silent

I kept silent when I was tortured by my enemy:
With iron and with steel, soul faint in agony –
The heroic stories are for children to believe.
I kept silent because I kept telling myself:
Has anyone, who entered the jungle and who was run over
    by the wild beast
Been stupid enough to open his mouth and ask for mercy?

Translated from the Vietnamese by Nguyen Huu Hieu

NGUYEN CHI THIEN

From Sundry Notes

(15)

I roll from prison camp to prison camp:
unwashed, foul-smelling clothes, a hirsute face;
so starved that all my ribs, my backbone show.
But mosquitoes, bedbugs, germs still care for me.

(16)

Hand over fist they toss
good people into jails to die
while shooting off their mouths:
"People are precious capital!"

(17)

Besides sheer famine and dire woe,
the age of Ho Chi Minh
looms large in these two shapes:
prisoner's graves and soldiers' tombs.

(20)

On Uncle Ho's own soil,
life's sadder than a tomb.
In the black night of his regime,
light flashes only when guns bark.

(30)

Flowers from hell – real blood has watered them,
blood mixed with animal sweat, with parting tears.
Blooming in prison, sickly, starved and cold,
they reek of damp and mold, look gray as mud.

(68)

Short measure get all sentiments in jail,
where friendship weighs less than a cigarette,
where loyalty, like a report card, spreads thin,
where self-respect a spoon of rice knocks down.

Translated from the Vietnamese by Huynh Sanh Thong

TO HUU

The State Of A Prisoner's Soul

To Huu: "These are thoughts..."

How heavy it is, the solitude of a prisoner!
Ear strained, heart boiling,
I listen passionately to the noises of life
which is flowing outside with an immense happiness!

Here – twilight, pallid gleams of the evening
slip furtively past the bars of the little window;
here – the coldness of four bare walls;
here – an alignment of planks on the ironwood floor.

Twittering of birds in the tide of a strong wind rising:
swift rustling of night bats, their wings beating;
tinkle of bells as a horse paws the ground by a well of cold water;
far below on the road the clatter of passing clogs.

Oh! today how the sap of life overflows
in all these familiar noises.
I hear the wind pouring through the boughs, through the tips of the leaves.
I hear the healthy vigour of a hundred species.
Half dreaming I hear how all things outside
murmur together gently in the vastness of space
gorging themselves on the nectar of life drunk on flowers and fruits
and with the fragrance of liberty which perfumes each one of a thousand days.

All these mirages of my innocent soul
suddenly for a brief minute make me forget how sad life is
there outside... how many imprisoned destinies
are crushed in depths of fathomless despair.
This evening in prison, bitterness in my heart,
I am only one among suffering humanity.
I am only a little bird, a young one,
thrown into a tiny cage in the midst of a great cage.
. . .
Far off in the wind comes the sound of a horn...

Cell No. 1
Thua Thien Prison,
19-4-1939

Translated from the Vietnamese by Elizabeth Hodgkin and Mary Jameson

U Sam Oeur

Exodus

Once the Blackcrows had usurped the power
they started to evacuate people from Phnom Penh;
they threw patients through hospital windows
(women in labor and the lame), drove tanks
over them then bulldozed them under.

The sun shone bright, as if it had come close to the earth.
The ground was dried and cracked.
Millions of panicked Phnompenhards jostled each other,
desperately overflowing along prescribed routes.*

Out! Out!!! *Phankphankphank*! My cousin's guts were hanging from his belly.
Over there! *pap — pap —*
The corpses floated face up, face down in the Bassac River –
those who refused to give up their *Orient* wrist-watches.

> Twenty meters a day
> for the first three days
> the journey without purpose;
> lost to wife and children,
> separated from your loved ones,
> repeated night and day,
> wandering in circles.
>
> There is crying and wailing
> and the elders are groaning –
> no one bothers with them;
> everyone stampeding
> to reach a destination,
> any destination
> away from Phnom Penh.

* *The population of Phnom Penh numbered 2,500,000 to 3,000,000. The evacuees were allowed to travel by prescribed routes only, which were so narrow that the people butted against each other, trampling the young, the sick, the elderly.*

Translated from Khmer by U Sam Oeur and Ken McCullough

U SAM OEUR

The Loss Of My Twins

Deep one night in October '76
when the moon had fully waxed,
it was cold to the bone;
that's when my wife's labor pains began.

I searched for a bed, but that was wishful thinking;
I felt so helpless. Two midwives materialized –
one squatted above her abdomen and pushed,
the other reached up my wife's womb and ripped the babies out.

What a lowing my wife put up
when she gave birth to the first twin.
"Very pretty, just as I'd wished, but those fiends
choked them and wrapped them in black plastic.

Two pretty girls . . .
Buddho!* I couldn't do a thing to save them!"
murmured my mother.
"Here, *Ta*!" the midwives handed the bundles to me.**

Cringing as if I'd entered Hell,
I took the babies in my arms
and carried them to the banks of the Mekong River.
Staring at the moon, I howled:

"O, babies, you never had the chance to ripen into life –
only your souls look down at me now.
Dad hasn't seen you alive at all, girls...
forgive me, daughters, I have to leave you here.

Even though I'll bury your bodies here,
may your souls lead me, your mom, brother, grandma
to a safer place, to a good safe world."

* *Buddho*: God!
***Ta*: colloquial for "Old Man" - used pejoratively.

Translated from Khmer by U Sam Oeur and Ken McCullough

U Sam Oeur

The Krasang Tree* At Prek Po**

for Joe Pohl

In '75 the *krasang* tree was green,
bore fruit for the soup of all the villagers.
By '79, the *krasang* tree had withered, its thorns
adorned with the hair of babies, its bark blood-stained.

In '75 the *krasang* tree was surrounded
by people seeking refuge.
By '79, the *krasang* tree was surrounded
by babies' skeletons, smashed

against its trunk by Utapats.***
The Utapats said: "To annihilate
grasses, uproot them, daily!" O, Grass!
What sin has grass committed?

After the Vietnamese invasion
I followed the Mekong home.
I stopped to rest here, exhausted, sick.
On the second floor of the abandoned ashram

I stretched out to sleep in pitch darkness,
but the smashed skulls out there made me tremble.
Half asleep, I heard the moaning souls
of children beg for explanation:

"Ma! *oeuy! oeuy! Ma!* / What had we done wrong?
The Utapats slaughtered us / grasping our feet to
smash us with no mercy / breaking our skulls
            against the *krasang* tree.

We had just been born / never had shelter
just at the time of war; / what did the Utapats want?
Why were the Utapats / against God's children?
            How dare the Utapats belittle God!"

That night, the smell of blood stayed with me.
At dawn, I went downstairs to find
rice husks spread over blood a meter deep:
evidence of a massacre more recent.

Then I heard the choked soul of the *krasang* tree,
drowned in the blood of infants. The Utapats
had killed its fruit with the fruit of our loins.
Neither had a chance to run away from them.

* *krasang: a tree which has long thorns on its bark and bears a sour nut-like fruit which villagers frequently add to soups.*
** *Prek Po: a village 50 km. north of Phnom Penh.*
*** *Utapats: general term used to refer to evil-doers.*

Translated from Khmer by U Sam Oeur and Ken McCullough

PUTU OKA SUKANTA

From Time

I

time despatched a whip
made from the teeth of a stingray's tail
a cutting edge, supple and strong
time took hold of it
and cracked the air with it
like a blacksmith pounding
a hammer into steel
it gagged my lips
and wiped the dripping blood
from the streams which creased my skin

where had the human values gone
the prison guard who lifted the broken body
shed tears
under the dark umbrella sprinkled with lights
ripped by a crescent moon rising from the grave

I hid behind the shadows
inside my own head
at that time
the time
when human life was as cheap as a gutter rat's
hunted down by hungry dogs.

III

how impatiently I awaited you
time
I measured the yard so many times
morning and afternoon, walking
I practiced breathing deep and long
while the key turned inside the lock

how impatiently I awaited you
time
as I counted the grains
of corn in my bowl or
soaked the rice to separate the grit

I waited for you night and day
during discussion sessions, studying without books
or pencils, from one head to another
I waited for you
as I thought of the tenderness
of a sweetheart who risked her own security
for a parcel and a few moments in the visitors' room

oh, how impatient I was
but it was you who taught me
how to prepare properly
to receive you

VI

you came – time
this morning with the appointed hour
for raising the red and white flag
under the mango tree
proclaiming the pancasila
and speeches – speeches
speeches
speeches
speeches

a mob of ants attacked my feet
and my body swayed

the commandant called me
he sprayed me with shit in the drains
and his boots played with me
like a ball

ah, those wretched ants
who don't understand the importance
of flag call and the pancasila
have sent me off to block N
without a sleeping mat
on half rations
and alone
alone
like the victim of a contagious disease
doing martial arts exercises
with the mosquitoes.

VIII

you took my hand
stared into my eyes
responded to my smile
and paid for my loss
because
you
have made known to me
a – release –

IX

time
it bears me over
the narrow bridge
as I leave behind the salemba gates
and head out into an open field
like a baby turtle, just hatched
waylaid by misfortune, on land and sea.

X

the sun turns the hands of the clock
and the days pass without our reckoning
so we set up our expectations
like a road builder fitting together the stones
for those who will pass across

a part of myself was shattered
in a way I'd never planned
I'm just a tiny speck
in the embrace
of time.

Translated from the Indonesian by Keith Foulcher.

PUTU OKA SUKANTA

Walking Along The Path

it's true, I've been walking a long time
from east to west, turning right, coming round
and going back to the east, before the sun
reaches the top of my head
when there is no assembly
I wait till the sun has crossed the barbed wire
netted above the wall
and walk again, barefooted,
till I feel the tremor the earth, our Indonesian earth,
kissing the soles of my feet
in counterpoint to the drumming of my heart.

I couldn't even estimate how many kilometers it's been
just to strengthen the muscles of the calves and stop the knee joints
from hardening up
I walk, making a path
across a small plot of ground, before the bell
closes the last door on defeat

it's true, I've been walking a long time
but my feet just go over and over the same piece of ground
while the clouds
so sweetly arm in arm with desire
go wandering across the whole wide world.

Translated from the Indonesian by Keith Foulcher

MILA AGUILAR

To A Foreigner

You accuse me of sloganeering
And being unpoetic
My writing lines like
"Damn the US-Marcos Dictatorship".

Friend, my reply is
You do not understand
The weight, the ocean depth
Of our class hatred.

Yesterday I heard
A comrade had been ambushed.
One of five bullets
Had smashed through his young heart.

When my ears caught
The uttered syllables of his name
The muscles of my jaw tightened
To the hardness of a gun butt.

My fingers curled up
To a firm trigger squeeze
And the heat of anger exploded
Like bullets out of my eyes.

Have you not heard
What the people do to the traitors
Who betray their precious ones?
They cut them up

Into pieces so small
You could hardly tell
They once had the force
To murder a Red fighter.

You are a foreigner indeed,
Foreign to the rhythm of our struggle.
In the face of class murder,
How can we be lyrical?

MILA AGUILAR

Pigeons For My Son

I gave the boy
a pair of pigeons
born and bred
in my harsh prison.
They had taped wings,
and the instructions were
specifically
to keep them on for weeks
until they'd gotten used
to their new cages.
He never liked
the thought of me
in prison, his own mother,
and would never
stay for long
to visit.
So perhaps I thought
of souvenirs.
But the tape from his pigeons
he removed one day,
and set them free.
You'd think
that would have angered me,
or made me sad at least
but I guess we're of one mind.
Why cage pigeons
who prefer free flight
in the vaster, bluer skies?

AMADO V. HERNANDEZ

A Man's Share Of The Sky

I was betrayed by an underhand agent,
who was out to incarcerate my spirit,
thinking that because the body is frail,
human feeling and purpose could be destroyed.

I was caged up in this place of stone
and steel, gunshots, ferocious guards;
cut off from the normal world,
who counted me dead, though I still lived and breathed.

At my eye's farthest reach, through that narrow window,
shines my share of the sky, full of tears –
meagre solace for an injured heart,
sorry banner for a man torn up by the roots.

The guard's look is as sharp as the lightning's edge;
no one but him comes near the padlocked door;
the cry of a prisoner in a nearby cell
sounds like an animal howling in a cave.

Daylight is a chain dragged by bloody feet,
night is a funeral shroud,
a coffin readied for a convict's grave;
the agent's claws are still felt, day and night.

Sometimes one hears the thud of footsteps,
the sound of rattling, clanking chains;
A thousand shadows are flung against the sun,
a thousand phantoms thrown out from the gloom.

Sometimes the night is shocked awake
by a siren's scream – an escape!
Blast of gunfire; sometimes a creaking bell
whimpers at the gallows: someone's being hung.

This is my world now, it belongs to me,
this prison that is the graveyard of the living,
ten, twenty, how many years? All the years
of my life will be buried here.

But the mind fears no pain,
the heart, still steadfast, beats.
Being jailed is a part of the fight;
this kind of bondage only toughens resistance.

Neither God nor man sleeps forever, the humiliated
are not humiliated forever;
every tyrant has his day of judgment
every Bastille has its day of vengeance.

And from here I glimpse tomorrow,
in that narrow span of sky wiped clean of tears,
foresee the rays of victory's golden dawn,
when, freed, I shall salute you, freedom.

Translated from the Tagalog by E. San Juan Jr.

JOSE MARIA SISON

From Fragments Of A Nightmare

4. As if midnight, the tight manacles
    And the demons were not enough,
    I am blindfolded and moved in circles.
    A series of boxes swallow me;
    A sprawling fort, a certain compound
    With a creaking-croaking gate
    And finally a cell of utter silence
    To which I am roughly plunged.
    The demons want me to feel
    Blind, lost, suffocating, helpless.

5. I remove the blindfold and find
    Myself in a musty tomb.
    I abhor the absence of windows,
    The sickly green and muteness
    Of the walls and the ceiling,
    The deep brown of the shut door,
    The dizzying flicker of the dim lamp
    And sparse air from an obscure vent.
    The pit of my stomach keeps turning
    And my lungs become congested.

7. I am forcibly shorn of my shirt
    And it is wound around my face.
    One more piece of cloth is tightened
    Across my covered eyes and nape.
    My hands are cuffed behind my back
    So tightly as to numb them.
    I am fixed on a wooden chair
    And made to wait for my fate
    In utter blindness and helplessness
    In the hands of some monster.

8. All of a sudden sharp fist blows
    Strike my floating ribs.
    Chest and solar plexus.
    Then the demons make barrages
    Of questions, threats and taunts
    with more barrages of blows.
    My silence, answer or comment

Always fetches harder blows,
The demons keep on threatening
to break my skull against the wall.

14. I hear water gushing against water,
The racket of plastic pails
And the screeches of frantic boots.
A small towel is put across my face
And mouth; and strong hands hold
My head and grasp my mouth.
Cascades of water dig into my nostrils
And flood my mouth, throat and lungs.
The torrents of water come with torrents
Of questions, threats and taunts.

15. The cuffs slash my wrists and ankles
As I strain for air again and again
Against the stinging rush of water.
I suffer for so many persons, groups,
Addresses, villages, mountains
That I do not know or do not want
To tell or confirm to the demons.
They are most vicious and persistent
In trying to extract hot leads,
More prey and more spoils.

16. For more than a thousand times,
The strength of my heart is tested.
As I struggle and scream for air,
American rock music screens my screams
Outside the torture chamber.
From time to time, a demon pokes
The barrel of a gun into my mouth;
Another keeps on jabbing his fingers
Into different parts of my body
To disrupt the rhythm of my resistance.

17. My struggles loosen the blindfold.
I can see a senior demon gloating,
Then a stocky demon sits on my belly.
As my body weakens and I grow dizzy,
The chief interrogator vainly tries
To hypnotize me by repeating words,
Suggesting that I am going, going
To sleep and rest my mind in his power.

I resist and keep my wits alive
By recalling the words of a battlecry.

19. I keep on thinking of seagulls
    Frail and magical above the blue ocean;
    And doves in pairs so gentle,
    One partner so close to the other.
    I am blindfolded and a vulture demon
    Comes to insult me with an offer:
    To be caged with my beloved
    In return for one free comrade.
    I grit my teeth and grunt at the demon
    And wish that I could do more to his face.

21. The torture does not cease
    But becomes worse a thousand times.
    The seconds, minutes, days, weeks
    Months and seasons fall
    Like huge blocks of lead
    On my brain and nerves,
    On my prostrate body on the rack,
    With my left hand and right foot
    Constantly cuffed to a filthy cot
    In a perpetuated process of violence.

22. Thick calluses grow where the irons
    Press against my flesh and bones.
    And I suffer the extremes
    Of heat and cold upon the change
    Of seasons and the part of a day.
    I see nothing beyond the dusty walls
    And the cobwebbed ceiling.
    Day and night, every ten minutes,
    A demon peeps through a small hole
    To make sure I remain in shackles.

23. Only bedbugs, mosquitoes, ants,
    Cockroaches, lizards and spiders
    Are my cohabitants in this part of hell
    I miss and yearn for my beloved
    And think of her own fate.
    I long for my growing children;
    I long for the honest company
    Of workers, peasants and comrades.
    I long for the people rising
    And the wide open spaces of my country.

27. I struggle against the tedium,
     The cumulative stress on my body and mind
     And the occasional lure of suicide.
     I keep on composing and reciting poems
     To damn the Devil and the demons.
     I keep on summoning the images
     Of my beloved suffering but enduring;
     Our free and fast-growing children;
     And the masses of avenging angels
     Armed with the sharpest of swords.

28. Every day that passes is a day won,
     Heightening will and endurance.
     I anticipate the Devil's pretense –
     Bringing me to his courts for a show
     And having the demon judges acclaim him
     As supreme lawmaker, captor, torturer,
     Prosecutor, judge and executioner.
     After so long on the rack, I can sit
     Beside my beloved before the demon judges
     And let the people know our ordeal.

29. To speak of torture in hindsight,
     To speak of one-hour punching
     So many meals and hours of sleep lost,
     Six hours of suffocation by water,
     Eighteen months on the rack
     And so many years of cramped seclusion,
     Is never to say enough of suffering.
     The Devil and the demons never tell
     The victim when a certain ordeal ends
     Even as they threaten more pain and death.

30. But still my pain and suffering is small
     As I think of those who suffer more
     The violence of daily exploitation
     And the rampage of terror on the land.
     I belittle my pain and suffering
     As I think of the people who fight
     For their own redemption and freedom
     And avenge the blood of martyrs.
     I belittle my pain and suffering
     As I hope to give more to the struggle.

December 1979

JOSE MARIA SISON

The Guerrilla Is Like A Poet

The guerrilla is like a poet
Keen to the rustle of leaves
The break of twigs
The ripples of the river
The smell of fire
And the ashes of departure.

The guerrilla is like a poet.
He has merged with the trees
The bushes and the rocks
Ambiguous but precise
Well-versed on the law of motion
And master of myriad images.

The guerrilla is like a poet.
Enrhymed with nature
The subtle rhythm of the greenery
The inner silence, the outer innocence
The steel tensile in-grace
That ensnares the enemy.

The guerrilla is like a poet.
He moves with the green brown multitude
In bush burning with red flowers
That crown and hearten all
Swarming the terrain as a flood
Marching at last against the stronghold.

An endless movement of strength
Behold the protracted theme:
The people's epic, the people's war.

1968

Usman Awang

Little Girl

Her body reminded me of
areca palm in quiet country
tall and thin
in heavy storms
broken branches fall around
but the palm stands erect
awaiting the morning sun.

So it was with this little girl
thin as areca palm
year after year meeting her father
across the barbed wire of a prison
imprisoned these many years
courageously fighting oppression
steady and faithful.

This little girl surprised me
calm and smiling broadly
politely turning down my help
'I don't need money, uncle,
just paper and books.'

Young in age
her soul matured by experience
not everyone grows strong this way
a unique steadiness that charms.

When I expressed sympathy and sadness,
feeling sorry for her,
once again she smiled and said:
'Don't be sad, uncle, steady your heart,
there are many children like me in the world.'

I became quite still
she calmed me, this little girl
pacifying waves of emotion
forbidding pity for her bitter experiences.

Is it not shameful for a grown man,
wanting to help suffering prisoners
to receive counsel from the child of one in prison
to be brave and steady?

Ten children like this
will destroy the purpose of a thousand prisons.

Translated from the Malay by Adibah Amin

Usman Awang

Father Utih

I

He has one wife – whom he embraces until death
five children who want to eat every day
an old hut where an inherited tale is hanging
a piece of barren land to cultivate.

The skin of his hands is taut and calloused
accustomed to any amount of sweat
O Father Utih, the worthy peasant.

But malaria comes hunting them
even though he offers a million prayers
and Mother Utih calls the village medicine man
for magic formulas, curses repeatedly chanted.

The medicine man with his reward goes home
with money and a pullet tied together.

II

In towns the leaders keep shouting
of elections and the people's freedom,
a thousand-fold prosperity in a sovereign state
a golden bridge of prosperity into the world hereafter.

When victory brightly shines
the leaders in cars move forward, their chests thrust forward
ah, the beloved subjects wave their hands.

Everywhere there are banquets and festivities
delicious roast chicken is served
chicken from the village promises prosperity

Father Utih still waits in prayer
where are the leaders going in their limousines?

Translated from the Malay by Adibah Amin

KEVIN GILBERT

Kiacatoo

On the banks of the Lachlan they caught us
at a place called Kiacatoo
we gathered by campfires at sunset
when we heard the death-cry of curlew
women gathered the children around them
men reached for their nulla and spear
the curlew again gave the warning
of footsteps of death drawing near
Barjoola whirled high in the firelight
and casting his spear screamed out 'Run!'
his body scorched quickly on embers
knocked down by the shot of a gun
the screaming curlew's piercing whistle
was drowned by the thunder of shot
men women and child fell in mid-flight
and a voice shouted 'We've bagged the lot'
and singly the shots echoed later
to quieten each body that stirred
above the gurgling and bleeding
a nervous man's laugh could be heard
'They're cunning this lot, guard the river'
they shot until all swimmers sank
but they didn't see Djarrmal's family
hide in the lee of the bank
Djarrmal warned 'Stay quiet or perish
they're cutting us down like wild dogs
put reeds in your mouth - underwater
we'll float out of here under logs'
a shot cracked and splintered the timber
the young girl Kalara clutched breath
she later became my great grandma
and told the story of my people's death
The Yoorung bird cries by that place now
no big fish will swim in that hole
my people pass by that place quickly
in fear with quivering soul
at night when the white ones are sleeping
content in their modern day dreams
we hurry past Kiacatoo
where we still hear shuddering screams

you say 'Sing me no songs of past history
let us no further discuss'
but the question remains still unanswered
How can you deny us like Pilate
refusing the rights due to us.
The land is now all allocated
the Crown's common seal is a shroud
to cover the land thefts the murder
but can't silence the dreams of the proud.

ROBERT WALKER

Life Is Life

The rose among thorns
may not feel the sun's kiss each mornin'
and though it is forced to steal the sunshine
stored in the branches by those who cast shadows,
it is a rose and it lives.

ROBERT WALKER

Solitary Confinement

Have you ever been ordered to strip
Before half a dozen barking eyes,
Forcing you against a wall –
ordering you to part your legs and bend over?

Have you ever had a door slammed
Locking you out of the world,
Propelling you into timeless space –
To the emptiness of silence?

Have you ever laid on a wooden bed –
In regulation pyjamas,
And tried to get a bucket to talk –
In all seriousness?

Have you ever begged for blankets
From an eye staring through a hole in the door,
Rubbing at the cold air digging into your flesh –
Biting down on your bottom lip, while mouthing 'Please, Sir'?

Have you ever heard screams in the middle of the night,
Or the sobbings of a stir-crazy prisoner,
Echo over and over again in the darkness –
Threatening to draw you into its madness?

Have you ever rolled up into a human ball
And prayed for sleep to come?
Have you ever laid awake for hours
Waiting for morning to mark yet another day of being alone?

If you've ever experienced even one of these,
Then bow your head and thank God.
For it's a strange thing indeed –
This rehabilitation system!

ERROL WEST

There is no one to teach me . . .

There is no one to teach me the songs that bring the Moon Bird, the fish or any
    other thing that makes me what I am.

No old women to mend my spirit by preaching my culture to me –
No old man with the knowledge to paint my being.
The spectre of the past is what dwells within –
I search my memory of early days to try to make my presence real, significant,
    whole.

I use my childhood memories of places, people and words to re-create my
    identity.
Uncle Leedham, a fine black man is my fondest memory –
He could sing, he could dance and play the mouth organ or gum leaf.

His broad shoulders carried me and, as I remember, I found it a great pleasure.
I owe him and his contemporaries a debt – and I'll pay –
But there is no one to teach me the songs that bring the Moon Bird, the fish or
    any other thing that makes me what I am.

Like dust blown across the plain are the people of the Moon Bird –
Whitey said, 'You'll be better over there, you will grow again!'
Oh, how wrong he was – why the graves of children run four deep – all victims
    of a foreign disease.
They had no resistance to the legacy of the white invasion – or so they must
    have thought
I am their legacy and I'll not disgrace them,

But there is no one to teach me the songs that brings the Moon Bird, the fish
    or any other thing that makes me what I am.
Inside, a warrior of ages rises up – my soul he possesses, his righteous
    indignation is the cup from which I drink –
I do not want blood – just opportunity – to be.

But even with him within there is no one to teach me the songs that bring the
    Moon Bird, the fish or any other thing that makes me what I am.

Though wretched the invaders were – for me they created a greater
    wretchedness for they, at least, spoke their language, understood their
    role, yet it was nothing to be sought.

My great-grandparents knew their culture and it could not be taken from them,
Through the minutes since their life it was taken from me – though my warrior
within says differently –

Even yet there is no one to teach me the songs that bring the Moon Bird, the
fish or any other thing that makes me what I am.

ERROL WEST

I feel the texture . . .

I feel the texture of her complexion with both hand and heart;
I shut my eyes; still I cannot divorce the loving memory of her touch, her
    influence on my life.

To separate from my only reality is impossible, as long as I live – is that not a
    fatalist's view considering her future?
Mining, digging, drilling, a cancer attacking the essence of my life; in unity
    our spirits scream Stop! Desist!
We can bear no more your attack.

Under better law this assault could not occur –
my brothers and sisters would stand, a human wall, a barrier against this
    vicious attack – yet now, with almost none to defend her you rip out her
    heart, her spleen and liver – mining, digging, drilling, a cancer attacking
    the essence of my life.

You destroy her lovely face and scar her gentle body – as we can see; to your
    disgrace – I shut my eyes; still I cannot divorce the loving memory of her
    touch, her influence on my life –

Songs of another time, were sung – and so she had remained – I know not those
    songs or the singers to face yet with them I am entwined –
There are the songs anew, the answer in them lies, I take nothing for myself, I
    wish to nourish and nurture – see she grows in strength.

South Asia

Faiz Ahmed Faiz

The Rain Of Stones Is Finished

(Elegy for Hassan Nasir, tortured to death in the Lahore Fort, 1959)

Today as I stared, suddenly a string snapped,
and the moon and sun were smashed in the sky.
No darkness is left in any corner, and no light –
behind me the road of fidelty lies broken,
    its lights extinquished, like my heart;
and nothing remains ahead. Friends, what will happen now?

Convoys of pain bearing cargoes of love must keep moving,
but someone else must now wave them forward.
And others must tend the garden where ardor blooms –
I can't: the dew of my eyes has dried: I won't weep again.
All rapture, the pure madness of passion, has ceased,
    and no one's left to bear the rain of stones.

That road behind me: it was the Beloved's street.
It is now the colour of her lips;
my blood, like a flag, has been unfurled there.
I have nothing left to give.

And a glass is being filled again.
Friends, let one of you now come forward,
for the cry has begun: "Who'll dare to drink this wine of love that
    is blood and poison? Who?"
This is the cry in the tavern after I'm gone.

Translated from the Urdu by Agha Shahid Ali

Faiz Ahmed Faiz

A Prison Nightfall

The night descends
step by silent step
down the stairway of stars.
The breeze goes by me
like a kindly whispered phrase.

The homeless trees of the prison yard
are absorbed, making patterns
against the sky.

On the roof's high crest
the loving hand of moonlight rests.
The starry river is drowned in dust
and the sky glows silver with moonlight.
In the dark foliage
shadows play with the wind
as a wave of painful loss
invades the heart.

Defiantly, a thought tells me
how sweet life is at this instant:
Those who brew the poison of cruelty
will not win, tomorrow or today.
They can put out the lamps
where lovers meet;
they cannot blind the moon!

Translated from the Urdu by Mahmood Jamal

FAIZ AHMED FAIZ

Prison Daybreak

Though it was still night
the moon stood beside my pillow and said:
                              'Wake up,
the wine of sleep that was your portion
is finished. The wineglass is empty.
Morning is here.'
                              I said goodbye to my beloved's image
in the black satin waters of the night
that hung still and stagnant on the world.
                              Here and there
moonlight whirled, the lotus dance commenced;
silver nebulas of stars dropped from the moon's white hand.
They went under, rose again to float, faded and opened.
For a long time night and daybreak swayed,
locked together in each other's arms.

                    In the prison yard
my comrades' faces, incandescent as candlelight,
flickered through the gloom. Sleep had washed them
with its dew, turned them into gold.
                              For that moment
these faces were rinsed clean of grief for our people,
absolved from the pain of separation from their dear ones.

In the distance a gong struck the hour;
wretched footsteps stumbled forward on their rounds,
wasted by near starvation, *maestros* of the morning shuffle,
lockstepped, arm in arm with their own terrible laments.
Mutilated voices, broken on the rack, awakened.

                    Somewhere a door opened,
another one closed; a chain muttered, grumbled
shrieked out loud. Somewhere a knife plunged
into the gizzard of a lock; a window went mad
and began to beat its own head.

This is the way the enemies of life,
shaken from sleep, showed themselves.
These daemons, hacked from stone and steel,
use their great hands to grind down the spirit,

slim as a feather now, of my useless days and nights.
They make it cry out in despair.
                    The prisoners,
all of us, keep watch for our saviour
who is on his way in the form of a storybook prince,
arrows of hope burning in his quiver,
                    ready to let them fly.

Translated from the Urdu by Naomi Lazard

Faiz Ahmed Faiz

Do Not Ask Of Me, My Love

Do not ask of me, my love,
that love I once had for you.
There was a time when
life was bright and young and blooming,
and your sorrow was much more than
any other pain.
Your beauty gave the spring everlasting youth;
your eyes, yes your eyes were everything,
all else was vain.
While you were mine, I thought, the world was mine.
Though now I know that it was not reality,
That's the way I imagined it to be;
for there are other sorrows in the world than love,
and other pleasures, too.
Woven in silk and satin and brocade,
those dark and brutal curses of countless centuries:
bodies bathed in blood, smeared with dust,
sold from market-place to market-place,
bodies risen from the cauldron of disease
pus dripping from their festering sores –
my eyes must also turn to these.
You're beautiful still, my love
but I am helpless too;
for there are other sorrows in the world than love,
and other pleasures too.
Do not ask of me, my love,
that love I once had for you!

Translated from the Urdu by Mahmood Jamal

KISHWAR NAHEED

We Sinful Women

It is we sinful women
who are not awed by the grandeur of those who wear gowns
who don't sell our lives
who don't bow our heads
who don't fold our hands together.

It is we sinful women
while those who sell the harvests of our bodies
become exalted
become distinguished
become the just princes of the material world.

It is we sinful women
who come out raising the banner of truth
up against barricades of lies on the highways
who find stories of persecution piled on each threshold
who find the tongues which could speak have been severed.

It is we sinful women.
Now, even if the night gives chase
these eyes shall not be put out.
For the wall which has been razed
don't insist now on raising it again.

It is we sinful women
who are not awed by the grandeur of those who wear gowns
who don't sell our bodies
who don't bow our heads
who don't fold our hands together.

Translated from the Urdu by Rukhsana Ahmad

M. GOPALAKRISHNA ADIGA

A Common Man

How dare you call me Common Man. Your dad
is common; in the company of my father
your grandfather and our great grandfathers who are dead.
Hey you, tell me if you know my name. Does your father own
this face, this stance and this lashless
God's-eye mind of mine? Faraway you sit in your
airconditioned room and without
knowing my name and ancestry you conduct
my funeral rites with your generalisations.
If you have any guts, come out
and look at my palm; look at the
unique mounts, crosses and lines. I will show you
how in this broken lantern the sooty wick
lifts up its burning head.

You are the wooden handle of the axe
which has forgotten the flowering, fruit-bearing tree.
For you everything is the same. A group
means a flock, a flock means sheep
and sheep means mutton. Where is the humanity
in you to call each one by name, feed
and fondle it with endearing words? You know
only to number us and fill up the trucks by the
meat factory. You know only to apply the
same brand name to all the cans. You dream
of tasting me only from the can.
For a piece of bread, you bastard, you
have allowed them to scrape off your nose and face.
You are the tailless fox for whom variety
is sour. You hold the foot rule and
scrape off everything until it becomes common.
You, worshipper of the shapeless black money's
jingle, what is the name of the machine
in your chest! Come on, breathe out.

Everything that can breathe has its own history,
its special smile, its own evolution
and direction. It will escape your map
and lift up its flag of individuality
until it can build a tower of light.

I may be an eczema-stricken farmer in torn clothes, part of a chorus,
or a come-what-may-I-don't-care
factory worker in sooty clothes,
or a limping thrusting-forward beggar on the street.

2

Did you call me a common man! You are mistaken.
Beware, I don't stretch my hands for the handcuffs.
I will bite and tear the noose around my neck
while I close my eyes and muse. Your pistol may
threaten me to march to its tune but I
will be dancing to a different tune in my mind.
I am a free-born soul.
You, worshipper of commonalities who has scraped
off your face to wear the mask of 'Hiranayaksha'!*

Your only ambition is to stick to your chair.
Therefore either you chizel off the faces of others
or keep them in jails. But look, look there
the great boar is sharpening his tusks
waiting for the proper time.
I am the 'Narasimha' caught up in a pillar,
I am also waiting
for a proper time.

* *Demon who cast Earth into the cosmic ocean, but Vishnu as Boar (Varaha) killed him and raised the earth on his tusk. Another cruel demon Hiranayakashipu was killed by Narasimha (man-lion), who burst from a pillar at sunset.*

Translated from the Kannada by Sumatheendra Nadig

Amarjit Chandan

Who Would Not Want It

Who would not want to
    sit in the company of dear ones
and sip Kashmiri tea, read
    the poems of Brecht and think of
    turning poetry into life
    and life into a poem.

Who would not want to
    drink mahua offered by the tribal girl
and languorously talk of
    one's first love
    or the colours of one's choice
    or just the simple truth that
    tears swim even in the eyes of a whore
and these tears are akin
    to the soft letters made with trembling
        finger-tips on the face of the earth.

Who would not want to
    talk on the bike on the long road ahead
    the broken slate of childhood
    and life with its iron teats
    just laugh it away and
    watch the long road shorten.

Who would not want to
    fire at those clocks
    that desert us in the countdown
    and go to the brokers of time.

Who would not want to
    once again turn
    the still waters of life
        into waves of the tossing sea.

Who would not want it?

Translated from the Punjabi by Nirupama Dutt

Amarjit Chandan

Name Any Saz

Name any saz:
Cuckoo, bells round a bullock's neck, life
Wine, sarod, bodies aglow in the dark, algozei.

Name any saz:
Handcuffs, shackles, guns
Prisoners' utensils.

Name any saz:
The trees wish for rest
But the breeze wants to blow
name any saz.

Saz: a musical instrument
Sarod: Indian version of an Afghan stringed instrument
Algozei: a pair of flutes played together

Translated from the Punjabi by the author

Dhruba Sen Gupta

The Charge – Treason

By the window books jostle
scraps of paper, random,
scattered.
These were the companions to your monotony.

From Bilaspur, your cousin wrote regularly
news of her gentle husband
and domineering mother-in-law
spread over the space of an inland form.

One day the neighbour's dog
chased your girlfriend Jaya
she didn't come to the house again.
Pain constricted you
as the clouds straitjacket the sun.

You were always gloomy
this city depressed you – you felt that
its entrails were twining around you
and like a tapeworm in its bowels
you wanted to jerk it into unease
see its whole body jackknife with pain
so that it would be forced to retch you
up, with your girlfriend Jaya
And the neighbour's grumpy mongrel
would be free to copulate with stray dogs
under the sun or the moon.

2/ Your mother cooked,
squatting by the fire
one day she couldn't straighten her back.
Your father, a retired Government servant,
scanned the advertisement columns daily
in search of part-time jobs.
Anger smouldered silently in your sister –
there were dark circles under her eyes.

Some nights the police cordoned off your house
in search of your absconding brother.

They turned the little room upside down –
the hush surrounding their noise struck you strangely...
in the neighbouring houses no lights came on
no windows opened
even out of common curiousity.

3/ In the examination hall you were told
that in a small village in Mograhat
they had tied Kajal to a tree and killed him.
Three days later they came to Kajal's house, and
told uncle to go to the morgue and identify him.
Neither uncle nor aunt cried out
but Kajal's younger brother gnashed his teeth.

A month later he left a note: "I am going away
to finish Kajal's work. Bless me".
Uncle died. For some time after
aunt was like clay –
now she has hardened into stone.
When you pass that house your head bows
and your feet hasten across the path.

4/ It is said that Professor Bhattacharya
is not normal any more. Torture
and suffering have crippled him.
They broke the flats of his feet and shattered his wrists,
did something to his eyes,
he cannot see very well and his tongue sticks
to the roof of his mouth.
The charge – Treason.

At regular intervals he is brought to court
for the hearing
then the same prison van takes him back again –
this has been going on for five or six years now.

Professor Bhattacharya taught physics –
how the electron which circles the nucleus
is practically weightless. Yet this
weightless thing, the electron,
can control the nature of the atom.
It is a question of numbers only.
While the neutron has no positive charge,
a change in the number of neutrons
can transform the nature of the atom.

You took notes and he smiled, whether
in pain or in contempt you did not know.
Towards the end he stopped coming.
Then one day you heard that in a
slum in Gulu-Ostagar Lane
the police had arrested him.
The charge – Treason.

5/ Sharbani and Rekha
taught in a slum school. One day
the Special Branch jeep just picked them up.
The charge – Treason.

Treason because they shouted slogans in a procession:
"We demand the release of political prisoners, removal of PD,
Misa, the Black Laws."
Treason because they were suspected of mingling with the masses
of wanting to share their lives.

6/ Curzon Park, July 20, 1974.
They trampled on Prabir's stomach with hobnailed boots.
This city learnt under the terror of the Black Maria,
the hail of merciless lathis,
that to speak the word 'Vietnam'
was treason.

There is treason in your song, treason in your play,
for you and I, and you and you and you
to meet is treason,
treason
treason
treason
to live in this country...

February 1975

Translated from the Bengali by Rati Bartholomew, Anjan Ghosh and Radha Kumar

SUBHAS MUKHOPADHYAY

Why He Didn't Come Back

For a long time now the lights have shone in the street
But
Why hasn't *baba* come back yet, *ma?*

When he left, he said
He'd come back early with his pay.
Whatever shopping we need for *puja*
Should have been done by now.

When he left, that's what he said.
But that man hasn't come back yet.

The boy sat with his book on the mat
Facing towards the window –
The pages of the history-book were open in front of him.

The clock ticks.
Water drips from the tap.
A cat with long whiskers
Jumps off the wall of a house.

Like a boy spoiled and pampered by his father,
The scribbled letters – obstinate and
Disobedient –
Won't move
Until *puja* clothes are bought.

But
Why hasn't *baba* come back yet, *ma?*

The cooking was finished long ago
And mother has changed for the evening.
She sits down to knit
But drops her stitches.

A rattling sound is heard –
The bolt slides back.
Who is it?
It's your boy, *ma.*

The boy stands at the street-door.
The news is being read now on the radio.
Why hasn't that man come back yet?

The boy steps out into the street.
There was a crowd at the corner;
A black van;
And the crack of many fireworks.

Which *puja* is it, today?
The boy goes out to see.

Then, very late at night,
Through streets thick with the smell of gunpowder,
After walking through many lanes and back-alleys,
Side-stepping death,
The father came back.

The boy did not come back.

Translated from the Bengali by Sibani Raychaudhuri and Robert Hampson

Subhas Mukhopadhyay

The Petition

With a million and one bows,
My lord, we present this request –
Please excuse us from rent this year,
Not a grain of rice have we harvested.

Our fields have dried up like our luck.
As far as our eyes can see
The canals are dry, the ponds are dry,
Only in our eyes is a salty sea.

Who can go, with hands out, to whom?
Everyone in the village is in the same condition.
For a few days we've been eating wild greens
After three nights of starvation.

What we are wearing
Does not keep us decently clothed.
We've sold all our pots and pans –
We've sold everything we owned.

In these hard times, great lord,
Please let us off the dues you demand.
Your bailiffs, we hope,
Will not try to seize our lands.

There are about a thousand of us
Tenants in this settlement.
We have decided together
How we might survive.

Our bellies burn, our fields burn.
Who is going to pay your taxes?
If you do not save us this time, my lord,
Flames will rise!

Translated from the Bengali by Sibani Raychaudhuri and Robert Hampson

AMRITA PRITAM

To Waris Shah

Today I asked Waris Shah:
Speak from your grave;
Open a new chapter
In the Book of Love.

A daughter of the Punjab once wept;
You wrote her long story for her.
Today millions of daughters weep,
Waris Shah. They're calling you.

O Friend of sorrow,
Look at the Punjab.
The village square heaped with corpses,
The Chenab flooded with blood!

Someone mixed poison
In the five rivers;
Their flow
Watered the Punjab.

Poison has sprouted
From this fertile land.
Look, how far the red has spread.
Curse how far the red has spread!

Poisoned air
Floated into the jungles
Turning all bamboo flutes
To snakes

Biting everyone's lips;
Their tongue tips rose up
And quickly all parts
Of the Punjab turned blue.

Song is crushed in every throat;
Every spinning wheel's thread is snapped;
Friends parted from one another;
The hum of spinning wheels fell silent.

Oars have left all boats
And float in the current;
Peepal branches with swings
Lie broken.

Where is the grove where love songs
Used to echo, where the flute?
All Ranjha's brothers
have forgotten how to play the flute.

Blood keeps falling upon the earth,
Oozing out drop by drop from graves.
The queens of love
Weep in tombs.

It seems all people have become Kaidos,
Thieves of beauty and love –
Where should I search out
Another Waris Shah.

Waris Shah!
Open your grave;
Write a new page
In the Book of Love.

* Waris Shah is the author of *hiir* ("Heer"), an epic in Punjabi written in the eighteenth century. Heer is the heroine; Ranja, the hero; and Kaido, the villain.

Translated from the Punjabi by Kiron Bajaj and Carlo Coppola

K. SATCHIDANANDAN

From The Times Of Torment

Poetry And The Police

They hand-cuff poetry.
Poetry's fingers turn into flames
and melt the manacle.
They raise their clubs
to beat poetry into a pulp.
Poetry scatters into words
and slips away from the batons.
They hang poetry high
on the ceiling's beams.
Poetry turns into a pipal tree
and goes out piercing the roof.
They bring red-hot iron
to brand poetry on its thighs.
The thighs turn into rains
and render the iron cold and kind.
Rifle-butts come marching
to batter poetry's cheeks.
The cheeks blow the snake-charmer's pipe
and make the rifles dance to its tune.
Bayonets try to pierce poetry's throat.
The throat turns into a sparrow
and sits twittering on the bayonets.
Bullets seek the heart of poetry.
The heart flies up to the clouds
and blossoms into a rainbow.
They boil poetry in a cauldron.
Its body turns into a drum
and is heard from the hill-top.
They advance knives
to pluck out the eyes of poetry.
The eyes shine in the firmament
with the Great Bear.

Translated from the Malayalam by the poet

SARVESHWAR DAYAL SAXENA

Red Cycle

All night
a red cycle
Stood aganst the barbed fence
forlorn and alone
Shrill whistle of the police blew
heavy boots thudded the ground.

In the morning
a child appeared
and played
with the cool dew-wet cycle bell.

Then
with screaming siren
a huge black van
roared to a stop –
The child
forgot his bell
Watching in fascination
the winking blue light on its roof ...

The black van took away the child.

For the first time
I watched the shadow of the window-bars
on the floor
And was
filled with terror.

Translated from the Hindi by Rati Bartholomew

SHAMSUR RAHMAN

Mother

She lived in a lonely village.
All day she worked at home, silently.
Hardly noticed the sun
throbbing in a summer sky
and rafts of clouds sailing by.
She did not notice time moving on.

Everything was familiar:
painted in gentle colours,
an intricate pattern woven carefully.
A pot of boiling rice, greens,
some fish: a plebeian meal
for her husband, a schoolteacher.

At times she would glance
at the creepers near the fence
or at the yellow bird on the jackfruit tree
wagging its tail endlessly
And time would move on.

A quick bath by the well
and she would comb her greying tresses
thinking of her son
in the local school
memorising multiplication tables.
She would think of her eldest son,
as she filled the jar with sweets
in pretty wrappings . . .
his large bright eyes
the city in which he studied.

Her footfalls would never be heard
outside this small world of her own:
she would never venture out.
It was a self-imposed exile:
a simple life of her own.
Only the memories of her dead parents
would sometimes rake up
pangs of nostalgia.

And then suddenly
one day her entire country reared its head
like a raging god.
News came in: of martyrdom and bloodsmeared soil,
the blood-spattered clothes of her son
drew her out of her village home.
She went.

She left behind her those creepers near the fence,
the river, the fields, and the familiar pond.
Today her footfalls can be heard
on the roads of the city:
down the narrow streets and the alleys.
Memories of her dead son
and the tears of her stricken heart
merge with the slogans
that reverberate.

Translated from the Bengali by Pritish Nandy

SHAMSUR RAHMAN

Signs Of Fear

One by one the signs of fear
are being wiped away smoothly.
Wounded walls of private houses,
stores, railway stations, students'
hostels, are healing like the holes
in a skull filling up with new flesh.
Signs of fear are smoothly disappearing
one by one from the towns and villages.

On the electric pole the industrious crow
sits once again with pieces of straw
in his beak – it is egg-laying
time for mama-crow.
The Rabindranath Tagore of the heart
is freed from the state prison now
and can be heard again
in Bangla's light and air –
his serene portrait radiant on our walls.
I take out the empty cage
and hang it out in the veranda
hoping for the return
of a bright green bird.
For the signs of fear are disappearing,
disapppearing one by one.

But still the blood in my veins,
in my brain, flows obedient to fear's rule.

Hens under the guava tree become
suddenly alert to the sound
of an explosion inside their head.
Near the haystack a rabbit shivers
stricken by the memory
of the touch of bare steel.
In their nightmares the leaves of trees
can still see the flames of some
burning ghats and shrivel black
in the hot ash-blown air.

A large hairy arm bursts in
through the window and smashes up
the household. The innocent rice-bowl
becomes the grinning face of a Colonel
and begins to bounce bodyless on the floor.
Suddenly my faithful dog pounces on me
with his bloodthirsty teeth on my neck.
My son howls with laughter
as he slits his brother's throat.
I see my sister's hanged body dangle
from the ceiling beam.
There is a blizzard in my room –
the snow tightening over my chest –
the coffin cloths are dancing
in the wind to the song of death!

I've tried hard. I've built
scarecrows and planted them
all over the field of my mind.
But the ghosts refuse to leave.
Everyday, at the end of day,
I feel tired, I feel tired,
tired of the hissing tentacles
of fear gripped around my being.

Will the white cow
ever come back to her shed
softly blowing dust at her feet
and tinkling her bell at sunset?

Translated from the Bengali by Farida Majid

LAXMIPRASAD DEVKOTA

Quatrain

Oh had I been some green and lovely vine
I would have sucked ambrosia and put out fine flowers;
glad-hearted song birds would have come to carol –
well, my country's turned ambrosial but this poetry's barbarous.

1958

Translated from the Nepali by David Rubin

LAXMIPRASAD DEVKOTA

Mad

Surely, my friend, I am mad,
that's exactly what I am!

I see sounds,
hear sights,
taste smells,
I touch things thinner than air,
things whose existence the world denies,
things whoses shapes the world does not know.
Stones I see as flowers,
pebbles have soft shapes,
water-smoothed at the water's edge
in the moonlight;
as heaven's sorceress smiles at me,
they put out leaves, they soften, they glimmer
and pulse, rising up like mute maniacs,
like flowers – a kind of moonbird flower.
I speak to them just as they speak to me,
in a language, my friend,
unwritten, unprinted, unspoken,
uncomprehended, unheard.
Their speech comes in ripples, my friend,
to the moonlit Ganga's shore.
Surely, my friend, I am mad,
that's exactly what I am!

You are clever, and wordy,
your calculations exact and correct forever,
but take one from one in my arithmetic,
and you are still left with one.
You use five senses, but I have six,
you have a brain, my friend,
but I have a heart.
To you a rose is a rose, and nothing more,
but I see Helen and Padmini,
you are forceful prose,
I am liquid poetry;
you freeze as I am melting,
you clear as I cloud over,
and then it's the other way around;

your world is solid, mine vapor,
your world is gross, mine subtle,
you consider a stone an object,
material hardness is your reality,
but I try to grasp hold of dreams,
just as you try to catch the rounded truths
of cold, sweet, graven coins.
My passion is that of a thorn, my friend,
yours is for gold and diamonds,
you say that the hills are deaf and dumb,
I say that they are eloquent.
Surely, my friend,
mine is a loose inebriation,
that's exactly how I am.

In the cold of the month of Magh I sat,
enjoying the first white warmth of the star:
the world called me a drifter.
When they saw me staring blankly for seven days
after my return from the cremation *ghats*,*
they said I was possessed.
When I saw the first frosts of Time
on the hair of a beautiful woman,
I wept for three days:
the Buddha was touching my soul,
but they said that I was raving!
When they saw me dance
on hearing the first cuckoo of Spring,
they called me a madman.
A silent, moonless night once made me breathless,
the agony of destruction made me jump,
and on that day the fools put me in the stocks!
One day I began to sing with the storm,
the wise old men sent me off to Ranchi.*
One day I thought I was dead,
I lay down flat, a friend pinched me hard,
and said, "Hey, madman, you're not dead yet!"
These things went on, year upon year,
I am mad, my friend,
that's exactly what I am!

I have called the ruler's wine blood,
the local whore a corpse,
and the king a pauper.
I have abused Alexander the Great,

poured scorn on so-called great souls,
but the lowly I have raised
to the seventh heaven on a bridge of praise.
Your great scholar is my great fool,
your heaven my hell,
your gold my iron, my friend,
your righteousness my crime.
Where you see yourself as clever,
I see you to be an absolute dolt,
your progress, my friend, is my decline,
that's how our values contradict.
Your universe is a single hair to me,
certainly, my friend, I'm moonstruck,
completely moonstruck, that's what I am!

I think the blind man is the leader of the world,
the ascetic in his cave is a back-sliding deserter;
those who walk the stage of falsehood
I see as dark buffoons,
those who fail I consider successful,
progress for me is stagnation:
I must be either cockeyed or mad –
I am mad, my friend, I am mad.

Look at the whorish dance
of shameless leadership's tasteless tongues,
watch them break the back of the people's rights.
When the black lies of sparrow-headed newsprint
challenge Reason, the hero within me,
with their webs of falsehood,
then my cheeks grow red, my friend,
as red as glowing charcoal.
When voiceless people drink black poison,
right before my eyes,
and drink it through their ears,
thinking that it's nectar,
then every hair on my body stands up,
like the Gorgon's serpent hair.
When I see the tiger resolve to eat the deer,
or the big fish the little one,
then into even my rotten bones there comes
the fearsome strength of Dadhichi's* soul,
and it tries to speak out, my friend,
like a stormy day which falls with a crash from Heaven.
When Man does not regard his fellow as human,

all my teeth grind together like Bhimsen's,*
red with fury, my eyeballs roll round
like a half-penny coin, and I stare
at this inhuman world of Man
with a look of lashing flame.
My organs leap from their frame,
there is tumult, tumult!
My breath is a storm, my face is distorted,
my brain burns, my friend, like a submarine fire,
a submarine fire! I'm insane like a forest ablaze,
a lunatic, my friend,
I would swallow the whole universe raw.
I am a moonbird for the beautiful,
a destroyer of the ugly,
tender and cruel,
the bird that steals the fire of Heaven,
a son of the storm thrown up
by an insane volcano, terror incarnate,
surely, my friend,my brain is whirling, whirling,
that's exactly how I am!

1. *A ghat is a stepped platform beside a river where Hindus take their daily baths and where the bodies of the dead are cremated.*
2. *Ranchi is the mental asylum in Bihar, northern India.*
3. *According to the Mahabharata, the magical "diamond-weapon" of Indra, the god of war, was made from a bone of the the legendary sage Dadhichi.*
4. *Bhimsen "the terrible" was the second of the five Pandava princes and was described in the Mahabharata as an enormous man of fierce and wrathful disposition.*

Translated from the Nepali by Michael James Hutt

GOPALPRASAD RIMAL

A Mother's Dream

Mother, will he come?

Yes son, he will come,
come spreading light like the morning sun;
at his waist you will see a weapon,
for his fight against injustice,
shining like the dew.
At first you will think him a dream,
you will grope with your hands to touch him,
but he will surely come,
more tangible than fire or snow.

Are you sure, mother?

When you were born,
I hoped to find his shadow in your soft face,
his beauty in your lovesome smile,
his soft voice in your baby talk,
but that sweet song has not made you its flute,
though in my youth I had dreamt
that you yourself would be him.
But he will come, whatever befalls us,
a mother speaks for all Creation,
I know this is no idle dream.

When he comes, you will lift your face from my lap,
cease listening to truth like some fantastic tale;
you will be able to see it,
to bear it and grasp it yourself.
Instead of drawing courage from me,
you will go to war alone,
consoling a mother's inconsolable heart,
and I shall no longer stroke your hair
as if you were a sickly child.

You will see him come as a storm,
follow him like a leaf in the wind,
see, he comes falling down from life's sphere,
pouring forth like moonlight,
our lifeless inertia squirms like a snake;
my son, rise up when he comes.

Will he come like dawn's softness to the throats of birds?
My heart trembles with hope.

Yes, son, he will surely come,
come spreading light like the morning sun,
but that you yourself would be him:
this was the dream of my youth.

Translated from the Nepali by Michael James Hutt

BHUPI SHERCHAN

This is a land of uproar and rumor

This is a land of uproar and rumor,
where deaf men wearing hearing aids*
are judges at musical contests;
and those whose souls are full of stones
are connoisseurs of poetry;
where wooden legs win races, and bayonets of defense
are held by plastered hands;
where, basket upon basket,
truckload after truckload,
souls are offered for sale
along the roads, in front of doors;
where the leaders are those who can trade in souls,
like shares on a stock exchange;
where the men who presume to lead our youth on
have faces wrinkled like roofing steel;
where the "wash and wear" creases of honor
are never spoiled by any malpractice,
and even the prostitute's terylene skin
cannot crease, whatever her crime;
where seeds which double production
are displayed at farmers' fairs
which fill with news of drought and famine;
where beer and whisky flow instead of sacred rivers*
and people come to our holiest shrines
less to receive the food of the gods,
more to consume the forbidden fruits
of Adam and Eve in the gardens behind;
where the sugar factory makes booze, not sugar,
and mothers of freedom give birth to soldiers instead of sons;
where the great poet must die an early death to pay his debts
and a poet, driven mad by the pain of his land,
must take refuge in a foreign hospice;
where Saraswati's lonely daughter
must live her whole life shriveled
by a sickness untreated in her youth;*
where a guide describes to a tourist
Nepal's contributions to other lands,
then departs, demanding his camera,
where young men sing the songs
of forts and foreign conquests,
marching in parades . . .

In this land I am forced to say,
clipping a *khukuri* to my tie and lapel,*
tearing open my heart:
compatriots, nation-poets of this land,
who sing the songs of my country's awakening,
respected leaders of my people:
if you wish, you may call me a slanderer, a traitor,
but this land is mine as well as yours,
my hut will stand on a piece of this land,
my pyre will burn beside one of our rivers;
I am forced to say, made bold by this feeling,
this is a land of uproar and rumor,
dig deep, and you find hearsay
heaped up beneath every home,
so this is a land of tumult and gossip,
a country supported by rumors,
a country standing on uproar:
this is a land of uproar and rumor.

1. *The English words "ear phone" are used in the Nepali original.*
2. *The original Nepali poem refers to the Bishnumati and the Bagmati, the two sacred rivers of the Kathmandu Valley. Similarily, the following line names the temples of Swyambhu and Pashupati.*
3. *The "great poet" referred to here is Lakshmiprasad Devkota, the poet who is driven mad is Gopalprasad Rimal, and "Saraswati's lonely daughter" is Parijat.*
4. *The khukuri is the ubiquitous Nepali knife that has become a military emblem and almost a national symbol. Sherchan perhaps intends to show that he does not lack patriotic feeling.*

Translated from the Nepali by Michael James Hutt

Latin America
&
The Caribbean

Marjorie Agosin

Torture

—For Rosa Montero and all those who told her their stories

Slowly and in secret
the roof of my silenced mouth burning
and I already naked and
so far away
conspiring to trap
my nipples, thin wires of terror.
Their small fingers, sloughed off scales of bitter wormwood
venture along that slow agony, through obscured
brightness between my legs
and they, the idle hangmen
pant while
the moon's blood
howls on the sickly metal surface,
they wipe my forehead
so that later they can empty the
scattered leaves of my story
and between gaps of time
seconds of air
electric spears and tears
explode like falling leaves of unhinged warriors
fingernails spread out over the floor in flames and menses,
teeth crushed by shocks and traitorous spittle
let go from the shore of my lips
now shorn of word, truth, light
now turned into something other,
even my hair splits, withers
among the ashes and fans out like doomed petals
naked I am forced to face
each one of them
to confess to them
secrets I never had,
uncertain living places
and before each silence,
black shrouds like those of mordant warlocks
coil round me to
consume the tongue that had nothing to tell,
to strip the tongue

that once knew about birds, light and onions
in a garden
and again the torment of glowing wires weaving me in
threads of ill omen, the soles of my feet, my
breasts shrunken by the terror of the
terrible green talons.
Now I am dead,
my name is Carmen, or Maria,
I am a woman
immersed in silence,
immersed in my nakedness,
an imprisoned
stone,
I am a dead woman who managed to survive
who told nothing
new
who in a matter of moments lost aromas, lilacs, yellow,
while sleeping next to other bodies defecating, dying
from pain and not from fear,
I am the woman who was blindfolded for a second, for a month
and forever
impaled by the
eternal ceremony of
torture.

Translated from the Spanish by Cola Franzen

MARJORIE AGOSIN

The most unbelievable part

The most unbelievable part,
they were people like us
good manners
well-educated and refined.
Versed in abstract sciences,
always took a box for the Symphony
made regular trips to the dentist
attended very nice prep schools
some played golf ...

Yes, people like you, like me
family men
grandfathers
uncles and godfathers.

But they went crazy
delighted in burning
children and books
played at decorating cemeteries
bought furniture made of broken bones
dined on tender ears and testicles.

Thought they were invincible
meticulous in their duties
and spoke of torture
in the language of surgeons and butchers.

They assassinated the young of my country
and of yours.
now nobody could believe in Alice through the looking glass
now nobody could stroll along the avenues
without terror bursting through their bones

And the most unbelievable part
they were people
like you
like me
yes, nice people
just like us.

Translated from the Spanish by Cola Franzen

María Eugenia Bravo Calderara

And I Cried

And they were torturing children, mother,
they were stretching their bones, mother,
and giving them electric shocks, mother.
Hour upon hour, mother,
interminable ages, then ages again, mother,

and their shrieks were all round me, mother,
and to blackest black the demented world, mother,
whirled giddy with grief.

And I cried as I have
never cried before, mother,
I cried in a frenzy, mother,
desperate to my last fibre, mother,
and the children screamed
in more and more anguish, mother,

and I cried mother,
as I will never cry again
as long as I live.

Translated from the Spanish by Dinah Livingstone

María Eugenia Bravo Calderara

On Exiles And Defeats

No. It was not the bad time in Chena,
nor the sudden grim prosecutions
in improvised war councils.
No. The rifle butt in my back
didn't defeat me,
nor investigation's black hood of horror
nor the grey hell of the stadiums
with their roars of terror.

No. Neither was it the iron bars at the window
cutting us off from life,
nor the watch kept on our house
nor the stealthy tread
nor the slide into the deep maw of hunger.

No. What defeated me was the street that was not mine,
the borrowed language learned in hastily set-up courses.
What defeated me was the lonely uncertain figure
in longitudes that did not belong to us.
It was Greenwich
longitude zero
close to nothing.

What defeated me was the alien rain,
forgetting words
the groping memory,
friends far away
and the atrocious ocean between us,
wetting the letters I waited for
which did not come.

What defeated me was yearning day after day
at Jerningham Road
agonising under the fog
at Elephant and Castle
sobbing on London Bridge.

And I was defeated step by step
by the harsh calendar;
and between Lunes-Monday and Martes-Tuesday
I had shrivelled into a stranger.

What defeated me was the absence of your tenderness, my country.

Translated from the Spanish by Cicely Herbert.

ARIEL DORFMAN

First Prologue: Simultaneous Translation

I'm not so different from the interpreters
in their glass booths
at endless international conferences
translating what the peasant from Talca
tells about torture
repeating in English that they put him on the cot
stating in the most refined and delicate French
that electric shock produces lasting transmissible effects
finding the exact equivalent for rape by dogs
pau d'arara I insulted the murderers
finding a phrase without emotion
that describes exactly the sensation
– please forgive any rhymes or rhythms you may find –
when the wall is at your back
and the captain begins to say the word fire,
trying to take the melodrama out of the sentences
trying to communicate the essence and the feeling
without giving in to the dark cloying current
of what they are really saying
they were torturing my son in the other room
they brought back our compañero unconscious
they put rats inside our compañero it's God's truth.
Not so different from them
with their voices their dictionaries their notes their
                                culture their going back home
in Geneva in New York in the Hague,
an intermediary, not even a bridge,
simultaneous translation for good pay
because we are specialists
and the incredible thing is that in spite of us
in spite of my river of interpretations and turns of phrase
something is communicated
a part of the howl
a thicket of blood
some impossible tears
the human race has heard something
and is moved.

Translated from the Spanish by Edith Grossman with the author

ARIEL DORFMAN

Corn Cake

My old lady had nothing
      to do with any of it.

They took her
because she was our mother.
She knew nothing
I mean
nothing about nothing.

      Think about it.
      Even more than the pain
      think how amazed she was.
      She never even knew
      there were people
         like them
      in this world.

Almost two and a half years
and she hasn't come back.
They came into the kitchen
and left the kettle boiling
on the stove.
When the old man came home
he found the kettle
         dry
steaming on the stove.
Her apron was gone.

      Think how she must have
         looked at them
      for two and half years,
      how she must have...
      think about the blindfold
      coming down
         over her eyes
      for two and a half years
      and those same men
      who shouldn't be in this world
      coming toward her
         again.

She was my mother.
I hope she never comes back.

Translated from the Spanish by Edith Grossman with the author

JAVIER HERAUD

In Praise Of Days
Destruction And Eulogy To Darkness

They promised us happiness
and we still have nothing.
Why promises
if when the time for rain comes
we have no more than sun and the dead wheat?

Why harvest and harvest again
if afterwards they take the corn,
the wheat, the flowers, the fruits?

To have our bit of rest
we don't want to wait on promises
and pleas:
We'll have to go back to the
beginning, start over again,
come back slowly spreading rain
over the fields, planting wheat
with our own hands, harvesting fish
with our unending mouths.
We don't want to take anything
we're not entitled to,
O happiness!
Better to have been sunk
and never have arrived,
for now we must do everything
with our own hands:
build words
like the trunks of trees,
neither beg nor weep
but end,
put an end to the dead earth with blows.

Translated from the Spanish by Robert Márquez

JAVIER HERAUD

Flies

OK fly,
you fly OK
you draw yourself in the air
tight banks quick turns
graph the walls
with your shadow
and you're laughing at me
and I don't even look at you
settle on my nose
take a trip on my head
settle on my shoulder
and I suppose it amuses you fly
when I try to flatten you
with my slow hand,
sure, settle on my bread
my toast, my books
they're just there for you.
You know,
they tell me you push
some heavy diseases
but I don't believe it
and when I go to piss
there you are again
fixing your wings.
Some fools buy swatters
or chase you
with an old newspaper
just to see you fall down dead –
that's a job for the idle,
fly killing
            you don't scare
the larger animals
or even dogs.
But I want you to get this:
If someday I could
I'd call in all the experts
in the world
I'd order them to put together
a flying machine your size
to finish you and all your girlfriends

for ever -
Because I have this recurrent hope
not to feed you
I don't want to see you
in my entrails
the day they cut me open
in the countryside
and leave my body under the sun.

Translated from the Spanish by Edward Dorn and Gordon Brotherston

Pablo Neruda

Letter To Miguel Otero Silva, In Caracas (1948)

A friend delivered me your letter written
with invisible words, on his suit, in his eyes.
How happy you are, Miguel, how happy we are!
No one's left in a world of stuccoed ulcers
except us, indefinably happy.
I see the crow pass by and it can't harm me.
You observe the scorpion and clean your guitar.
We live among wild beasts, singing, and when we touch
a man, the substance of someone in whom we believed,
and he crumbles like rotten pastry,
you in your Venezuelan patrimony rescue
whatever can be salvaged, while I defend
the live coal of life.
                    What happiness, Miguel!
You wonder where I am? I'll tell you
– giving only details *useful* to the government –
that on this coast full of wild stones,
sea and countryside merge: waves and pines,
eagles and petrels, foam and meadows.
Have you seen from very close up and all day long
how the seabirds fly? It seems as if
they carried the world's letters to their destinations.
Pelicans cruise by like windships,
other birds that fly like arrows and bring
the messages of deceased kings, of princes
entombed with turquoise threads on the Andean coasts,
and gulls made of round whiteness,
that constantly forget their messages.
How blue life is, Miguel, when we've put into it
love and struggle, words that are bread and wine,
words that they cannot yet dishonor,
because we take to the streets with shotgun and songs.
They're lost with us, Miguel.
What can they do but kill us, and even so
it's a poor bargain for them, they can only
try to rent a flat in front of us and shadow us
to learn to laugh and weep like us.
When I wrote love lyrics, which sprouted

from all my pores, and I pined away,
aimless, forlorn, gnawing the alphabet,
they told me: "How great you are, O Theocritus!"
I'm not Theocritus: I took life,
stood before it, kissed it until I conquered it,
and then I went through the mine galleries
to see how other men lived.
And when I emerged with my hands stained with filth and grief
I raised and displayed them on gold chains,
and I said: "I'm not an accomplice to this crime."
They coughed, became very annoyed, withdrew their welcome,
stopped calling me Theocritus, and ended up
insulting me and sending all the police to imprison me,
because I didn't continue to be preoccupied exclusively with metaphysical
    matters.
But I had conquered happiness.
Ever since I've awakened to read letters
that seabirds bring from afar,
letters delivered wet, messages that little by little
I keep translating leisurely and confidently: I'm
meticulous as an engineer in this strange craft.
And suddenly I go to the window. It's a square
of transparency, the distance of grasses
and pinnacles is pure, so I keep working
amid things that I love – waves, stones, wasps –
with an intoxicating marine cheerfulness.
But no one likes us to be happy, to you they assigned
a fool's role: "But don't overdo it, relax,"
and they tried to pin me in an insect collection amid the tears,
so that I'd drown and they could make their speeches on my grave.
I remember a day on the sandy nitrate
pampa, there were five hundred men
on strike. It was the scorching afternoon
of Tarapacá. And when their faces had drawn
all the sand and the dry bloodless desert sun,
I saw old melancholy approach my heart,
like a wineglass of hatred. That critical hour,
in the desolate salt marshes, in that frail minute
of struggle, in which we could have been defeated,
a pale little girl from the mines
recited with a plaintive voice composed of crystal and steel
one of your poems, one of your old poems that rolls between the wrinkled
    eyes
of all the workers and farmhands of my country, of America.

And that fragment of your song suddenly beamed
on my mouth like a purple flower
and ran down to my blood, filling it again
with a surging happiness born of your song.
And I thought not only of you but of your bitter Venezuela.
Years ago, I saw a student whose ankles bore
the scar of the chains that a general had put on him,
and he told me how chain gangs worked on the roads
and people disappeared in the prisons. Because that's how our America has
        been:
a prairie with devouring rivers and constellations
of butterflies (in some places, emeralds are thick as apples),
but always, all night long and along the rivers
there are bleeding ankles, near the petroleum before,
today near the nitrate, in Pisagua, where a dirty despot
has buried the flower of my country so that it will perish, and he can market
        the bones.
That's why you sing, that's why, so that dishonored and wounded America
will make its butterflies flutter and will harvest its emeralds
without punishment's ghastly blood, clotted
on the hands of hangmen and merchants.
I realized how happy you'd be, beside the Orinoco, singing,
for sure, or perhaps buying wine for your home,
occupying your place in the struggle or in happiness,
broad shouldered, like the poets of our times
– with light-coloured suits and walking shoes.
Ever since, I've been thinking that sometime I'd write you,
and when the friend arrived, chock-full of your stories
that fell from his entire suit and were
scattered under the chestnut trees in my garden,
I told myself: "Now," yet I still didn't sit down to write you.
But today has been too much: not just one but thousands
of seabirds passed by my window, and I collected
the letters which no one reads and which they carry
around the world's seacoasts, until they lose them.
And then, in each one I read your words
and they were like those that I write and dream and sing,
and so I decided to send you this letter, which I sign off now
in order to gaze through the window at the world that is ours.

Translated from the Spanish by Jack Schmitt

ALICIA PARTNOY

To My Daughter
(Letters From Prison)

I.

Listen:
My throat befriends the winds
to reach you
dear gentle heart, new eyes.
Listen:
place your ear to a sea shell,
or to this infamous prison phone,
and listen.

The reason is so simple,
so pure,
like a drop of water
or a seed
that fits in the palm of your hand.
The reason is so very simple:
I could not
keep from fighting for the happiness
of those who are our brothers our sisters.

II.

To write you,
my sun caramel, my *chiquita*,
I would have to ...
I would have to gather so much tenderness ...
And your mother, my love,
your mother has hardened,
her soul is made of stone,
she almost never cries ...
except when she writes to you,
my sun caramel,
my moon crystal.

III.

Today I cast off the lines
imprisoning my dreams
and I arrive at your golden
sun-drenched shore.
My dear daughter, I am a sailor
on a ship of hopeful dreams
with one port of call:
your soft face and your voice.
To buckle your shoes,
to let loose your laughter,
to walk by your side
through a better world ...
For these tasks
I know what is needed:
my hands and my tenderness,
my freedom and my voice.
To let loose your laughter,
to buckle your shoes,
to tear down the walls
that block out the sun ...
It is for these tasks
I am preparing
my word, my life,
my fist and my
    song.

Translated from the Spanish by Richard Schaaf, Regina Kreger, and Alicia Partnoy

César Vallejo

A man goes by with a loaf on his shoulder . . .

A man goes by with a loaf on his shoulder
After that, how can I write about my double?

Another sits down, scratches himself, picks a flea from his armpit, kills it
How can I have the nerve to talk about psychoanalysis?

Another, with a stick in his hand, has assaulted my chest
Should I immediately talk to the doctor about Socrates?

A lame man goes by, holding a child by the hand
After that, how can I read André Breton?

Another, shivers with cold, coughs, spits blood
Will it ever again be possible to refer to the Inner I?

Another searches in the mud for bones, for peel
After that, how do I write about The Infinite?

A bricklayer falls from the roof, dies before lunchtime
Can I then introduce the trope, the metaphor?

A shopkeeper steals a gramme from a customer
Do I go on to talk about the fourth dimension?

A banker fiddles his balance sheet
How can I have the face to weep at the theatre?

A pariah sleeps with his foot on his back
Should I promptly talk to a nobody about Picasso?

Somebody goes to a burial, sobbing
Is that the right moment to join the Academy?

Someone cleans a gun in his kitchen
How can I have the nerve to speak of The Beyond

Someone goes by, counting on his fingers
How can I talk about the Not-I without screaming?

Translated from the Spanish by Anthony Edkins

Claribel Alegría

Once We Were Three

It was winter with snow
it was night
today is a green day
of birds
of sunlight
a day of ashes
and laments
the wind pushes me
it drags me over the bridge
over the cracked earth
over the dry gully
overflowing plastic and tins.
Death takes life
here in Deyá
the gullies
the bridges
my dead lurking
at every corner
the innocuous railings
of a balcony
the blurred reflections
of my dead
smile at me in the distance
they take their leave
departing the cemetery
to form a wall
my skin becomes
transparent
they knock at my door
they gesticulate.
The bridge was stone
it was night
arms linked
to the sway of a song
our breath rose
from our mouths
in little crystallised clouds.
It was winter with snow
there were three of us
today the earth is dry

it reverberates
my arms drop
I am alone
my dead mount guard
they signal to me
they assail me on the radio
in the newspapers
the wall of my dead
is rising
it stretches from Aconcagua
to Izalco.
They maintain the struggle
they mark out the route
the bridge was stone
it was night
no one could tell
how they died
their tormented voices
were jumbled
they died in prison
tortured.
My dead are rising
they are angry
the streets are deserted
my dead still wink at me
I am an expropriated cemetery
they are too many to bury.

Translated from the Spanish by Amanda Hopkinson

TOMÁS BORGE

Letter To Ana Josefina

Today on your second birthday
your father remembers
the shudder
the moment of love
when he and your mother
decided
to bring you to life

This means
you were not foretold
by the cards
you were not born
through an error of the clock
or through importunate
canoodling

I have not forgotten the day
it all began
your mother and I shared
the feeling
the tabernacle
on a warm August night
We were sure of the miracle

Afterwards
when you became
a wave
inside your mother's body
we were alert
to enjoy
your whispering hands

The day you were born
– 12th of April 1975 –
they tried to assassinate me

But I was so protected
by your newness
there was no room
for death

Later
I was arrested
and enemies wrote
scars
on my ribs
and my soul's
frontiers

Hooded and handcuffed
for nine months
in a lichen-clad
cubby-hole
I watched
the procession
of darkness

In solitary
but now with the right
to clench my fists
I clung to your memory
I needed to be worthy
of you my daughter
deserve you

If I had grovelled
on my knees
I would ask you
to write me off
But I was and will be
loyal to catechism
and heresies

Although without merit
– I am barely
a grain of maize –
I want you to feel
proud of the man
who embraced
your mother

Yes, your mother is an oasis
She washed
your clandestine nappies
to the point of exhaustion
And her life is a torch

a strong bolt
a lake of poppies

I will forever be
thirsty for your love
but your mother
must always
come first
special
as communion bread

She is like
those Managua evenings
in summer
like doves' kisses
skimming the fresh waters
of all those inland seas

I don't know if I'll die
when the cocks crow
this coming winter
But if my hands grow cold
and my eyes lose their teasing gleam
their tenderness
I shall live on

I shall go on
if you are generous
if in your heart
egoism finds no room
and with your sweetness and your rage
you stand firm
against injustices

Then
the moment when your mother and I
became a single body
to bring you into being
will make sense
The light we wanted to strike
will shine

Tipitapa Prison, 12th April 1977

Translated from the Spanish by Dinah Livingstone

ERNESTO CARDENAL

The Women From Cuá Arrived

And the women from Cuá also came to the great mass rally.
The wife of Jacinto Hernández who fell at Kuskawás.
The wife of Bernardino.
                              Amanda Aguilar.
A delegation from Cuá.
                    They came with children also.
They recalled their sorrows, the "Events at Cuá."
At the Cuá which never told where the guerrillas were.
                    Amanda Aguilar knew a poem about Cuá.
Amanda Aguilar was a pseudonym, her name is Petrona Hernández.)
They were taken with their children to the command post of Cuá.
          "Some of us were pregnant."
They were left homeless.
Angelina Díaz said:
          "We went from place to place through the countryside."
And Bernardino's widow:
          "Battered and dirty, blindfolded, they carried him off."
A story one can never forget, said Juana Tinoco.
She told of the tortures to their little children.
          Their little children screaming in that command post.
          "It was so they'd tell who we were giving food to."
And Bernardino's widow:
"He had a sick son, and was comforting him in our little loft.
The guards arrived. And they yelled that he should come down.
          He said: I'm just tending to my son!
The lieutenant told me:
          Say good-bye to that husband of yours, you'll never see him again.
I went following after him."
Bernardino Díaz Ochoa, the one who said:
          "We're not birds meant to live off the air,
          we're not fish meant to live off the sea,
          we're men meant to live off the earth."
When they took Bernardino away it was cornhusking time.
And Bernardino's wife also recounted:
"They pulled out his tongue with a barnacle clamp.
They stuck nails in his ears.
They'd asked him: How many guerrillas come here? Do you know Tomás
                                             Borge?
When they killed him, the guardsmen were drinking raw booze."
          There day and night were always night.

Until the revolution of the boys triumphed.
Then it was as if they pulled off their hoods.
Amanda Aguilar brought food to the guerrillas.
These things the ones from Cuá related.
Humbly dressed they came
with a placard that read: The women of Cuá, Present!
This was the journalistic report
about the arrival of the delegation of peasant women from Cuá.

Translated from the Spanish by Marc Zimmerman

ERNESTO CARDENAL

A Museum In Kampuchea

We went into a museum that used to be a high school
but under Pol Pot the high school became
                    the biggest prison in Cambodia.
The classrooms divided into little cells.
Here one only came to die.
More than 20,000 prisoners passed through here
                    of whom only 17 survived,
the ones who hadn't yet been killed when the liberating
                                        troops arrived.
            This was Pol Pot's "Democratic Kampuchea".
Here are the photos taken of them on entering.
                    They took photos of them all.
Some with their hands tied, others wearing chains
                                        and iron collars.
        The worst thing to see was the horror in their faces.
You could see they weren't looking at the camera, but at death
            and the torture before death.
But even more shocking was a smiling face:
a girl, or teenage boy, someone innocent, unaware
evidently of what was going to happen to them.
            And photos of mothers with babies.
Some crude device for pulling out fingernails.
Tongs for tearing off nipples.
            A great many different kinds of tools ...
The tank where they were held underwater.
The posts where they were hanged.
The cell where Pol Pot's Minister of Information was also held
            before being killed.
More than 100 mass graves where they buried them
                                have been found.
The infants buried with their milk bottles and pacifiers.
And the skulls, large piles of skulls
                that nobody wants to see.
        They killed 3 of the 8 million inhabitants.
They destroyed the factories, the schools, the medicines.
They'd jail someone for wearing glasses.
            The towns remained deserted.
The whole world knew about this.
How can it be that now, since Kampuchea was liberated,
the North American press doesn't speak badly of Pol Pot?

Finally we went outside.
                    There were flowers outside.
In a clean puddle a white duck fluttered
            bathing itself in the water and sun.
The young women who passed by on the street
looked like pagodas.

Translated from the Spanish by Jonathan Cohen

Somoza Unveils The Statue Of Somoza In Somoza Stadium

It's not that I think the people erected this statue
because I know better than you that I ordered it myself.
Nor do I pretend to pass into posterity with it
because I know the people will topple it over someday.
Not that I wanted to erect to myself in life
the monument you never would erect to me in death:
I erected this statue because I knew you would hate it.

Translated from the Spanish by Stephen F. White

OTTO RENÉ CASTILLO

Apolitical Intellectuals

One day,
the apolitical
intellectuals
of my country
will be interrogated
by the humblest
of our people.

They will be asked
what they did
when their country was slowly
dying out,
like a sweet campfire,
small and abandoned.

No one will ask them
about their dress
or their long
siestas
after lunch,
or about their futile struggles
against "nothingness,"
or about their ontological
way
to make money.
No, they won't be questioned
on Greek mythology,
or about the self-disgust they felt
when someone deep inside them
was getting ready to die
the coward's death.
They will be asked nothing
about their absurd
justifications
nurtured in the shadow
of a huge lie.

On that day,
the humble people will come,
those who never had a place

in the books and poems
of the apolitical intellectuals
but who daily delivered
their bread and milk,
their eggs and tortillas;
those who mended their clothes,
those who drove their cars,
those who took care of their dogs and gardens,
and worked for them,
and they will ask:
"What did you do when the poor
suffered, when tenderness and life
were dangerously burning out in them?"

    Apolitical intellectuals
of my sweet country,
you will have nothing to say.

    A vulture of silence
will eat your guts.
Your own misery
will gnaw at your souls.
And you will be mute
in your shame.

Translated from the Spanish by Francisco X. Alarcón

OTTO RENÉ CASTILLO

Police Jail

1.

The police jail in my country
is colored martyr grey
and winter grey.
The cry of suffering
has sounded against time
and against the hate
inside its walls,
built alongside the anguish of the people.

It's a frontier of poison thorns.
The man of the people
                    knows it
and rebels against it,
because there,
              for many years,
the poor man's voice was battered,
the flower of his dreams was tortured,
and a lonely tower of laments
and bitter lilies
was raised up by the pride
                        of the hangman.

The police jail in my country
is, in truth, dismal.

The unfolding of so many hopes
was broken there.
Many men died
holding the absence of food and their children
in the sweet hollows
                    of their hands.
They died on schedule,
holding on tight in their tortured delirium
to a warm landscape of corn
and thinking of the birds
                        flying
freely through the blue sky
of Guatemala.

2.

Oh...how painful
it is to have to speak of all this!
But the police jail
          in my country
invades the land
          of clear
laughter,
      raises its hand
of terrifying ivy
          into the heart
of the wind
       and dirties
our clean dialogue with life.
That's how the people know
its color is grey
and so sad.

3.

That's why children run from policemen,
accusing them with their simple fear.

That's why the people point out the jail,
spitting with hate.

Translated from the Spanish by Stephen Kessler

ROQUE DALTON

The Consolations Of Soul Saving

I

(1932)

Agustín Farabundo Martí,
letting it pass when the priest
with whom he had refused to confess
embraced him,
walked on to the execution wall.

Suddenly he turned
and called to Chinto Castellanos,
the Presidential Secretary, who had stayed up with him through the night
chatting and smoking cigars
in the room where the dead lie in state.

– Embrace me – he whispered in his ear –
it irritates me that the last embrace I take away
from life should be with such a scheming priest.
– And why me? – asked Chinto.
– Ah – replied Farabundo – because you are going to be one of us,
in time you'll see.

And he faced the firing squad.

II

(1944)

To execute Víctor Manuel Marín
they had to prop him up by his armpits
on wooden sawhorses
(those they put the ironing board on).

During the torture they broke his arms
and legs and a few ribs,
plus they tore out one eyeball
and crushed his testicles.

The same priest who couldn't get Farabundo to confess
went up to Víctor Manual, and said:
'My son, I come to console your spirit.'

And that one replied between his busted teeth
and swollen lips:
'It's my body that weakens, not my spirit.'

Then they shot him.

III

(1973)

Every time I read in the society pages
of *Diaio de Hoy* or *Prensa Gráfica*
those pompous obituaries
costing two hundred *colones* or more
informing us a bourgeois died
consoled with the last rites
of our Catholic religion,
I think of all those two deaths mean to us:
that they refused the consolations of those soul-savers.

Translated from the Spanish by Richard Schaaf

Roque Dalton

Hitler Mazzini: Comparison Between Chile In 1974 And El Salvador In 1932

It doesn't surprise me that they slander
the honorable Military Junta of Chile.

Communists are like that:

They say the military has killed
in some four months
more than eighty thousand Chileans.

That's an exaggeration
since concrete evidence shows
no more than some
forty thousand were killed.

It was the same with El Salvador in 1932.
The communists say General Martínez
killed in less than a month
more than thirty thousand peasants.
That, too, is an exaggeration:
no more than twenty thousand were verified dead.

The rest
were considered disappeared.

Translated from the Spanish by Richard Schaaf

ROQUE DALTON

Like You

Like you I
love love, life, the sweet smell
of things, the sky-blue
landscape of January days.

And my blood boils up
and I laugh through eyes
that have known the buds of tears.

I believe the world is beautiful
and that poetry, like bread, is for everyone.

And that my veins don't end in me
but in the unanimous blood
of those who struggle for life,
love,
little things,
landscape and bread,
the poetry of everyone.

Translated from the Spanish by Jack Hirschman

ALAÍDE FOPPA

Prayer 1

Give me, Lord,
a deep silence
and a thick veil
over my face.
Thus may I become
a sealed world,
a darkened island.
I'll painfully excavate myself
as through hardened earth,
to reach my furthest depths.
Once I'm bled white,
my life will become
lithe and clear.
Then, like a sonorous and translucent river
my trapped song
will flow free.

Translated from the Spanish by Amanda Hopkinson

ANGEL CUADRA

This Man

We will never know how many Cubans have lost their lives
in the sea, escaping from the island by way of the coast.

There is a man moving through the night.
Perhaps no one will ever know about his small tragedy.
For days and weeks he has dreamed about this fear,
spent sleepless hours reviewing his terrors and his hopes.
He has smiled cordially,
pondered slogans, made political concessions
and secretly wrestled with his impotence.
He had to pass through those daily reefs, and so he did.
He was a simple man who went to the movies
and walked the streets under an ordinary name.
It's just that in him burned a light,
a very little light, painful, in his heart and temples.
He carried no weight in that sea
of great affairs where he was dragged
closer every day toward disaster.
And on this night, a night like any other,
this man shouldered his terrors and his hopes.

The moon, which is always mentioned in these cases,
revealed him on the coast,
and this man's light was shining out.
Every possible eye, every accusing finger
was raised in the darkness to denounce his flight.
In his solitude he had become a great man, a fugitive,
this simple man who did not leave his name,
and we will never know where
the ocean quenched his little light,
now that he has left the coast
where the winds sing through flutes of salt.

Translated from the Spanish by Catherine Rodríguez-Nieto

Angel Cuadra

Brief Letter To Donald Walsh
Translator Of My Poems (In Memoriam)

My friend:
In what language shall we begin our conversation?
How can I begin to celebrate
the support your voice gives me
in sending out my songs, drenched in your accents,
to live in this world?
And not know what the warmth of your hand is like in friendship;
only this music shining from the soul,
stretching like a bridge between us:
you in your country open to the stars,
I behind bars of rancor,
dying since the dawn.
Yet even so we meet.
The hands of friends
brought your name to me with the morning dew.
And you are here, and I am talking to you.

Because I've learned that not everything is hatred.
I want to declare another word,
sow it as it were in furrows
of goodness and of hope.

There are some men who crush my words,
tear me to pieces for producing beauty,
bring my poem to trial
and sentence it to run the gauntlet:
the drops of blood my poem sheds
form a constellation among the stars.

But there are other men who rescue me
and save my poems like unransomed light,
who gather up its pieces of suffering clay
and, like Prometheus, lend me fire for it.
The fire of love, I proclaim it now,
that is the word I will defend
in martyrdom, among the thorns.
My poem, the grape of pain
for which I bleed and grow.

And you exist, Donald Walsh.
I knew nothing of your musical being,
of that gemstone clear and high, transparent.
Don't leave now
that I have found days dawning in my heart
that were sent me by your hand.
Don't leave now
that we begin to speak in a language
that unites the souls of Whitman and Marti.
And on the streets of all the world
– without bars, without bitterness or fear
– you and I will walk together, speaking
the word of Love that has existed since before the age of man.

22 March 1980, Boniato Prison

Donald Walsh died a few days before the arrival of this poem, which was enclosed in a letter from Cuadra written in April 1980.

Translated from the Spanish by Catherine Rodríguez-Nieto

ERNESTO DÍAZ RODRÍGUEZ

The Little One

If a child wants you
to tell him
what is
a little one's life,
tell him first
that there are other things
much more beautiful
such as the flowers
when spring
dresses
in a thousand colors.
Show him the sky,
the seagull
and the butterfly...
the snowy costume
of his feathers
over the waves.

If the child cries,
if later he asks you
to tell him what
a prisoner's
life is like...
tell him there are things
even more beautiful!
The white rose,
the white star,
and the colors
of his flag.

If a child wants
you to tell him
what a prisoner's
life is like:
sing a song,
make up a game...!
But don't tell
the little one
what the prisoner's life
is like.

Translated from the Spanish: translator unknown

ANGEL PARDO

Fracture

Night shatters, letting springtime escape
while brief seconds take refuge in cold pores
deprived of their hours.

Day hides in a dry belly
full of the emptiness of breathless air
and mixes with the gastric juices of will.

The moisture of waiting
dries out the throat, cracks the lips,
sets the teeth to gnawing on a mass of nothingness
tasting only like a mouthful of good-byes.

Night shatters . . .
day crumbles . . .
autumn as well.
Teeth fall out
gums break open
and while night is away
a roof tile is split asunder
by a single ray of sunlight.

November 25, 1980
17 days

Take Me With You

My lips have not drunk,
nor has my mouth tasted,
nor have my teeth chewed
the sweet ambrosia of delirium.

I want to partake of your life,
I want to drink of your vine,
I want to sink in your depths.

Embrace me, embrace me,
take away my summertime,
embrace me, embrace me,
oh, take me with you.

My lips have not drunk,
nor has my mouth tasted,
nor have my teeth chewed
the sweet ambrosia of delirium.

Slake my anxiety,
give me your being,
embrace me, embrace me,
take away my summertime,
embrace me, embrace me,
oh, take me with you.

I want to consume you in my hunger,
I want to feel you in my blood
in the fury of your burning flesh.

Embrace me, embrace me,
take away my summertime,
embrace me, embrace me,
take me with you until I awaken.

December 4, 1980
26 days

Rays Of Faith

Seconds are made dizzy as earth spins around,
while minutes are lost in hours
and days run around in wakeful nights.

Months shrink,
the world contracts
and new ideas spew forth.

A comet shoots through the galaxy
trailing satellites
while earth keeps on turning around.

The corner of a star
shines from the mouth of a dare
and in the distant sky
a cross holds up the power line
through which rays of faith run their course.

December 6, 1980
28 days

Globule In The Void

A globule tumbles into the void
and spews forth flecks of vomit
at the immensity of its thoughts.

Like an atom recomposing
a melody of stars,
El Turquino* stretches out
and wets his throat with the moisture
of the nearby Cauto**.

Amid the taste of forest thickets,
history is charred in the quarries
of his monolithic frame
whose spine and shoulders
carry the weight of all humanity.

Nothing stops;
the sun keeps on rising in the east
setting fire anew at each instant
to the torches of flames
shining like hymns on the Olympus of the Antilles,
pointing westward always.

December 8, 1980
30 days

* *Highest mountain in Cuba*
** *Country's longest river.*

Translated from the Spanish by Barbara E. Joe

ARMANDO VALLADARES

Planted In My Chair

I am planted in my wheelchair
with the impotence of a tree
of deep roots
that let me open
my arms into branches
but don't let me
walk in the roads
of the forests that call me.
This horizon of reeds and rocks tortures me
and the blue bevy
of yellow butterflies
that I want to reach
beyond these prison bars
where the sun belongs to everyone
with the pain and trembling of these arm-branches
where the blood-sap burns
stretched toward the impossible
in an absurd effort
while my root-feet
dry up ... and fuse
with the iron
of my wheelchair
I am almost a tree
but a sad tree
What impotence
to be unable to run

Translated from the Spanish: translator unknown

ARMANDO VALLADARES

Wings Will Grow One Day

Wings will grow some day
on my wheelchair
I will be able to fly over parks
carpeted with children and violets.

My chair will be a winged dream
without the deranging obsession of bars
and I will be able to climb the rainbow
and alight on a quiet mountain

My chair will be a dream without eyes
a metal swallow above the earth.

Translated from the Spanish: translator unknown

Jorge Valls Arango

Sweet Fish

Mother,
my last outcry
hangs from a steel strut
(behind the window
like dead hens,
dead, black hens;
and some strange inverted moons,
daughters of chrome and sulphur...).
A tiger cub is crouching on my nape
gnawing marrow,
gnawing marrow...
and vessels of fog, transparent,
carrying a sweet riddled fish
looking on with anguished eyes –
flesh surrendered,
releasing a warm little thread of blood –,
a sweet fish pierced
by all my thorns.
Mother of the sweet fish,
the invaded crevices
whistle in your ears,
and you are pierced
from boat to boat by the distilled bile.
Mother,
of ash and sand and dying ember,
of ground and pressed thistle
and of crushed stone
and of spitting wind
among swirls of rebelliousness
I am made.
The sweet fish is all
my flashing eyes watch
as they wildly roll around;
the sweet fish with staring eyes
and the thin, gaping mouth.

*Translated from the Spanish by James E. Marannis & Emilio E. Labrada,
with Louis Bourne*

KAMAU BRATHWAITE

Stone

for Mikey Smith
stoned to death on Stony Hill, Kingston 1954-1983

When the stone fall that morning out of the johncrow sky

it was not dark at first . that opening on to the red sea humming
but something in my mouth like feathers . blue like bubbles
carrying signals & planets & the sliding curve of the
world like a water pic. ture in a raindrop when the pressure. drop

When the stone fall that morning out of the johncrow sky

I couldn't cry out because my mouth was full of beast & plunder
as if I was gnashing badwords among tombstones
as if the road up stony hill . round the bend by the church
yard . on the way to the post office . was a bad bad dream

& the dream was like a snarl of broken copper wire zig
zagging its electric flashes up the hill & splitt. ing spark & flow.
ers high. er up the hill. past the white houses & the ogogs bark.
ing all teeth & fur. nace & my mother like she up. like she up.

like she up. side down up a tree like she was scream.
like she was scream. like she was scream. ing no & no.
body i could hear could hear a word i say. ing . even though
there were so many poems left & the tape was switched on &

runn. ing & runn. ing &
the green light was red & they was stannin up there &
evva. where in london & amsterdam & at unesco in paris &
in west berlin & clapp. ing & clapp. ing & clapp. ing &

not a soul on stony hill to even say amen

& yet it was happening happening happening .
the fences begin to crack in i skull .
& there were loud booodooooooooooooooooooogs like
guns goin off   .   them ole time magnums .

or like a fireworks a dreadlocks was on fire .
& the gaps where the river comin down
inna the drei gully where my teeth use to be smilin .
& i tuff gong tongue that use to press against them & parade

pronounciation . now unannounce & like a black wick in i head & dead .

& it was like a heavy heavy riddim low down in i belly . bleedin dub .
& there was like this heavy heavy black dog thump. in in i chest &
pump. in

murdererrrrrrrrrrrrrrrrrrrrrrrrrrrrrrrrrrrrrrrrrrrrrrrrrrrrrrrrrrrrrrrrrrrrrrrrrrrr

& i throat like dem tie. like dem tie. like dem tie a tight tie a.
round it. twist. ing my name quick crick. quick crick .
& a nevva wear neck. tie yet .

& a hear when de big boot kick down i door . stump
in it foot pun a knot in de floor . board .
a window slam shat at de back a mi heart .

de itch & ooze & damp a de yaaad
in mi sil. ver tam. bourines closer & closer .
st joseph marching bands crash. ing & closer .

bom si. cai si. ca boom ship bell . bom si. cai si. ca boom ship bell

& a laughin more blood & spittin out

lawwwwwwwwwwwwwwwwwwwwwwwwwwwwwwwwwwwwwwwwwwwwwwwwd .

i two eye lock to the sun & the two sun starin back black
from de grass

& a bline to de butterfly fly. in

•
& it was a wave on stony hill caught in crust of sun. light

•
& it was like a matchstick schooner into harbour muffled in the silence
of of it wound

•
& it was like the blue of speace was filling up the heavens
with it thunder

& it was like the wind was grow. ing skin
the skin had hard hairs . hardering

•
it was like marcus garvey rising from his coin .
stepping towards his people crying dark

& every mighty word he trod. the ground fall dark & hole
be. hine him like it was a bloom x. ploding sound .

my ears were bleed. ing sound

•

& I was quiet now because i had become that sound

the sun. light morning washed the choral limestone harsh
against the soft volcanic ash. i was

& it was slipping past me into water. & it was slipping past me
into root. i was

& it was
slipping past me into flower. & it was ripping upwards

into shoot. i was

& every politrician tongue in town was lash.
ing me with spit & cut. rass wit & ivy whip & wrinkle jumbimum

it was like warthog . grunt. ing in the ground

& children running down the hill run right on through the spash
of pouis that my breathe. ing make when it was howl & red &

bubble
& sparrow twits pluck tic & tap. worm from the grass

as if i man did nevva have no face. as if i man did nevva in this place

•

When the stone fall that morning out of the johncrow sky

i could not hold it brack or black it back or block it off or limp
away or roll it from me into memory or light or rock it steady
into night. be

cause it builds me now with leaf & spiderweb & soft & crunch &
like the pow.
derwhite & slip & grit inside your leather. boot &

fills my blood with deaf my bone with hobbledumb & echo.
less neglect neglect neglect neglect &

lawwwwwwwwwwwwwwwwwwwwwwwwwwwwwwwwwwwwwwwwwww

•

i am the stone that kills me

MARTIN CARTER

I Come From The Nigger Yard

I come from the nigger yard of yesterday
leaping from the oppressor's hate
and the scorn of myself;
from the agony of the dark hut in the shadow
and the hurt of things;
from the long days of cruelty and the long nights of pain
down to the wide streets of tomorrow, of the next day
leaping I come, who cannot see will hear.

In the nigger yard I was naked like the new born
naked like a stone or a star.
It was a cradle of blind days rocking in time
torn like the skin from the back of a slave.
It was an aching floor on which I crept
on my hands and knees
searching the dust for the trace of a root
or the mark of a leaf or the shape of a flower.

It was me always walking with bare feet,
meeting strange faces like those in dreams or fever
when the whole world turns upside down
and no one knows which is the sky or the land
which heart is his among the torn or wounded
which face is his among the strange and terrible
walking about, groaning between the wind.

And there was always sad music somewhere in the land
like a bugle and a drum between the houses
voices of women singing far away
pauses of silence, then a flood of sound.
But these were things like ghosts or spirits of wind.
It was only a big world spinning outside
and men, born in agony, torn in torture, twisted and broken like a leaf,
and the uncomfortable morning, the beds of hunger stained and sordid
like the world, big and cruel, spinning outside.

Sitting sometimes in the twilight near the forest
where all the light is gone and every bird
I notice a tiny star neighbouring a leaf
a little drop of light a piece of glass
straining over heaven tiny bright

like a spark seed in the destiny of gloom.
O it was the heart like this tiny star near to the sorrows
straining against the whole world and the long twilight
spark of man's dream conquering the night
moving in darkness stubborn and fierce
till leaves of sunset change from green to blue
and shadows grow like giants everywhere.

So was I born again stubborn and fierce
screaming in a slum.
It was a city and coffin space for home
a river running, prisons, hospitals
men drunk and dying, judges full of scorn
priests and parsons fooling gods with words
and me, like a dog tangled in rags
spotted with sores powdered with dust
screaming with hunger, angry with life and men.

It was a child born from a mother full of her blood
weaving her features bleeding her life in clots.
It was pain lasting from hours to months and to years
weaving a pattern telling a tale leaving a mark
on the face and the brow.
Until there came the iron days cast in a foundry
Where men make hammers things that cannot break
and anvils heavy hard and cold like ice.

And so again I became one of the ten thousands
one of the uncountable miseries owning the land.
When the moon rose up only the whores could dance
the brazen jazz of music throbbed and groaned
filling the night air full of rhythmic questions.
It was the husk and the seed challenging fire
birth and the grave challenging life.

Until to-day in the middle of the tumult
when the land changes and the world's all convulsed
when different voices join to say the same
and different hearts beat out in unison
where on the aching floor of where I live
the shifting earth is twisting into shape
I take again my nigger life, my scorn
and fling it in the face of those who hate me.
It is me the nigger boy turning to manhood
linking my fingers, welding my flesh to freedom.

I come from the nigger yard of yesterday
leaping from the oppressor's hate
and the scorn of myself.
I come to the world with scars upon my soul
wounds on my body, fury in my hands.
I turn to the histories of men and the lives of the peoples.
I examine the shower of sparks the wealth of the dreams.
I am pleased with the glories and sad with the sorrows
rich with the riches, poor with the loss.
From the nigger yard of yesterday I come with my burden.
To the world of tomorrow I turn with my strength.

This Is The Dark Time, My Love

This is the dark time, my love.
All round the land brown beetles crawl about.
The shining sun is hidden in the sky.
Red flowers bend their heads in awful sorrow.

This is a dark time, my love.
It is the season of oppression, dark metal, and tears.
It is the festival of guns, the carnival of misery.
Everywhere the faces of men are strained and anxious.

Who comes walking in the dark night time?
Whose boot of steel tramps down the slender grass?
It is the man of death, my love, the strange invader
watching you sleep and aiming at your dream.

MARTIN CARTER

Letter 1

This is what they do with me
Put me in prison, hide me away
cut off the world, cut out the sun
darken the land, blacken the flower
stifle my breath and hope that I die!

But I laugh at them –
I laugh because I know they cannot kill me
nor kill my thoughts, nor murder what I write.
I am a man living among my people
Proud as the tree the axeman cannot tumble –
So if my people live I too must live!
And they will live, I tell you they will live!
But these ...
I laugh at them.
I do not know what thoughts pass through their minds.
Perhaps they do not know to think at all –
tigers don't think, nor toads nor rooting swine
but only man, just listen and you know.

In Kenya to-day they drink the blood of black women.
In Malaya the hero is hunted and shot like a dog.
Here, they catch us and lick their tongues like beasts
who crouch to prey upon some little child.

But I tell you
Like a tide from the heart of things
Inexorably and inevitably
A day will come.

If I do not live to see that day
My son will see it.
If he does not see that day
His son will see it.
And it will come circling the world like fire.
It will come to this land and every land
and when it comes I'll come alive again
and laugh again and walk out of this prison.

Britain
Ireland
USA

PAT ARROWSMITH

English Political Prisoner

Stretched out on my tough-haired bedspread
(the straight limbed wooden chair too stiff and hostile),
patched with faded stains of saturation
from god knows what unsavoury previous source,
the cave top arches over me,
squat window lours down at me,
glares behind its heavy frown of bars.
Brick walls enclose me,
thinly camouflaged by scrawled-on skin of paint.
Beneath me lies the dust-ribbed splintery floor.
In front, the massive studded door stands guard.

Yet I feel guilty – it is all so easy.
The hours pass in steady, dull tranquility.
I read books and papers, letters from my comrades.
Cocooned in music from the radio I'm permitted
I hardly hear the din outside my cell.

No warders drag me off to be interrogated,
order me to confess or else be killed.
No one sticks poles and bottles up my genitals,
forces me to stand stock-still for days on end;
roasts me in a specially designed oven,
holds my head down under water till I burst;
shoots electric shock waves through my nipples,
chains me in a filthy cage for years;
gives me grit and maggots for my dinner,
injects drugs in me till I go insane.

For I am not in prison in Rhodesia,
incarcerated on an island off Vietnam;
being cured of deviations in Siberia,
interned indefinitely in Northern Ireland;
held for questioning by the Chile Junta,
detained untried in fascist Spain.

No, I am English. This is England, land of justice,
of peace, democracy, equality, fair-play.
We are temperate, tolerant, urbane and placid,
enjoy free speech and free association –
there are no political prisoners, they say.

Holloway Prison, 1974

BRENDAN BEHAN

Loneliness

The blackberries' taste
after rainfall
on the hilltop.

In the silence of the prison
the train's cold whistle.

The whisper of laughing lovers
to the lonely.

Translated from the Irish Gaelic by Ulick O'Connor

LINTON KWESI JOHNSON

Sonny's Lettah

(Anti-Sus Poem)

                                        Brixtan Prison
                                        Jebb Avenue
                                        Landan south-west two
                                        Inglan

Dear Mama,
Good Day.
I hope dat wen
deze few lines reach y'u,
they may find y'u in di bes' af helt.

Mama,
I really doan know how fi tell y'u dis,
cause I did mek a salim pramis
fi tek care a lickle Jim
an' try mi bes' fi look out fi him.

Mama,
Ah really did try mi bes',
but none-di-les'
mi sarry fi tell y'u seh
poor lickle Jim get arres'.

It woz di miggle a di rush howah
wen everybady jus' a hus'le an' a bus'le
fi goh home fi dem evenin' showah;
mi an' Jim stan-up
waitin' pan a bus,
nat causin' no fus',
wen all an a sudden
a police van pull-up.

out jump t'ree policeman,
di' hole a dem carryin batan.
Dem waak straight up to mi an' Jim.
One a dem hol' aan to Jim
seh him tekin him in;
Jim tell him fi let goh a him
far him noh dhu not'n
an him naw t'ief,
nat even a but'n.
Jim start to wriggle

Di police start to giggle.

Mama,
mek Ah tell y'u whey dem dhu to Jim
Mama,
mek Ah tell y'u whey dem dhu to him:

dem t'ump him in him belly
an' it turn to jelly
dem lick him pan him back
an' him rib get pap
dem lick him pan him he'd
but it tuff like le'd
dem kick him in him seed
an' it started to bleed

Mama,
Ah jus' could'n' stan-up deh
an' noh dhu not'n:

so mi jook one in him eye
an' him started to cry
mi t'ump one in him mout'
an' him started to shout
mi kick one pan him shin
an' him started to spin
mi tump him pan him chin
an' him drap pan a bin

an' crash
an de'd.

Mama,
more policeman come dung
an' beat mi to di grung;
dem charge Jim fi sus,
dem charge mi fi murdah.

Mama,
doan fret,
doan get depres'
an' doun-hearted.
Be af good courage
till I hear fram you.

I remain
your son,
Sonny.

SAUNDERS LEWIS

The Carcass

'Many ask, Welshman among them, why it should be allowed to live.'
Article in Y *Llenor*, Summer 1941

The carcass of Wales is lying here, sorely abused,
　　With not many to weep for her misfortune,
Her conqueror's wretched slave-girl – yesterday found
　　To his fancy – today, a turd.

To lick her disgrace and muck her about underfoot
　　They gather together, the shabby herd
Of magistrate swine, grunting above her blood,
　　And the frenzied bitches of parliament.

What is the stench that's moving within her flesh?
　　Tapeworms, a swarm of officials
Growing fat on the death of a poor motherland;

And on her forehead, see – a black toad
　　Croaking before the day of judgement
A quaking summons to the shameless desecration.

Translated from the Welsh by Joseph P. Clancy

SAUNDERS LEWIS

A Word To The Welsh

You Welsh, my kinsfolk,
Who have nurtured dreams of luxury on a Welshwoman's milk and breast,
And have garnered memory and conscience and all the guilt of adolescence
And the power to judge good and evil
From father and mother's word-stock and the voices of church or chapel,
Since without those there is no Welsh,
Consider now and judge,
You Welsh-speaking Welsh:
The government of the realm is announcing your end
And that there'll be no Welsh-speaking Wales;
Murder has been the goal of the government
For six centuries,
And today it sees it achieved.
The killing the Conquest did not attempt,
That the treason of the Union could not bring about,
That the thousand years of poverty,
Lacking dignity, lacking learning, lacking manners,
Did not manage,
Today pleasure and the business of pleasure with its greed and its babble in
     every kitchen and parlour of our land,
Under government patronage,
Is destroying our families and their faith,
Is accomplishing our death.

Rape is a tyrant's deed, *summa iniuria*,
The attribute of an unjust government,
'Customary after arrogance, a long death' -
Unless a shock and a challenge come to the nation of Wales, and a sudden
     awakening,
And a declaration to the world
That there is blood in her veins,
And she will not die without witnesses,
Be they but three.

Translated from the Welsh by Joseph P. Clancy.

EOGHAN MACCORMAIC

Acquaintance Renewed

Walking up the wing tonight
I saw a face I hadn't seen in years,
ten years, almost, less a month or two
and the face had changed. Older,
the silver shade of age on the hairs
and crows feet stamping years on the
fold at the side of the eyes, marking time.
They hadn't changed, still staring,
watching, a bit less assured maybe,
and that poutinglower lip, like a bed
hanging out of a window, gave him away.
I mind him younger, at forty, a bull
of a man standing over my naked frame.
I was eight stone ten, he had half as much
again, and clothes, boots and other screws
to help him drag me from my cell. He
tried, I mind, to break my shoulder
with the door frame. Shoulders break easier
than conviction and dignity weighs less
than all the clothes he wore. The bastard
tried and failed that day but he hurt me
all the same. Saw him eyeing me tonight
but I wouldn't give him the satisfaction
of recognition. Funny how his kind seem
to think we're almost old comrades,
the blanket screw and Blanketman, the
link being their infliction of what we endured.
Symbiotic. Know now how survivors
of Auschwitz feel when old ghosts
come into view.

Eoghan MacCormaic

A Reflection Across The Yard

Across the yard from this wing
sits an identical row of cells
It's occupied by Loyalists
and some will say they can tell
the difference by the windows
– ours are sparse and bare
theirs are lined with personal goods
while over here we share.

We don't have much in common
it's always them and us
we rarely meet and seldom talk
we've nothing to discuss
And looking out our windows
both sides are framed in bars
but they see Taigues while we see Huns
and neither side see the stars.

At night when all the cells are lit
and I stand up by the door
I can look across and see them
like they see me I'm sure
And times I wonder what they think
when they look across and see
Do we ever cross their minds at all
and what do they think of me?

PADRAIC PEARSE

The Rebel

I am come of the seed of the people, the people that sorrow,
That have no treasure but hope,
No riches laid up but a memory
Of an Ancient glory.
My mother bore me in bondage, in bondage my mother was born,
I am of the blood of serfs:
The children with whom I have played, the men and women with whom I have
    eaten,
Have had masters over them, have been under the lash of masters,
And, though gentle, have served churls;
The hands that have touched mine, the dear hands whose touch is familiar to
    me,
Have worn shameful manacles, have been bitten at the wrist by manacles,
Have grown hard with the manacles and the task-work of strangers,
I am flesh of the flesh of these lowly, I am bone of their bone,
I that have never submitted;
I that have a soul greater than the souls of my people's masters,
I that have vision and prophecy and the gifts of fiery speech,
I that have spoken with God on the top of His holy hill.

And because I am of the people, I understand the people,
I am sorrowful with their sorrow, I am hungry with their desire:
My heart has been heavy with the grief of mothers,
My eyes have been wet with the tears of children.
I have yearned with old wistful men,
And laughed or cursed with young men;
Their shame is my shame, and I have reddened for it,
Reddened for that they have served, they who should be free,
Reddened for that they have gone in want, while others have been full
Reddened for that they have walked in fear of lawyers and of their jailers
With their writs of summons and their handcuffs,
Men mean and cruel!
I could have borne stripes on my body rather than this shame of my people.

And now I speak, being full of vision;
I speak to my people, and I speak in my people's name to the masters of my
    people.
I say to my people that they are holy, that they are august, despite their chains,
That they are greater than those that hold them, and stronger and purer,
That they have but need of courage, and to call on the name of their God,

God the unforgetting, the dear God that loves the peoples
For whom He died naked, suffering shame.
And I say to my people's masters: Beware,
Beware of the thing that is coming, beware of the risen people,
Who shall take what ye would not give. Did ye think to conquer the people,
Or that Law is stronger than life and than men's desire to be free?
We will try it out with you, ye that have harried and held,
Ye that have bullied and bribed, tyrants, hypocrites, liars!

OSCAR WILDE

The Ballad Of Reading Gaol

V

I know not whether Laws be right,
Or whether Laws be wrong;
All that we know who lie in gaol
Is that the wall is strong;
And that each day is like a year,
A year whose days are long.

But this I know, that every Law
That men have made for Man,
Since first Man took his brother's life,
And sad world began,
But straws the wheat and saves the chaff
With a most evil fan.

This too I know – and wise it were
If each could know the same –
That every prison that men build
Is built with bricks of shame,
And bound with bars lest Christ should see
How men their brothers maim.

With bars they blur the gracious moon,
And blind the goodly sun:
And they do well to hide their Hell,
For in it things are done
That Son of God nor son of Man
Ever should look upon!

The vilest deeds like poison weeds
Bloom well in prison-air:
It is only what is good in Man
That wastes and withers there:
Pale Anguish keeps the heavy gate,
And the Warder is Despair.

For they starve the little frightened child
Till it weeps both night and day:
And they scourge the weak, and flog the fool,
And gibe the old and grey,
And some grow mad, and all grow bad,
And none a word may say.

Each narrow cell in which we dwell
Is a foul and dark latrine,
And the fetid breath of living Death
Chokes up each grated screen,
And all, but Lust, is turned to dust
In Humanity's machine.

The brackish water that we drink
Creeps with a loathsome slime,
And the bitter bread they weigh in scales
Is full of chalk and lime,
And Sleep will not lie down, but walks
Wild-eyed, and cries to Time.

But though lean Hunger and green Thirst,
Like asp with adder fight,
We have little care of prison fare,
For what chills and kills outright
Is that every stone one lifts by day
Becomes one's heart by night.

With midnight always in one's heart,
And twilight in one's cell,
We turn the crank, or tear the rope,
Each in his separate Hell,
And the silence is more awful far
Than the sound of a brazen bell.

And never a human voice comes near
To speak a gentle word:
And the eye that watches through the door
Is pitiless and hard:
And by all forgot, we rot and rot,
With soul and body marred.

And thus we rust Life's iron chain
Degraded and alone:
And some men curse, and some men weep,
And some men make no moan:
But God's eternal Laws are kind
And break the heart of stone.

And every human heart that breaks,
In prison-cell or yard,
Is as that broken box that gave
Its treasure to the Lord,
And filled the unclean leper's house
With the scent of costliest nard.

Ah! happy they whose hearts can break
And peace of pardon win!
How else may man make straight his plan
And cleanse his soul from Sin?
How else but through a broken heart
May Lord Christ enter in?

And he of the swollen purple throat,
And the stark and staring eyes,
Waits for the holy hands that took
The Thief to Paradise;
And a broken and a contrite heart
The Lord will not despise.

The man in red who reads the Law
Gave him three weeks of life,
Three little weeks in which to heal
His soul of his soul's strife,
And cleanse from every blot of blood
The hand that held the knife.

And with tears of blood he cleansed the hand,
The hand that held the steel:
For only blood can wipe out blood,
And only tears can heal:
And the crimson stain that was of Cain
Became Christ's snow-white seal.

VI

In Reading gaol by Reading town
There is a pit of shame,
And in it lies a wretched man

Eaten by teeth of flame,
In a burning winding-sheet he lies,
And his grave has got no name.

And there, till Christ call forth the dead,
In silence let him lie:
No need to waste the foolish tear,
Or heave the windy sigh:
The man had killed the thing he loved,
And so he had to die.

And all men kill the thing they love,
By all let this be heard,
Some do it with a bitter look,
Some with a flattering word,
The coward does it with a kiss,
The brave man with a sword!

BENJAMIN ZEPHANIAH

Dis Policeman Keeps On Kicking Me To Death

Ina de distance of de night
you see dem moving round
investigating and crime-making
within any town,
creeping persons wid no hearts
dem control who dem please
dem only like fe see you
when you de pon you bending knees.
Some of us will fight dem, we fight dem
some of us fight back
informers will sleep wid you
den stab you ina yu back
dis regime is racist we know
dis regime is bent
dis regime is like a worthless penny
dat's unspent.

Dis policeman keeps on hitting me and pulling out my locks
he keeps on feeding me unlimited brock-lacs
dis policeman is a coward he gets me from behind
he can jail my body but him cannot jail my mind.

Like a bat from hell he comes at night
to work his evil plan
although he goes to church on Sunday
he's a sinner man,
like a thief in the dark he take me to de
place where he just left
and when him get me in der
he is kicking me in der
he is kicking me to death.
Dis policeman, dis policeman
dis policeman keeps on kicking me to death.

I got me up and took me to de place fe human rights
a notice on de door said 'Sorry we are closed tonight'
so I turn round and took myself to see dis preacher guy
who told me 'bout some heaven
dat was in de bloody sky,
now I don't wa' to kid myself

but I don't think I'm free
if I'm free den why does he
keep fucking kicking me.

I tell you I'm not joking
you should see dem over der
dey have no respect for either
living or welfare,
dis policeman is a creep
I tell you he is mad
I am trying to do good
while he exhibits bad.
I am living in de ghetto
trying to do my best
when dis policeman tells me
I'm under damn arrest.

Him beat me so badly
I was on the floor
him said if I don't plead guilty
him gwan kick me more
I was feeling sick, I pleaded
RACIST ATTACK
and another policeman come to finish me off –
dis one was BLACK.

In dis war we have traitors
who don't think to sell you out
in dis war der are people who refuse
to hear de shout
for human rights to be regarded
as a basic right
still dis policeman kicks me
every day and every night.

Like a bat from hell he comes at night
to work his evil plan
although he goes to church on Sunday
he's a sinner man
like a thief in de dark he takes me to
de place where he just left
and when him get me in der
he is kicking me to death.
Dis policeman, dis policeman
dis policeman keeps on kicking me to death.

BENJAMIN ZEPHANIAH

Strange Truth

It's strange de way I think I am free
when really I am not,
It's strange de way dat I stay cool
when fires burning hot,
it's strange de way my mind relaxes when my bills are paid,
it's strange de way I keep on going, but till now I've stayed.
It's strange de way I write poems because I have no gun,
it's strange de way you read dem
but I am sure you will like some,
it's strange de way I have no friends but everyone's friendly,
it's strange de way I feel unsafe wid state security.
Well that's all strange, but stranger still, is I love peace,
but I would kill,
a monk I am, a monk at heart
but I would tear a state apart,
it's strange dat I should fight for peace,
it's strange dat I can't trust de priest,
it's strange, so strange that there's no chains
but slavery still affects our brains.

Jimmy Santiago Baca

I Will Remain

To Tello Hinojosa (xinoxosa)

I don't want to leave any more or get transferred
       to another prison because this one is too tough.
I am after a path you cannot find by looking at green fields,
       smelling high mountain air that is clear and sweetly
Odorous as when you fall in love again and again and again.
I am looking for a path that weaves through rock
       and swims through despair with fins of wisdom.
A wisdom to see me through this nightmare,
       not by running from it; by staying to deal blow for blow.
I will take the strength I need from me,
       not from fields or new friends. With my old friends fighting!
Bleeding! calling me crazy! And never getting the respect I desire,
       fighting for each inch of it ....
I am not one of those beautiful people,
       but one of the old ones, a commoner of the world
You can find in taverns, seaports carrying bamboo baskets with fish,
       drinking coffee in a donut shop, weeping in the dark
In a two-for-five ramshackle hotel room,
       dreaming and walking along a city street at dawn.
To move about more freely, to meet and talk with new people,
       to have silence once in a while, to live in peace,
Without harassment of cops pulling you in as a suspect,
       these are very beautiful thoughts.
But I will remain here where the air is old and heavy, where life is grimy,
Full of hate at times, where opportunities are rare,
       anger and frustration abundant,
Here in this wretched place I most wish to leave
       I will remain.
I stay because I believe I will find something,
       something beautiful and astounding awaits my pleasure,
Something in the air I breathe,
       that will make all my terrors and pains seem raindrops
On a rose in summer, its head tilted in the heat
       as I do mine.
Here on this island of death and violence,
       I must find peace and love in myself, eventually freedom,
And if I am blessed, then perhaps a little wisdom.
I stay here searching for gold and ivory in the breast of each man.
I search for the tiny glimmering grains in smiles and words
       of the dying, of the young so old old, of the broken ones.

JIMMY SANTIAGO BACA

Against

I saw the moon at first one blue twilight,
standing, blowing drops of breath into cold air,
standing in my prison jacket, 4:30,
in the compound, circled with high granite walls,
not a stir, but glare of spotlights, the silent
guard towers and stiff-coated guards above them all,

A big bloated desert moon, there,
how held up, such a big moon? Such a passionate tear!
How, against the velvety spaciousness of purple sky,
how does it hold itself up, and so close to me! To me!

Tell me! What should it mean,
that a moon like a wolf's yellow eye
should stare into my eye directly?
My finger, had I raised my arm,
could have punctured it like a peach and on my head
sweet juice drips, I could have pushed my finger in,
retrieved the seed of its soul, the stern hard pupil,
and placed it upon my tongue, sucked its mighty power

of dreams! Dreams, for how I needed them,
how I howled inside, sweeping great portions of thoughts
away with steel blue blades of the hour,
this, the time of my imprisonment.

I split days open with red axes of my heart,
the days falling like trees
I chopped up into each hour
and threw into the soul's fire.

I had not known the desert's power back then.
I had not known the black-footed demons
pecking each lightray as if it were straw.
I had not known my dreams, diamond hard,
could break at the silence of dragging winds;
no, nor that a pebble could come to mean
a world, unlocking fear....

I looked into that moon, amazed, never
having seen a moon so much mine,
gathering my plundered life into its arms,

Moon! Moon! Moon! that twilight morning,
on the way to the kitchen to have some coffee,
thinking of my ten years to do in prison,
bundled up in my jacket, my boots feeling good and firm,
walking on under the guard's eye, blinded and blank-eyed,
to my escape, my freedom just then,
the guard's ears clogged, deaf,
when the moon said, "You are free,
as all that I have, winds, mountains, you are free ....

JIMMY SANTIAGO BACA

The New Warden

He sat in the cool morning.
He had a handful of seeds in his palm.
He sat there contemplating
Where he would plant them.
A month later he tore the kitchen down
And planted apple seeds there.
Some of the convicts asked him why:
"Apples," he said, "is one of America's
great traditional prides. Remember
the famous ballad Johny Apple Seed?"
Nobody had heard of it, so he set up
A poetry workshop where the death house had been.
The chair was burned in a great ceremony.
Some of the Indian convicts performed
Ancient rituals for the souls of those executed in the past.
He sold most of the bricks and built
Little ovens in the earth with the rest.
The hospital was destroyed except for one new wing
To keep the especially infirm aged ones.
And funny thing, no one was ever sick.
The warden said something about freedom being the greatest cure
For any and all ailments. He was right.
The cellblocks were razed to the ground.
Some of the steel was kept and a blacksmith shop went up.
With the extra bricks the warden purchased
Tents, farming implements and bought a big yellow bus.
The adjoining fields flowed rich with tomatoes, pumpkins,
Potatoes, corn, chili, alfalfa, cucumbers.
From the nearby town of Florence, and as far away as Las Cruces,
People came to buy up loads and loads of vegetables.
In one section of the compound the artists painted
Easter and Christmas and other holiday cards, on paper
Previously used for disciplinary reports.
The government even commissioned some of the convicts
To design patriotic emblems.
A little group of engineers, plumbers, electricians
Began building solar heating systems, and sold them
To elementary schools way under cost. Then,
Some citizens grew interested. Some high school kids
Were invited to learn about it, and soon,

Solar systems were being installed in the community.
An agricultural program opened up.
Unruly convicts were shipped out to another prison.
After the first year, the new warden installed ballot boxes.
A radio and TV shop opened. Some of the convicts' sons
And daughters came into prison to learn from their fathers'
Trades and talking with them about life.
This led to several groups opening up sessions dealing with
Language, logic, and delving into past myths and customs.
Blacks, Mejicanos, Whites, all had so much to offer.
They were invited to speak at the nearby university
Discussing what they found to be untouched by past historians.
Each day six groups of convicts went into the community,
Working for the aged and infirmed.
One old convict ended up marrying the governor's mother.

Joy Harjo

For Anna Mae Pictou Aquash, Whose Spirit Is Present Here And In The Dappled Stars (for we remember the story and must tell it again so we may all live)

Beneath a sky blurred with mist and wind,
                      I am amazed as I watch the violet
heads of crocuses erupt from the stiff earth
                            after dying for a season,
as I have watched my own dark head
                    appear each morning after entering
the next world
          to come back to this one,
                    amazed.
It is the way in the natural world to understand the place
                        the ghost dancers named
after the heart/breaking destruction.
                Anna Mae,
                  everything and nothing changes.
You are the shimmering young woman
                who found her voice,
when you were warned to be silent, or have your body cut away
from you like an elegant weed.
          You are the one whose spirit is present in the dappled stars.
(They prance and lope like colored horses who stay with us
        through the streets of these steely cities. And I have seen them
        nuzzling the frozen bodies of tattered drunks
                on the corner.)
This morning when the last star is dimming
                and the buses grind toward
the middle of the city, I know it is ten years since they buried you
        the second time in Lakota, a language that could
                free you.
I heard about it in Oklahoma, or New Mexico,
        how the wind howled and pulled everything down
    in a righteous anger.
      (It was the women who told me) and we understood wordlessly
the ripe meaning of your murder.
     As I understand ten years later after the slow changing
          of the seasons

that we have just begun to touch
> the dazzling whirlwind of our anger,
we have just begun to perceive the amazed world the ghost dancers
> entered
>> crazily, beautifully.

In February 1976, an unidentified body of a young woman was found on the Pine Ridge Reservation in South Dakota. The official autopsy attributed death to exposure. The FBI agent present at the autopsy ordered her hands severed and sent to Washington for fingerprinting. John Trudell rightly called this mutilation an act of war. Her unnamed body was buried. When Anna Mae Aquash, a young Micmac woman who was an active American Indian Movement member, was discovered missing by her friends and relatives, a second autopsy was demanded. It was then discovered she had been killed by a bullet fired at close range to the back of her head. Her killer or killers have yet to be identified.

Joy Harjo

We Must Call A Meeting

I am fragile, a piece of pottery smoked from fire
made of dung,
the design drawn from nightmares. I am an arrow, painted
with lightning
to seek the way to the name of the enemy,
but the arrow has now created
its own language.
It is a language of lizards and storms, and we have
begun to hold conversations
long into the night.
I forget to eat.
I don't work. My children are hungry and the animals who live
in the backyard are starving.
I begin to draw maps of stars.
The spirits of old and new ancestors perch on my shoulders.
I make prayers of clear stone
of feathers from birds
who live closest to the gods.
The voice of the stone is born
of a meeting of yellow birds
who circle the ashes of a smoldering volcano.
The feathers sweep the prayers up
and away.
I, too, try to fly but get caught in the cross fire of signals
and my spirit drops back down to earth.
I am lost; I am looking for you
who can help me walk this thin line between the breathing
and the dead.
You are the curled serpent in the pottery of nightmares.
You are the dreaming animal who paces back and forth in my head.
We must call a meeting.
Give me back my language and build a house
Inside it.
A house of madness.
A house for the dead who are not dead.
And the spiral of the sky above it.
And the sun
and the moon.
And the stars to guide us called promise.

Etheridge Knight

Hard Rock Returns To Prison From The Hospital For The Criminal Insane

Hard Rock / was / "known not to take no shit
From nobody," and he had the scars to prove it:
Split purple lips, lumbed ears, welts above
His yellow eyes, and one long scar that cut
Across his temple and plowed through a thick
Canopy of kinky hair.

The WORD / was / that Hard Rock wasn't a mean nigger
Anymore, that the doctors had bored a hole in his head,
Cut out part of his brain, and shot electricity
Through the rest. When they brought Hard Rock back,
Handcuffed and chained, he was turned loose,
Like a freshly gelded stallion, to try his new status.
And we all waited and watched, like a herd of sheep,
To see if the WORD was true.

As we waited we wrapped ourselves in the cloak
Of his exploits: "Man, the last time, it took eight
Screws to put him in the Hole." "Yeah, remember when he
Smacked the captain with his dinner tray?" "He set
The record for time in the Hole - 67 straight days!"
"Ol Hard Rock! man, that's one crazy nigger."
And then the jewel of a myth that Hard Rock had once bit
A screw on the thumb and poisoned him with syphilitic spit.

The testing came, to see if Hard Rock was really tame.
A hillbilly called him a black son of a bitch
And didn't lose his teeth, a screw who knew Hard Rock
From before shook him down and barked in his face.
And Hard Rock did *nothing*. Just grinned and looked silly,
His eyes empty like knot holes in a fence.

And even after we discovered that it took Hard Rock
Exactly 3 minutes to tell you his first name,
We told ourselves that he had just wised up,
Was being cool; but we could not fool ourselves for long,
And we turned away, our eyes on the ground. Crushed.
He had been our Destroyer, the doer of things
We dreamed of doing but could not bring ourselves to do,
The fears of years, like a biting whip,
Had cut deep bloody grooves
Across our backs.

ETHERIDGE KNIGHT

The Idea Of Ancestry

1

Taped to the wall of my cell are 47 pictures: 47 black
faces: my father, mother, grandmothers (1 dead), grandfathers (both dead), brothers, sisters, uncles, aunts,
cousins (1st & 2nd), nieces, and nephews. They stare
across the space at me sprawling on my bunk. I know
their dark eyes, they know mine. I know their style,
they know mine. I am all of them, they are all of me;
they are farmers, I am a thief, I am me, they are thee.

I have at one time or another been in love with my mother,
1 grandmother, 2 sisters, 2 aunts (1 went to the asylum),
and 5 cousins. I am now in love with a 7-yr-old niece
(she sends me letters written in large block print, and
her picture is the only one that smiles at me).

I have the same name as 1 grandfather, 3 cousins, 3 nephews,
and 1 uncle. The uncle disappeared when he was 15, just took
off and caught a freight (they say). He's discussed each year
when the family has a reunion, he causes uneasiness in
the clan, he is an empty space. My father's mother, who is 93
and who keeps the Family Bible with everybody's birth dates
(and death dates) in it, always mentions him. There is no
place in her Bible for "whereabouts unknown."

2

Each fall the graves of my grandfathers call me, the brown
hills and red gullies of mississippi send out their electric
messages, galvanizing my genes. Last yr / like a salmon quitting
the cold ocean-leaping and bucking up his birthstream / I
hitchhiked my way from LA with 16 caps in my pocket and a
monkey on my back. And I almost kicked it with the kinfolks.
I walked barefooted in my grandmother's backyard / I smelled the old
land and the woods / I sipped cornwhiskey from fruit jars with the men /
I flirted with the women / I had a ball till the caps ran out
and my habit came down. That night I looked at my grandmother
and split / my guts were screaming for junk / but I was almost

contented / I had almost caught up with me.
(The next day in Memphis I cracked a croaker's crib for a fix.)

This yr there is a gray stone wall damming my stream, and when
the falling leaves stir my genes, I pace my cell or flop on my bunk
and stare at 47 black faces across the space. I am all of them,
they are all of me, I am me, they are thee, and I have no children
to float in the space between.

Janice Mirikitani

Awake In The River

The desert place. The child knew no other home.

The tortoise crawls in the hot sun. The special sun, like imprisoned, never seeming to move over the flat, flat land. Darkness falls suddenly like a velvet cloth. With it the cold, when the tortoise sleeps.

The child ran barefoot all the time, digging her toes deep into the sand, like a clawed reptile. Unlike them, she could not go beyond the barbed wire.

> Sleep,
> her mother sang,
> the sun will sap
> blood through your pores
> and make you weak.
> Sleep
> in the desert.

When the soldiers came each day, jaws like iron, picking up the men to take them to distant potato fields, she would run after her grandfather, sitting in the back of the army truck with the others, silent. Teeth gripped. Swallowing rage. Her small legs barely would reach the gate as the truck disappeared through the dust.

> Rebellion
> waits outside the gate,
> slowly gathering
> like sounds of angry snowgeese
> or water from the mountain
> springing free.
> Ocean's throat
> calls the awakening.

The children found the tortoise, big, dull shelled, making a slow journey through the desert. They named it Muhon-nin because it would not retreat into its shell, put it in the garden the men had grown from stones and succulents. Making beauty from adversity.

Old men would carve from dead wood in the shade of barracks, resurrecting old images of fierce gods. Women made feasts from rations to feed strength. Weaving songs with hidden messages.

Nenneko, nenneko ya	sleep little one
nashite naku yara	why do you cry?

Let the tortoise go, the women would say. It is wrong to imprison any living thing.

Kodomo ga	children
nemutte iru	sleeping
	frozen time
	entombs the race
	when will we wake?

The child, always digging, stepped deep onto a nail. Blood pouring from the bottom of her body. Mother in fear, whispering... For those who do not feign sleep, a strange life will follow. Turmoil threatens. Freedom's still a distant harvest.

The tortoise escaped. The children wept.

Kame kame	Tortoise takes
nigeru wa	each step
	inevitable as time
	full with spawn,
	a new age
	to the shore
	where it will bury eggs.

Her mother washed her feet each day. The child slept, knowing she would run under another sky.

Born in the desert
cord knotted to woman/belly
by barbed wire.
Womb blazing
Beyond bondage.
The sun spreads
in the sand
touching the lip
of the sea,
rising.

The men kept their war inside. Pulling weeds by roots. Figures bent, not broken, wind rounding their backs. Grandfather wears his wait like a shell. Sleep in the desert, he warned.

Tortoise, empty,
worn,
plunges to the deep.
In the steady
pounding of the waves,
offsprings wake.

Mother steady singing by the crib.

Sleep in the desert.
Awake in the river.

ADRIENNE RICH

North American Time

I
When my dreams showed signs
of becoming
politically correct
no unruly images
escaping beyond borders
when walking in the street I found my
themes cut out for me
knew what I would not report
for fear of enemies' usage
then I began to wonder

II
Everything we write
will be used against us
or against those we love.
These are the terms,
take them or leave them.
Poetry never stood a chance
of standing outside history.
One line typed twenty years ago
can be blazed on a wall in spraypaint
to glorify art as detachment
or torture of those we
did not love but also
did not want to kill

We move   but our words stand
become responsible
for more than we intended

and this is verbal privilege

III
Try sitting at a typewriter
one calm summer evening
at a table by a window
in the country, try pretending

your time does not exist
that you are simply you
that the imagination simply strays
like a great moth, unintentional
try telling yourself
you are not accountable
to the life of your tribe
the breath of your planet

IV
It doesn't matter what you think.
Words are found responsible
all you can do is choose them
or choose
to remain silent.   Or, you never had a choice,
which is why the words that do stand
are responsible

and this is verbal privilege

V
Suppose you want to write
of a woman braiding
another woman's hair –
straight down, or with beads and shells
in three-strand plaits or corn-rows –
you had better know the thickness
the length   the pattern
why she decides to braid her hair
how it is done to her
what country it happens in
what else happens in that country

You have to know these things

VI
Poet, sister: words –
whether we like it or not –
stand in a time of their own.
No use protesting   *I wrote that
before Kollontai was exiled
Rosa Luxemburg, Malcolm ,*

Anna Mae Aquash, murdered,
before Treblinka, Birkenau,
Hiroshima, before Sharpeville,
Biafra, Bangladesh, Boston,
Atlanta, Soweto, Beirut, Assam
– those faces, names of places
sheared from the almanac
of North American time

VII
I am thinking this in a country
where words are stolen out of mouths
as bread is stolen out of mouths
where poets don't go to jail
for being poets, but for being
dark-skinned, female, poor.
I am writing this in a time
when anything we write
can be used against those we love
where the context is never given
though we try to explain, over and over
For the sake of poetry at least
I need to know these things

VIII
Sometimes, gliding at night
in a plane over New York City
I have felt like some messenger
called to enter, called to engage
this field of light and darkness.
A grandiose idea, born of flying.
But underneath the grandiose idea
is the thought that what I must engage
after the plane has raged onto the tarmac
after climbing my old stairs, sitting down
at my old window
is meant to break my heart and reduce me to silence.

IX
In North America time stumbles on
without moving, only releasing
a certain North American pain.

Julia de Burgos wrote:
That my grandfather was a slave
is my grief;   had he been a master
that would have been my shame.
A poet's words, hung over a door
in North America, in the year
nineteen-eighty-three.
The almost-full moon rises
timelessly speaking of change
out of the Bronx, the Harlem River
the drowned towns of the Quabbin
the pilfered burial mounds
the toxic swamps, the testing-grounds

And I start to speak again

1983

Biographies

M. GOPALAKRISHNA ADIGA (1918-1992)   has come to be regarded as one of the major figures in modern Kannada literature. Publishing his first collection in 1946 his poetry developed with the history of post-independence India and has exerted a potent and liberating influence on other writers. Perhaps his single most important volumes are *Song of the Earth* (1959) and *Vardhamana* (1975), both of which are highpoints in the modernist movement in Kannada poetry. He published translations of Whitman's *Leaves of Grass* and of Ibsen and more recently was appointed Visiting Fellow at the Indian Institute for Advanced Studies in Simla. He died in 1992.

ADONIS ('Ali Ahmad Sa'id)(b.1929)   was born in a village in northern Syria. From 1956 to 1986 he lived in Beirut where he founded the avant-garde magazine *Mawaqif* and became known and honoured as one of the most influential Arab poets of the modern era. In both his poetry and his criticism he has radically changed Arabic poetics, developing new rhythms and forms and extending the classical heritage of his poetry to reach the realities of contemporary Arab society. As with Darwish the experience of being in a beseiged Beirut stunned him into writing superb poetry and the sequence *The Desert* is one of a number of long poems of his that are major contributions to late twentieth century poetry. His work is collected in (2) volumes and he has been widely translated, particularly into French but increasingly into English as well. In 1986 he left Beirut and now lives much of the time in Paris.

MARJORIE AGOSIN (b.1954)   educated both in the United States and her native Chile she is professor of Latin American literature at Wellesley College. Her own work is dominated by themes of human rights, its zones of pain and the elegaic celebration of both living and dead. In particular she has written about the experience of terror in Chile and the women of the Plaza de Mayo in Buenos Aires, mothers of disappeared children. She writes with an almost hallucinatory intensity of this real-life grimness and has many books of poetry and prose. Much of her work has been translated into English including *Zones of Pain* (!988), *Women of Smoke* (1988) and *Sargasso* (1993) and she has edited a number of books including the fine anthology of poetry by Latin American women *These Are Not Sweet Girls* (1994).

MILA AGUILAR   a graduate of the University of the Philippines English Department, she was arrested in 1984 and charged with being a leading member of the Communist Party. Although the charges against her were later reduced to possession of subversive literature, she was not released until after the defeat of Marcos in 1986. A pamphlet of her work was released by the Free Mila D. Aguilar Committee in 1984 and a book of her poems *A Comrade is as Precious as a Rice Seedling* by the Kitchen Table: Women of Color Press in New York. As well as a poetry of prison experience, hers is a poetry of feminist commitment and militant class consciousness.

AI QING (b.1910) spent three years in Paris in 1929 and became active in progressive literary circles on his return to China. In 1932 he was imprisoned but with the rise of Mao he became China's foremost poet acting as associate editor for *People's Literature*. However in 1957 he was charged with being a rightist by the Party and was sent to work in the provinces on col-

lective farms. All the poems he wrote during the next 20 years were lost and he was not rehabilitated until 1975. He is clearly one of the finest modern poets of China - but there is a distance between his work (influenced by Whitman among others) and the younger post war-
generation of *Misty* poets.

ANNA AKHMATOVA (1889-1966)   one of the great poets of a very great generation of
Russian poets who came to maturity before and during the Revolution with three books published by 1917. Her first husband, the poet Nikolai Gumilyov was tried and executed in 1921
and their son was frequently imprisoned in his adult life. Almost without exception she
remained in Russia all her lifetime, and remained in the consciousness of Russian people, living through the terror of the '30s, the war and bombardment of Leningrad (though she was
evacuated to Tashkent in 1941) and the Zhdanov inspired repression of the post-war years
which was directed particularly at her. Her early lyrics gave way to long-considered meditations and much of her poetry, early or late, lived in people's memories as witness, respite or
solace and as inspiration for the generation of younger poets.

NIZAMETDIN AKHMETOV (b.1949)   a Bashkir Russian poet who grew up in Tashkent
and became involved with protests at the status of the Crimean Tartars and their treatment
under the Soviet regime. Sentenced to 20 years in prison he began writing poetry and became
further involved in human rights issues. He was transferred to a psychiatric hospital, part of
an abuse that became common policy in Soviet Russia. After a campaign in the West he was
finally freed in 1987 and went to live in Germany. In 1991 he returned to Russia and now
lives with his wife in the town of Chita east of the Urals.

GÜLTEN AKIN (b. 1933)   was born in Yozgat, east of Ankara, an area to which she often
returns in her poetry. She studied law and has practiced as a barrister throughout Anatolia
for much of her life. Between 1956 and 1991 she published ten books of poetry. She was
awarded the Turkish Language Academy's prize for poetry in both 1961 and 1971, and is one
of Turkey's leading women poets. Her work is founded on the lives and language of ordinary
people and a strong knowledge of peasant and rural backgrounds. Very little of her work has
as yet been published in English translation.

CLARIBEL ALEGRÍA (b.1924)   is Salvadorean by parentage and culture though she was
born in Nicaragua. She has published many volumes of poetry, testimony, fiction and essays
and is very widely translated: three books and a pamphlet of her poetry are available in
English, as are two novels and some shorter fictions. At various times in her childhood and
adult life she has been in political exile or had her work censored and, together with a constant and almost radiant sense of affirmation, her writing also often denounces government
atrocities. *Ashes of Izalco*, a novel written with her husband and literary collaborator Darwin J.
Flakoll, is based on the massacre of thirty thousand campesinos in El Salvador in 1932.

PAT ARROWSMITH   worked full-time in the peace movement for ten years and for the
past twenty years has been on the staff of Amnesty International where she is presently
Assistant Editor. She has been a political prisoner eleven times, sentenced most often for non-
violent direct actions protesting nuclear war and other acts of civil disobedience and was
twice adopted by Amnesty as a prisoner of conscience. Her prison experience and passionate
commitment to pacifist non-violence are reflected in the poems collected in the volume *Nine
Lives* published in 1990.

ARSENAL POEMS   these poems were given to the imprisoned dissident Victor Fainberg in the Arsenal prison psychiatric hospital in Leningrad in the early '70s by a "thief of honour" who had written out the collection of eighty poems in one night on stolen hospital paper. It is difficult to tell whether the poems (unusually for Russian poems they are unrhymed) are the work of one or more hands, and we are publishing them as translations of anonymous poems since no further information seems to have emerged.

KOFI AWOONOR (b. 1935)   is one of Ghana and Africa's finest poets, whose reputation has grown since the publication of his first book in 1964 through the *Collected Poems* of 1987 and a subsequent collection. Ezekiel Mphahlele has characterised his verse as "the truest poetry of Africa" and he holds the rhythm and feel of traditional oral poetry in his own English voice. A novelist (*This Earth, My Brother* 1971 and *Comes The Voyager At Last* 1992) and affirming critic of Ewe poetry and Sub-Saharan culture (on both of which he's written significant books of essays), he was until recently Ghana's ambassador to the United Nations. Imprisoned in Ussher Fort Prison in Accra for many months during 1976, his poetry of that experience was collected in *The House by the Sea* (1978) and reprinted in the collected poems. At present he lives in Accra.

GENNADY AYGI (b.1934)   was born in the Chuvash Republic and the themes of his writing are often related to the language, culture and religion of the Chuvash people, though he himself has written in Russian since 1960. In the foreword to the English translation of the book he wrote for his daughter (*Veronica's Book* Polygon 1989), he writes of a 'sacred femininity' and of the violence and cruelty directed against his culture by collectivisation. He has emerged as one of the most distinctive Russian writers of the generation whose voices were darkened by the Brezhnev years. His voice is perhaps unique, modernist and yet rooted in tradition, fractured and yet immensely cohesive.

JIMMY SANTIAGO BACA (b.1952)   from Chicano and Native American backgrounds he ran away from an orphanage when he was eleven and lived on the streets for the next nine years. He taught himself to read and write while in solitary confinement in a maximum-security prison in Arizona, having been refused permission to study by the prison authorities. From *Immigrants in Our Own Land* (1979; repr. 1990) and *Martin & Meditations on the South Valley* (1987) through *Black Mesa Poems* (!989) he has become one of the most exciting and visionary poets of contemporary America. He was a recipient of the 1989 International Hispanic Heritage Award. Denise Levertov has said that his poetry is written with unconcealed passion, drawing on personal and community realities. His poems trace a visionary biography of place and show an intense concern for the disenfranchised.

REZA BARAHENI (b.1935)   rose to prominence as a writer in post-Mossadegh Iran. In 1973 under the Shah he was imprisoned and tortured over the course of 102 days by officers of SAVAK the state security police. His poems of torture, collected in the book *God's Shadow*, are among the most objective and terrifying written by any poet this century. A book of his essays has also been published in English as *Crowned Cannibals*. After his release he went to America and returned to Teheran in 1979 where he continues to live and write under the Islamic Republic. A critic as well as a poet and novelist he came to England in 1992 as a visiting professor, when one of the editors had the honour of meeting him.

BRENDAN BEHAN (1923-1964)   born in Dublin, he is internationally renowned for his work in English and the play he wrote in Irish as *An Ghiall* and translated as *The Hostage* . His poetry was written in Irish and collected after his death. A member of the IRA he was sentenced to three years borstal in 1939 and in 1942 to fourteen years in prison by a military court in Dublin. He leapt to fame in 1956 with the play *The Quare Fellow* in a production by Joan Littlewood and published an autobiography in two volumes - *Borstal Boy* in 1958 and *Confessions of an Irish Rebel*, posthumously, in 1965. Living by reputation and bravado he was also absurdly generous and, underneath it all, perhaps more courteous than his outbursts of violence might would tend to suggest. It can be said that he drank himself to his early death.

BEI DAO (Zhao Zhenkai)(b.1949) born in Beijing the same year as the People's Republic, his life and that of his generation was shattered by the Cultural Revolution. One of the foremost underground poets of the 1970s and editor with Mang Ke of the subsequently banned literary journal *Today* his poetry has both reflected and helped determine the course of contemporary Chinese poetry. At the time of the Tiananmen Square massacre Bei Dao was out of China. He has not been able to return since and at present he is living in exile in Sweden. His wife and daughter have had to remain in China. Three books of his poetry and a collection of short prose fictions have been translated into English.

SHERKO BEKAS (b.1940)   grew up in the city of Sulaymaniya in southern Kurdistan (Iraq) and was educated there and in Baghdad. Closely associated with the Kurdish Liberation Movement he has been forced to live in exile in Sweden since 1987, as have a number of other Kurdish writers. He has come to be seen as the best loved contemporary poet of Kurdish culture expressing both the facts of exile and the hopes of national independence. Some of his poems were published in an anthology of contemporary Kurdish poetry and other translations await publication. His father also was a much loved Kurdish poet .

HORST BIENEK (1930-91)   born in Gleiwitz, Upper Silesia. In 1951 he was arrested, sentenced to 25 years forced labour and deported to the prison camp of Vorkuta in Soviet Siberia. He was freed in an amnesty in 1955, after when he lived mainly in Munich. Much of his poetry dwells on the rise of fascism he saw as a child and memories of the prison years he experienced as an adult, worlds in which people had become objects: valueless, anonymous and disposable. He has written a number of novels, at least two of which have been translated into English, as have selections of his poetry in the Penguin Modern European Poets series and more recently from Unicorn Press in north America.

BO YANG (b.1920)   born in Kaifeng, Honan Province he moved to Taiwan in the 1950s and began writing fiction and later very individual newspaper articles in which he attacked unhealthy aspects of Chinese culture. In 1968 he was arrested by the Kuomintang government and accused of fomenting dissent. Under threat of death he was eventually sentenced to twelve years in prison and kept on Green Island off the southeast coast of Taiwan until his release in 1977. A prolific writer he has published over 150 volumes of fiction, essays , poetry, reportage and history. His prison poems have been published in English translation , as have a volume of short fictions and the satirical essays he wrote under the title of *The Ugly Chinaman* after his release.

TOMAS BORGE (b.1930)   imprisoned for complicity in the murder of the dictator Somoza Garcia in 1956, Borge was later a co-founder of the FSLN. In 1976 he was again imprisoned in Managua and kept in solitary confinement. Released in 1978 when the Sandinistas overthrew the authority of the National Palace, he subsequently became Minister of the Interior in the Sandinista government. In addition to his poetry (collected in *La ceremonia esperada*) Borge has written a memoir of Carlos Fonseca, an autobiographical memoir, and other prose, much of which has been translated in the United States and published by Curbstone Press.

KAMAU BRATHWAITE (b.1930)   born in Bridgetown, Barbados he studied history at Pembroke College, Cambridge and wrote a doctoral thesis on the development of Creole society in Jamaica. He taught in Ghana for seven years and later at the University of the West Indies. In 1966 he helped found the Caribbean Artists Movement in London. Much of his poetry is collected in the two trilogies *Rights of Passage, Masks, Islands* and *Mother Poem, Sun Poem, X/Self*. As his sense of musical rhythm and historical tension deepened other books have offshot from these: *Middle Passages* in 1992 and recently a deeply moving elegy on the death of his wife. Undoubtedly a writer of international stature he was awarded the coveted Neustadt Prize in 1994. His poem *Stone* was written in memory of the Jamaican poet Mikey Smith, stoned to death in 1983 and much lamented.

MARÍA EUGENIA BRAVO CALDERARA   was a university teacher at the time of the coup in Chile in 1973. She was taken to the National Stadium in Santiago where with many others she was imprisoned and tortured. Her first poems from prison were kept by her mother who buried them in her garden until later they were able to be sent to Switzerland in a diplomatic bag. Since the mid 1970s she has lived in London, able to visit her mother country only in 1990. Love and exile and the memory of prison have been at the core of her poetry, a bilingual volume of which was published in London in 1991 as *Prayer In The National Stadium*.

BERTOLT BRECHT (1898-1956)   born in Augsburg Brecht began publishing from his very early twenties and lived through the rise of Hitler and Nazism when his work was often unavailable in his own country. He went into exile in 1933, firstly to Denmark and was then forced to flee Europe spending the years 1941-47 in the USA. In 1949 he helped establish the Berliner Ensemble in East Berlin where he lived until his death. His Complete Works have been through a number of editions in German and his Collected Plays, Poetry, Diaries, Journals and other Prose have been published in English in numerous volumes. He is without doubt one of the most important playwrights of the twentieth century while his poetry, remarkable not least for its wide range, is hugely influential both in and beyond the German-speaking world.

BREYTEN BREYTENBACH (b.1939)   from a poor Afrikaans background he established himself as one of the leading poets and artists of the avant-garde *Sestigers* group. He left South Africa in 1959 and spent much of the next decade in Paris writing and painting. Increasingly politicised in exile he entered South Africa clandestinely in 1975, was arrested under the Terrorism Act and sentenced to nine years in prison. He was released in 1982 and returned to Europe where he still lives, in Paris. All of his autobiographical prose and prison writings and much of his early poetry has been translated into English and he is acclaimed as a cosmopolitan writer of world importance.

EDITH BRÜCK (b.1932)   from a Hungarian Jewish family she survived a childhood in concentration camps (a subject she returns to often in her work) and then lived in Israel following the liberation of the camps, before finally settling in Italy in 1954. For much of the time since then she has lived in Rome. She has worked as a filmmaker and playwright, as well as being a poet and novelist, struggling to gain the recognition that her uneasy work deserves. Unfortunately, little of her work has been published in translation .

DENNIS BRUTUS (b.1924)   born in Harare, he grew up in South Africa. In 1962 he was dismissed from his teaching post for his anti-apartheid activities and thereafter was arrested, shot in the stomach and imprisoned. In 1966 he left the country and much of the rest of his life has been spent teaching in the United States where he was granted political asylum in 1983 despite previous attempts to deport him. A prolific poet his early work and prison poems are collected in *A Simple Lust* (1973) and *Stubborn Hope* (1983). He has remained committed in his later work – whether lyric or angered – to the struggle for just rights and is rightly regarded as a major figure in contemporary South African literature.

ION CARAION (1923-1985)   one of the finest of post-war Romanian poets he was of a generation to have lived through both Fascist and Communist dictatorships. Arrested and sentenced to death in 1951, he was kept in solitary confinement for two years, followed by 11 years in prison. His wife Valentina Caraion was sentenced to 15 years in prison for having typed his poems. Freed in the political thaw of 1964, but published with great difficulty and suspicion under Ceausescu, he went into self-exile with his family in 1981. His poetry is a unique and very contemporary melting together of surrealist elements (though he is not a surrealist) and existential inquiry (though he is not an existentialist) and he is among the most original of recent Romanian poets. He once wrote that "poetry is pure danger" and that is perhaps not far from the truth of his life. His two books in English translation are *Poems* (1981) and *The Error of Being* (1994).

ERNESTO CARDENAL (b.1925)   ordained a Trappist monk in 1965 he set up a community of religious and peasants in the Solentiname islands in Lake Nicaragua where he established poetry workshops. The community was destroyed by the National Guard in 1977 and Cardenal went into exile. On the overthrow of Somoza, Cardenal became Minister of Culture in the revolutionary Sandinista government. He is one of the best known Latin American poets and his work has for many years been widely translated into English, including most recently the 600 page epic *Cantico Cosmico*.

MARTIN CARTER (b.1927)   born and educated in Guyana he became active in the early nationalist movement and was imprisoned for some months in 1953 when Britain imposed direct rule. His *Poems of Resistance* came out in 1954. He has published eleven books of poetry altogether, most recently *Poems of Succession* in 1977 and *Poems of Affinity* in 1980. He is widely respected as a historian and a politician, becoming Minister of Public Information and Broadcasting after independence and then representing Guyana at the United Nations.

OTTO RENÉ CASTILLO (1936-1967) following years of political agitation and exile Otto Rene Castillo was captured by a unit of the Guatemalan Army in the remote highland of his country. He was then savagely tortured and burnt to death at the stake. His urgent and redemptive poetry bears absolute witness to the commitment of revolutionary struggle in Central America and the qualities of his language stayed in the memories of contemporary and younger writers beyond the fact of his barbaric death. His poetry is translated in the two volumes *Tomorrow Triumphant* and *Let's Go!*

C.P. CAVAFY (1863-1933)   spent most of his life in Alexandria, a city of the greatest importance to him (though crucial years of his childhood were also lived in England). Outwardly uneventful - he was employed for many years in the Egyptian Ministry of Public Works - he slowly developed a poetry that has an unerring mythic sensibility coupled with an astute cynicism about politics. Esoteric and yet deeply rooted (resembling Fernando Pessoa in many ways) and with a distaste for rhetoric. Conservative and yet frank and avant-garde in his treatment of homosexual themes. He was never imprisoned, never indeed actively political. And he published no volume of poetry in his lifetime, rather preferring to distribute self-made copies or pamphlets to friends. Nonetheless he became widely recognised after his death as a very great modern poet and has been translated into many languages, his collected poems being in English in a number of different versions.

PAUL CELAN (1920-1970)   born in Czernowitz in the Bukovina he grew up in a mixed Jewish-German-Romanian culture. Both of his parents were killed in an internment camp of the Holocaust. Celan managed to live through this time, eventually settling in Paris in 1948 from where – writing in German – most of his mature work was done. One of the very best European poets of the period after 1945 his is a poetry of extreme and paradoxical precision. His work was shattered into being by the death camps which remained in his poetry to the end. He died, a suicide by drowning, in 1970. His work has been translated widely into English (particularly by Michael Hamburger) and many symposia/critical attentions have given him honour. He himself translated into German Blok, Mandelstam, Esenin, Michaux and Shakespeare among others.

AMARJIT CHANDAN (b.1946)   after graduating from Panjab University he joined the Maoist Naxalite movement and spent two years in prison and in solitary confinement. Subsequently he worked for various Punjabi magazines before migrating to England in 1980. Editor of many anthologies, including collections of British Punjabi writing, and translator of among others Neruda, Ritsos, Hikmet, Brecht and Cardenal, so far 3 collections of his own poetry have been published, together with a chapbook in English translation. He lives in London but travels widely, writing and lecturing. In a brief statement he has written "I think man is an exile everywhere. That's his fate. The real home of a man is where he has dignity, a possible hope or a desperate optimism."

EGHISHE CHARENTS (1899-1937) the foremost poet of Soviet Armenia, by the time he was twenty he had lived through the October Revolution and the period of the Turkish massacres and had written two outstanding long poems – the anti-war *Dantesque Legend* and the pro-revolutionary *Frenzied Masses*. Very active in the '20s but increasingly bitter at the course the revolution took, his own poetry developed a more taoist approach to Armenian politics and history, and this increasing dissidence through the '30s led to his imprisonment in 1937. He died under unclear circumstances in his prison cell. The mature poems of his last years were not properly edited and published for a further fifty years after his death. A large selection of his poetry was published in English translation in 1986.

FRANK MKALAWILE CHIPASULA (b.1949) Malawian poet, editor and fiction writer, at present he is Associate Professor of Black Literature at the University of Nebraska. He has edited the major anthology *When My Brothers Come Home* , a collection of poems from Central and Southern Africa (1985) and co-edited with Stella P. Chipasula the wonderful *African Women's Poetry* in the Heinemann series (1995). His own poetry is most recently collected in *Nightwatcher, Nightsong* (1986) and *Whispers in the Wings* (1991). Highly respected as a poet and critic his work is frequently concerned with the positive expression of human rights or with outrage at their abuse as with the poem 'A Hanging' where he refers to an execution in Zomba Central Prison.

JOSÉ CRAVEIRINHA (b.1922)   the leading Mozambican poet, he worked as a journalist in his home city Maputo. In 1966 he was arrested and held in Machava Prison where he was tortured because of his work and his sympathy for FRELIMO. His poetry, at first angry and defiant and latterly quieter and more melancholic, has been recognised for its passion and balance and in 1991 he was awarded the Camões Prize. He has said "I do not believe that it is possible to write poems without enjoying the taste of words." His poems have appeared in translation in numerous anthologies.

ANGEL CUADRA (b.1931)   started writing at an early age and became involved in literary life in the Cuba of the '50s, training also as a lawyer and opposing the corrupt and anti-democratic Batista regime. With Castro's seizure of power Cuadra entered a brief period of recognition and popularity but in 1967 he was arrested and sentenced to fifteen years in prison, during which time he was made a non-person and his poetry disappeared from view. He did not stop writing however, and two books were published abroad. Released in 1982 he was not allowed to leave Cuba for a further three years – after which he went to Miami, joining the Cuban community in exile. A substantial choice of his poetry and essays (*The Poet In Socialist Cuba*) were published in English translation in 1994.

DAI WANGSHU (1905-1950)   born near Hangzhou he was a figure of great importance in the development of the New Poetry in China and in the literary renaissance of the May Fourth Movement. His ideas on poetry and culture were original and challenging, a major influence on his contemporaries and on later generations. He translated Lorca, Baudelaire,Yesenin, Eluard and others (he stayed in France in the early '30s) but his great gift was to adapt his own deep roots in Chinese tradition. In 1938 he moved to Hong Kong and in 1941 was arrested by the Japanese and imprisoned for a number of months during which time his health was severely impaired. He stopped writing in 1945 and died in 1950. A communist in his youth, radical in his renewal of cultural roots, his was not an overtly political poetry but one of immense cultural integrity that has given strength to the best poets of the past decade.

ROQUE DALTON (1935-1975)   born in San Salvador. In 1955 he shared the Central American Poetry Prize with Otto Rene Castillo. That same year he joined the Communist party and was imprisoned and forced into exile on several occasions. For thirteen years he lived in exile in other Central American countries and in Eastern Europe and Vietnam. In 1973 he tried to return to El Salvador and live clandestinely – but in May 1975 he was murdered by a faction of his own revolutionary group. A novelist and critic as well as a major poet, his work eschews the dogmatics of socialist-realism and succeeds in combining a visionary poetic and a visionary politics. Much of his work has been or is being published in English in the United States, including the novel Miguel Mármol and two selections from the poetry.

MAHMOUD DARWISH (b.1942)   was born in al-Barweh, a village in Palestine but in 1948 his family had to flee their home. Returning to Palestine but unable to go back to his destroyed village Darwish was like "a refugee in my own country", a feeling reinforced by his imprisonment and house arrest at the hands of the Israeli authorities. Until 1971 he worked as a journalist in Haifa and then moved to Beirut where he stayed until 1982. His poetry of the Beirut experience is among the most important poetry of recent years. His work has been translated in numerous anthologies and single volumes, including *Victims of a Map* (with Adonis and Samih al-Qasim, in translations by Abdullah al-Udhari in 1984) and most recently *Memory For Forgetfulness* (University of California Press 1995) which is an extended reflection on the 1982 Israeli invasion of Lebanon and the meaning of memory and exile.

ROBERT DESNOS (1900-1945)   from an early, close and very rich association with surrealism and automatic writing Desnos broke with Breton in 1930 and sought to write a poetry closer to rhythms of ordinary language and fused with a matter-of-fact mysticism, more in the tradition of Villon. In the 1930's he worked for French Radio and wrote numerous film scripts. During the Occupation he was active in the resistance and as a journalist. He was arrested and sent to Buchenwald in April 1944 and he died in the Terezin cconcentration camp shortly after its liberation. A lovely poet whose later work radiates openness and warmth, a large selection of his work was published in English in 1992 in the United States.

NOÉMIA DE SOUSA (b.1927)   was born in Maputo and educated in Mozambique, Brazil and Portugal. She worked as a journalist between 1951 and 1964, publishing her poetry in various journals. She was the first African woman to achieve an international reputation as a contemporary poet and her work has appeared in numerous anthologies from Mario de Andrade's *Caderno de poesia negra de expressao portuguesa* of 1953 to the Heinemann anthology *African Women's Poetry* published in 1995. During the liberation war in Mozambique she fled to France and, though returning briefly after the war, she still lives in Europe.

LAXMIPRASAD DEVKOTA (1909-1959)   one of the great figures of modern Nepali and world poetry. Writing prolifically in all the principal genre of prose and verse, treating themes from Sanskrit drama equally with present-day complexities, in forms ranging from the quatrain to the epic, Devkota left behind at his death a huge body of work, some of it unpublished, some of it mislaid, all of it elemental to the renaissance of Nepali literature. His life a series of money problems and personal sorrows, depressions and - though he was not particularly political - of chosen exile, his work though shines with deep humanity and the warmth of breaking convention, the clemency of his language indicative of the balance of his inner life.

ERNESTO DÍAZ RODRÍGUEZ   born into a family of fishermen in Cuba, Diaz Rodriguez opposed the Batista dictatorship but was then imprisoned under the communist regime of Fidel Castro, at first for fifteen years in Combinado del Este Prison in Havana but then for a further twenty-five when convicted of conspiring from prison to overthrow Castro. Some of the poems he wrote from prison for children are wonderful for their simplicity and open regard for life. In the words of his fellow poet and political prisoner Andres Solares "to speak of Ernesto Diaz Rodriguez is to speak of poetry and hope." A bilingual selection of his poetry was published in Madrid in 1978.

BLAGA DIMITROVA (b.1922)   emerging to a position of dissidence, a sort of heretical ethics in the face of the dogmas of communism and a continual calling for cultural openness, her poetry has for many years been a force of witness for and affirmation of what had been marginalised in Bulgarian culture. These same concerns led her also to write passionately about the Vietnam War (and to translate a volume of Vietnamese poetry). This role which brought her a great deal of popularity in Bulgaria did not sink her poetry under a weight of morality but fed her language and voice with purpose. In 1992 she became the Vice-President of Bulgaria following the breakdown of dictatorship. One novel and so far two volumes of her poetry have been published in English translation. She is without doubt one of the finest of contemporary Bulgarian poets.

MAK DIZDAR (1917-1971)   a post office worker who joined the Partisan resistance during the Second World War, Mak Dizdar is reckoned among the greatest of contemporary Bosnian poets. Steeped in the medieval literature of Bosnia-Hercegovina (a very strong influence on his poetry), his best and most linguistically dazzling book is the *Stone Sleeper* of 1966 where his very individual style attains its greatest intensity and vigour. Much of his life was spent in Sarajevo editing journals and newspapers, researching the roots of south Slavic literature and establishing the beautifully anachronistic modernity of his own work .

LEILA DJABALI (b.1933)   was among the young intellectuals imprisoned in the 1950s by the French colonial authorities for her part in the Algerian independence struggle. Further information was not available to the editors at the time of this book going to press.

TAHAR DJAOUT (1954-1993)   after studying mathematics in Algiers Djaout worked as a journalist with *Algérie-Actualité* from 1976 onwards and published at first poetry and then more continuously prose fiction and essays. At the onset of the brutal quasi-civil war in Algeria Djaout continued writing. In May 1993 he was shot dead as part of the assassination policy of the FIS in which many intellectuals were murdered: the poet Youssef Sebti was also killed, in December 1993, while on his way to work. In the poem we have included, written more than twenty years ago, Djaout both celebrates the independence of his country and elegises the writer Mouloud Feraoun who was assassinated in circumstances not dissimilar to those of his own death as if in a repetition of cycles of violence.

ARIEL DORFMAN (b.1942)   citizen of Chile and supporter of Salvador Allende, he was forced into exile in 1973. Best known for his novels and the play *Death And The Maiden*, which deals with torture, he also wrote a very moving collection of poems on the pain and outrages suffered by the Chilean people during the Pinochet dictatorship. This book, part of which was brought out by Amnesty in London, has been published as *Last Waltz in Santiago* by Penguin in New York. Much of his prose fiction and cultural criticism has been translated (he also now sometimes writes in English) and his novels have become internationally known and praised. Since leaving Chile he has lived mostly in the USA where he teaches and where he is also considered to be a major critic.

PAUL ÉLUARD (1895-1952)   active in French dadaist circles and later an important presence in the surrealist movement, Éluard was a prolific poet right through his life. In 1938 he broke with Breton and Surrealism and joined the Communist Party, and during the war he was in the Resistance, remaining in Paris throughout the German Occupation and constantly changing address to avoid arrest. The clandestine poetry he wrote at that time gave him national recognition: copies of the poem *Liberté* were dropped from Allied planes over occupied France. Éluard also wrote love poetry of great quality. His complete writings have been published in two volumes by Editions de la Pleiade.

FAIZ AHMED FAIZ (1911-1984)   major Urdu poet of great lyric expression whose works are widely known and loved. Born in Sialkot in an undivided Punjab, he served in the British Indian Army and following the 1947 Partition he lived in Pakistan and became editor of The Pakistan Times. In 1951 he was arrested and spent four years in prison mostly in solitary confinement under the threat of death. In the next years the popularity of his poetry – based on a rich mesh of radical politics and traditional aesthetics – grew. A period of exile in Beirut only served to widen this popularity and he was deeply mourned in many places at the time of his death. He is now widely published in English in a variety of translations, although his work is not as well known in North America and Britain as it might be.

JERZY FICOWSKI (b.1924)   of a generation that lived through both Fascist and Communist dictatorships, Ficowski fought in the struggle against Nazi occupation of Poland and in the post-war years refused to capitulate to Stalinist totalitarianism. According to Zbigniew Herbert he has in his poems on the Holocaust "achieved something that would have seemed impossible: he has given artistically convincing shape to what cannot be embraced by words; he has restored to the faceless their human face, their individual human suffering, that is to say, their dignity." A dissident and published by underground presses, he has also written fine short stories and essays. He is the main editor and biographer of Bruno Schulz (who was shot by a Gestapo officer in the ghetto) and an expert on Polish Gypsy culture. In the late '70s he co-edited Zapis and he was a member of KOR. A pamphlet of his poems was published in London in 1981 by the Menard Press under the title *A Reading of Ashes*.

ALAÍDE FOPPA (1916-1980?)   was born in Barcelona of an Argentine father and a Guatemalan mother. After travelling widely she lived in Guatemala until forced into exile in Mexico after the overthrow of the Arbeuz government. A distinguished translator and critic and poet, lecturer in Italian literature, editor of feminist reviews, leading member of Amnesty International and supporter of the indigenous women of Guatemala, she was disappeared and presumed murdered by the security forces whilst on a visit to Guatemala late in 1980. Much of her poetry was published in Mexico during her lifetime and reprinted after her death, and she has been included in various anthologies published in Britain and the United States.

ERICH FRIED (1921-1988)   was born and grew up in Vienna, managing to get out in 1938, after his father had been killed by the Gestapo, and came to London from where he tried to help other victims escape. After the war he worked in the German Service of the BBC. Always a writer of the radical left he became popular with German youth in the 60's and frequently travelled to Germany to give readings (books of his political and love poems were bestsellers). He was always deeply supportive of fellow exiles in London, where his stature as a writer and the potential of his influence have perhaps never been fully recognised. An important translator, particularly of Shakespeare but also of Dylan Thomas and Sylvia Plath, his own poetry has been translated into English (*100 Poems Without A Country* and *Love Poems* among others) as has a volume of short stories.

KEVIN GILBERT (1933-1992)   born at Condobolin on the banks of the Lachlan River he was for the first twenty years of his life "on the receiving end of White Australia's apartheid system." Leaving school he took seasonal work and got by as he could. All his cultural warmth and truths came from his wider black family and he came to believe strongly in the great spirituality of the Aboriginal peoples. In 1957 he was sentenced to life imprisonment following the murder of his wife. He was released in 1972 and in 1973 wrote *Because a White Man'll Never Do It* , a major political work. His editions of *Living Black*(1978) and *Inside Black Australia*(1988), collections of oral histories and Aboriginal poetry respectively, are much reprinted and now used widely as textbooks. His own poetry was collected in *People Are Legends* (1979) and in the posthumous *Black From The Edge* of 1994.

NATALYA GORBANEVSKAYA (b.1936)   took a prominent part in the civil rights movement in the 1960's, helping to found and edit the samizdat journal *Chronicle of Current Events* and protesting the trial of Sinyavsky and Daniel. In August 1968 along with six friends she demonstrated in Red Square against the Soviet invasion of Czechoslovakia and was arrested and beaten up and subsequently detained in a 'special' psychiatric hospital where she was given forced drug therapy. This experience was documented in a number of books published in the West, together with translations from her poetry, and a campaign on her behalf led to her eventual release. In 1975 she emigrated and has since been living in Paris and working as deputy editor of *Kontinent*. She has published seven books of her own poetry and a number of translations, from Polish poets in particular. Self-effacing and for years effaced in her own country her work has since 1990 begun to be published in Russia.

GU CHENG (1956 -1993)   the youngest of the generation of Misty poets, Gu Cheng's entire family was exiled in 1969 and he worked for four years as a swineherd before being returned to Beijing. His poetry was in profound opposition to the values and language of the Cultural Revolution, but was radically influential in the development of Chinese poetry during the 1980s. In 1988 he went to live in exile in New Zealand where in terrible circumstances related only partly to their exile, he killed his wife and then took his own life in October 1993. The appalling violence and tragedy of these acts left a deep mark on many of their friends and fellow-writers. The prose and verve of his poetry looks back to Lu Zhun and other writers of the 1930s and should remain a seminal influence in Chinese poetry.

DHRUBA SEN GUPTA   We have been unable to gather details of this contemporary poet from West Bengal and would be grateful to hear more.

JOY HARJO (b.1951)   is a member of the Creek tribe and has said that this heritage provides for her work "the underlying psychic structure, within which is a wealth of memory." She also talks of memory as "a delta in the skin." She has published two highly praised collections *She Had Some Horses* (1983) and *In Mad Love And War* (1990) and is one of the finest poets of her generation. A contributing editor to a number of journals and active in community service she has traveled widely through the United States giving readings and taking part in workshops, has taught Native American literature and written scripts for television. Her poetry is fed with cultural memory and the innate sense that writing is a means of survival, personally and communally.

JAVIER HERAUD (1942-1963)   born in Miraflores, Lima, he attended the Universidad Catolica and was awarded a national poetry prize for his second book. After visiting Moscow and Cuba he joined the guerrilla movement *Ejercito de Liberacion Nacional* on his return to Peru and was shot dead by government security forces at the age of 21, killed like so many of the best of his contemporaries at a very young age. His poetry has real qualities of innocence and openness – an idealistic vision that may not have lasted. His death was a sacrifice that made of him a martyr, with all the problems that process entails. His collected poems were published in 1964.

ZBIGNIEW HERBERT (b.1924)   one of the most widely known and translated of post-war Polish poets, Herbert grew up with the experience of the Nazi occupation and began to write under the subsequent Stalinist regime. His refusal to take part in official literary life delayed the publication of his first book until 1956 but his stature was immediately apparent. His *Report From The Beseiged City* (1983) is probably the finest book of poetry from Poland under martial law (its first edition was published by internees in the Rakowiecka Prison in Warsaw). His poetry has increasingly born witness to the truths of things in their exact detail, because the withholding of truth is a major strategy of power (for all governments, everywhere) and thus he sees the naming of complexities as a way of resisting oppression. He is thought of as one of the finest living European poets. Four books of his poetry and two books of his essays have been translated into English.

AMADO V. HERNANDEZ (1903-1970)   worked as a journalist in the 1930s, joining the guerrilla resistance to Japanese occupation in the war. After 1942 he became a labour organiser and later spent six years in jail as a suspected communist subversive. He is one of those who revolutionised Filipino culture and his influence on the work of younger writers has been both genuine and rich, despite attempts by governments in his late years and after his death (he was proclaimed a "National Artist" by President Marcos in 1972) to co-opt his name and distort the sense of his work.

MIGUEL HERNÁNDEZ (1910-1942)   a goatherd from a young age he came to know Pablo Neruda and the circle of great contemporary Spanish poets in Madrid. In 1936 he enlisted in the Republican cause and fought at Teruel but after the war was imprisoned and kept in appalling conditions. He died in prison in 1942 of tuberculosis. There is a tenderness and freedom about the prison and war poems that not only made his work loved at the time but also served as a link to other realities for Spaniards during the subsequent years of dictatorship under Franco. His poems have been published in North America and Ireland and a first volume in Britain is due later in 1995.

NAZIM HIKMET (1901-1963)   one of the very greatest of modern Turkish poets, from the 1920s Nazim Hikmet revolutionised Turkish poetry in its language, its humanity and its aesthetics and in the openness of his verse and the human warmth of his struggle, sending waves far beyond the edges of his own language. Put in prison on a number of occasions, in 1938 he was sentenced to 35 years for inciting the Turkish army to revolt. In 1950 he was released and spent the last years of his life in exile in Sofia, Warsaw and Moscow. His work has been translated into English (and published in Britain, America and India) from the early 1950s on until the present and remains a deep source of clear uncynical inspiration. The epic masterpiece *Human Landscapes from My Country*, which Hikmet wrote in prison, appeared in English in 1982.

HO CHI MINH (1890-1969)   was born in a small village in central Vietnam   and inherited his father's wanderlust, but on a global scale. In 1920s Paris he became affiliated with the Communist Party and linked this to his obsession with the fate of his country. In 1942 he was arrested by Chinese forces and for over a year moved from prison to prison in appallingly disease-ridden conditions. During this time he wrote, in the language of his jailers, a diary of poems. The power of his leadership and vision played a huge role in securing the independence of Vietnam from French and later American intervention – though the regime of which he was head in its turn imprisoned not a few of its own citizens and writers.

VLADIMÍR HOLAN (1905-1980)   was one of the great Czech poets of the century. A friend of Frantisek Halas his poems of the war years were full of antifascist feeling. In 1948 under the Communist regime he was accused of 'decadent formalism' and until 1963 his work was largely ignored and little published. Much of his most powerful work including the long *A Night With Hamlet* was done while the least attention was being paid him. His whole life –that of a very reclusive man – was given over to poetry. By the time the Prague Spring was forced back the stature of his work was too formidable to be ignored and his fifty years of poetry is an astonishing body of meditation on suffering and harsh necessity and their unspoken mysteries. A *Selected Poems* was published in the Penguin Modern European Poets series and *Mirroring* has appeared more recently in America.

GYULA ILLYÉS (1902-1983)   the son of a machinist on a landed estate he began publishing his poetry in the 1920s and edited two of the most influential leftist literary journals of the period. In 1936 his classic prose study *People Of The Puszta* was published and he also wrote a biography of Petofi whose fiery commitment he shared. He survived the war in Budapest but the dictatorship and terror of the communist years disillusioned him. While it would be wrong to label him a dissident (and certainly he was not imprisoned by the regime), the poems he wrote in the early 1950s, including *A Sentence On Tyranny*, could not be published at the time and are very outspoken about freedom and survival. It is surprising given the translations explosion of recent years that there is only one book of his poems in English – and that from 25 years ago. Certainly he is regarded as one of the major Hungarian poets of the century.

ANTONIO JACINTO (1924-1991)   was born in Luanda and was a pioneer in the movement for cultural nationalism. He was arrested as an MPLA militant and sentenced to fourteen years in the Tarrafal Prison in the Cape Verde Islands. Released in 1972 he went back to Angola and returned to the active ranks of the MPLA. In 1986 he was the first African poet to be awarded the Noma prize (for his prison collection *Sobrevivir em Tarrafal*) and his poetry is now widely recognised both for its lyricism and for the quality of its commitment – its singing of beauty and its struggle for freedom.

LINTON KWESI JOHNSON (b.1952)   born in rural Jamaica he came to London in 1963 to join his mother in Brixton. Subjected to considerable racism at school he subsequently joined the Black Panthers and began writing poetry. He was closely involved with the Race Today Collective and his poetry has always been concerned with political action: the mainstay of his creative source is the experience of black people in British society. Equally he has linked poetry to popular music (often his work has been recorded and he has in the past toured with various bands) and the rhythms of natural speech clearly enrich his own work. His published poetry includes *Dread Beat An' Blood* (1975), *Inglan Is A Bitch* (1980) and *Tings An Times* (1991).

ATTILA JÓZSEF (1905-1937)   one of the greatest proletarian poets of this century and a rare poet of the lyric intellect, Jozsef never knew his father and was brought up in poverty by his mother, in Budapest and villages of the Hungarian countryside. Disdained by the fascist establishment of the '30s yet rejected by the Communist Party for his unorthodox attempt to integrate Freudian and Marxist perspectives, he became increasingly isolated and prone to breakdown and died a suicide falling under a train. If his poetry was taken up by the communist regimes of post-war Hungary, its real tribute is of the libertarian left and its protest the lack of freedom. It was his achievement in the last four imbalanced years of his life to create a lyric poetry of such balance and new order. The sheer verve of his poetic voice had lasting effects on Hungarian letters over many years. A number of poets have attempted the difficult task of translating him into English.

KATSETNIK 135633 (b.1917)   is the 'name' given him in Auschwitz which the Polish born writer Yechiel Dinur subsequently chose to write under. Its stark derivation is from the initials KZ (German pronounciation KaTzet) together with the number every concentration camp inmate had branded into the flesh of their left arm. After being liberated from Auschwitz he went to Israel where he has lived ever since. His many novels, which include the highly successful *House of Dolls*, have been translated very widely from the original Hebrew. In 1961 he made a celebrated public intervention at the Eichmann trial in Jerusalem. His most recent work *Shivitti* is a non-fictional account of a controversial treatment (pioneered in the 1970s in Amsterdam and using the drug LSD) to overcome the terror of his Auschwitz internment and the traumas of survival.

PARVIZ KHAZRAI   is an Iranian poet and dramatist now living in France. Since receiving his poem the editors have lost contact with him and are unable to provide further information.

KIM CHI HA (b.1941)   was sentenced to death, commuted to life imprisonment, for activities supposedly inimical to the government of South Korea. He was held in prison for a number of years and severely tortured. His poetry reflects both this experience and the intense surveillance that Korean culture and society have periodically suffered from. His plain direct poetry cannot be separated from his life, nor that life from the culture of his country. In English *Cry of the People And Other Poems* was published in Tokyo in 1974, a selected poems *The Middle Hour* in New York in 1988 and *The Gold-Crowned Jesus And Other Writings* in 1978. In recent years he has lived with less overt political involvement, and more quietly away from Seoul.

ETHERIDGE KNIGHT (1931-1991)   born in Mississippi, he served in the Korean War, where he was wounded. Discharged from the army and falling back into addiction, he was charged with armed robbery in 1960 and spent eight years in prison. It was in prison that he began to write poetry. He composed 'The Idea of Ancestry' while in one of his many stays in Solitary Confinement. Disoriented and feeling that he was suffocating, recalling his geneology was his means of reconnecting with himself and allowing himself to breathe a little more from the belly. Knight is a street-smart poet who writes from a great range of emotions. *The Essential Etheridge Knight* was winner of the 1987 American Book Award.

KO UN (b.1933)   his life is marked by immense changes: from 1952 for ten years he was a Buddhist monk and lived a life of Zen meditation but through the '60s he became increasingly involved with the Korean struggles for human rights. He has been arrested many times and served several prison terms. His response to constricted freedom in his country has been to realise that life has immeasurable value when under threat. This has been particularly clear in his poetry written since the traumatic Kwangju Uprising of May 1980. He is immensely prolific and the affirming angers of his work are expansive in ways perhaps akin to the poetry of Ernesto Cardenal, and as tied to Korean values as Cardinal's are to Nicaraguan.

RACHEL KORN (1898-1982) born in a village in East Galicia and living in Lvov until 1941 she fled to the Soviet Union and then emigrated to Canada. A Yiddish poet since 1919, much of what she has written has its roots in the sufferings, wanderings and memories of East European Jewry and the destruction of their vibrant culture during the Holocaust. From 1948 until her death she lived in Montreal, widely translated and anthologised and in the words of Elie Weisel "a great lady of Jewish and world literature." Two books of her poetry in English have been published in Canada and some of her short fiction is available in a recent translation of Yiddish women's short stories.

ABDELLATIF LAÂBI (b.1942) novelist and poet who published his first novel in 1969 and edited the literary journal *Souffles*. This was banned and in 1972 Laabi was arrested for "crimes of opinion". Tortured and isolated in prison, he was amnestied in 1980 following an international campaign but was deprived of his passport and work for another four years. In 1985 he left Morocco and has since lived in exile in Paris. Essayist and human rights activist, Laabi is also a superb translator of contemporary Arabic poetry into French. The pervasiveness of barbarism in his work is always balanced by an upwelling of the undeniable power of hope.

PRIMO LEVI (1919-1987) trained as a chemist Primo Levi joined a partisan group near his home city of Turin and was sent to Auschwitz after being captured. He managed to survive - his knowledge as a chemist perhaps saving him - and he worked as a chemist on his return to Italy. A novelist, short-stort writer and essayist he wrote one of the most lucid and sane and extraordinary accounts of the experience of the death camps (*If This Is A Man*). His poetry also, collected in the volume*Shema*, talks of the Holocaust. He was given many prizes for his prose and fiction, but in his last years he became increasingly depressed and fell to his death, almost certainly a suicide, from the stairwell of his home in 1987. As well as his *Collected Poems* and *If This Is A Man* Levi's novels and shorter fiction, including *The Wrench* and *The Periodic Table*, have been translated into English.

SAUNDERS LEWIS (1893-1984) regarded as perhaps the greatest of Welsh language writers of this century for his plays and fiction, Saunders Lewis was essentially a poet, despite the slimness of his poetic output. His work grew out of the Welsh non-conformist tradition and he was instrumental in setting up Plaid Cymru being its president in its early years. In 1936 he committed a symbolic act of arson and was tried for conspiracy to blow up a reservoir in North Wales. He was imprisoned for nine months in Wormwood Scrubs and on his release was deprived of his university position and endured a number of years of penury and hardship. His collected plays have been translated into English in four volumes by Joseph Clancy and in 1993 his *Selected Poems* also became available.

LIAO YIWU (b. 1958) born in Yanting, Sichuan Province, he gained recognition for his poetry in his early twenties. However in 1985 he fell out of favour with the government, who considered him a ring-leader of China's underground poetry movement. Harrassed by the authorities for several years, he was about to flee China when he was arrested in March of 1990. He has been denied all visits by his wife and his son, who was born while he was in prison, and his wife was detained for copying out the poem *Slaughter*, part of which is included in this anthology.

EOGHAN MacCORMAIC (b.1956)   born in Derry he was arrested in 1976 and served a fifteen year sentence in Long Kesh. Like a number of Republican prisoners (both men and women) he became a poet while in the H Blocks, during the intense years of protests and hunger strikes which culminated in the death of Bobby Sands (himself a poet) and stimulated a process of shared cultural consciousness and sharpened vision. Significantly he became fluent in Irish over this period and is now pursuing Irish Studies at University College Galway and his commitment to Republicanism remains intact and strong. His poems have appeared in journals and in the collection *H Block* published in Sheffield in 1991.

OSIP MANDELSTAM (1891-1938)   an Acmeist who once said that he wrote out of a 'craving for world culture' and also said that 'classical poetry is the poetry of revolution' Mandelstam at first welcomed the Revolution but was increasingly silenced under Stalin. His first three books of poetry were highly praised, but it is his work of the 1930s, the Moscow and the Voronezh Notebooks, written after five years silence and through periods of prison and exile - where he creates memorable lyric sustenance in the face of terror – that is his finest achievement. Arrested in 1934 and again in 1938 he is thought to have died near Vladivostok on his way to the gulags. His poetry remained in many people's minds for years and the continued existence of his late poetry is due to the tenacious memories of his friends – in particular his wife Nadezhda whose own prose on the Stalinist years is among the finest witness to that terrifying time.

JACK MAPANJE (b.1944)   born in Kadango Village, Malawi, he taught in secondary school before completing his Phd in linguistics. His first book *Of Chameleons and Gods* was published in 1981. On its second reprint it was banned by the government of Malawi and Mapanje was detained in Mikuyu Prison for over three years, although no charges were brought against him. In 1988 he received the Rotterdam International Poetry Award (for poets in prison) and he was released in May of 1991 after prolonged protest from writers and activists. His second book of poems *The Chattering Wagtails of Mikuyu Prison*, relating his prison experience, was published in 1993. At present Jack Mapanje lives with his family in Yorkshire.

CZESLAW MILOSZ (b.1911)   one of the leaders of the avant-garde movement in Polish poetry in the 1930s, in the Resistance during the German occupation he edited an anti-Nazi anthology of poetry. He was a diplomat after the war but broke with the communist government of Poland in 1951, living for 10 years in Paris before going to the University of California. The author of numerous prose works(*The Captive Mind, The Issa Valley, Native Realm, The Seizure of Power*) and collections of criticism(*Visions from San Francisco Bay, Emperor of the Earth: Modes of Eccentric Vision)* it is perhaps as a poet of severe but lyric intensity whose imagery is rooted in his native Lithuania that he is best known. He was given the Nobel Prize in 1980 and is widely seen as among the most important poets of modern Polish and world literature. Much of his poetry is available in English translation, most notably the *Collected Poems* of 1988.

JANICE MIRIKITANI   a third generation Japanese American born in California, she was interned as an infant with her family in an American concentration camp in Arkansas during the Second World War. She has published two collections of poetry in California (*Awake in the*

River in 1978 and *Shedding Silence* 1987) and in Britain her *New and Selected Poems* was published in 1995 by Virago Press. She has also edited anthologies of poetry and prose and been published herelf in numerous journals in Japan and America. At present she is Director of Programs at Glide Church, a multi-cultural, multi-service urban centre and church in San Francisco. Her poetry, which ranges from angry political involvement to tenderness and eroticism, has been highly praised by Maya Angelou among others.

MITTA VASLEYE (1908-1957)   born in the village of Asla Arabus, he worked as a teacher of his native Chuvash language. In 1937 he was arrested on an unfounded charge of 'nationalism' and spent seventeen years in Soviet labour camps and prisons and in exile. His lyric poetry only comprises a slim volume yet the fraternity of his Socratic voice and the restrained perfection of all that he wrote make him one of the finest modern Chuvash poets after Sespel Mishi. Released from prison he died in the village of his birth during the spring festival *Agadui* with the words "the poet who dies on his native soil is happy." Gennady Aygi has described him as a spiritually gifted poet whose work left a brotherly testament to his people. As with many imprisoned writers the exact date of composition of many of his poems is uncertain.

RITA MPOUMI-PAPPAS (b.1906)   trained as a Montessori teacher and ran a school for infants on Syros. Her first book of poems was published in 1930 and she is a poet of great productivity. Her book *A Thousand Murdered Girls* is about young women in the Greek resistance during World War II who were   court-martialled and executed when they refused to sign declarations of repentance.The poems are closely based on what the women wrote and said before they were killed. She has written for Greek progressive newspapers and is a poet of renown. With her husband (the poet Nikos Pappas) she translated an anthology of world poetry.

SUBHAS MUKHOPADHYAY (b.1919)   born in Krishnanagar in West Bengal, a longtime member of the Communist Party of India and a trade union organiser, he was jailed from 1948-1950 during the period of insurrectionary communism. Later he became president of the India branch of the Afro-Asian Writers Association and a member of the board of Sahitya Akademi. With his first collection *Padatik* (1940) he gained considerable popularity and became one of the most widely read poets in Bengal. Always remaining close to a left wing line in a poetry that has deepened over time, he has published volumes of both poetry and prose and translations of among others Pablo Neruda. At present he is living in Calcutta.

ÁGNES NEMES NAGY (1922-1991)   her first volume of poetry was published in 1946 and the book of selected poems *The Horses And The Angels* (1969) brought together three further collections. A brilliant essayist and critic (both of her own and others' poetries) and translator of, among others, Rilke and St. John Perse, Racine, Moliere, and Brecht, her own work is stark and concrete and, in the words of her translator, one walks into her poems as into "an abrupt change of climate." While she was neither imprisoned nor strictly speaking censored, her work has at its heart an unmistakably straitened Hungarian identity and a rigorous sense of the individual constrained yet richly defined by history. Her collected poems were published as *Between* in 1981.

KISHWAR NAHEED (b.1940)   has published seven volumes of poetry, various translations and a book of essays discussing women's rights in Pakistan. In her position as a writer and her role as an editor she has faced very strong male-dominated opposition (as an editor she has been charged with various offences on thirty diferent occasions) and has stood up against the increasing persecution of women under the regime of Zia ul-Haque and the promulgation of the Hudood Ordinances in 1979. Her language is known for its range and its energy and she writes with great professional dedication and constant verbal challenge. She is one of the few poets in Urdu to have written prose poetry that broke with conventional forms and thus also eroded traditional images. Two books of her poetry have been published in English translation in Lahore and her work is well represented in the anthology *We Sinful Women* (ed.&tr. by Rukhsana Ahmad) and published in London in 1991.

AHMED FOUAD NEGM (b.1929)   spent his early years in the Egyptian countryside, until the death of his father when Negm was six. Early hardships forced him to a variety of jobs : domestic servant, laundry boy, footballer, hawker, tailor, construction worker and railway labourer. In 1959 he was arrested for trade union activities and his first collection of poems *Scenes from Life and Prison* was smuggled out of prison. His lyrics, based on the poverty of ordinary people and attacking corrupt official life, are deeply influenced by the oral traditions of the *fellaheen* and also by Qur'anic recital, and by his collaboration with the great blind singer Sheikh Imam. One of the very few Arabic lyricists whose work has genuinely reached out across the Arab world despite official obstruction, harrassment, torture and detention over the past two decades. In 1989 he was convicted for 'invading' Ain-Shams University campus and 'assaulting' the police.

PABLO NERUDA (1904-1973)   publication of his first book of poetry brought him immense popularity and during his life he became a genuinely public poet for his country and continent. Yet he retained a great range and diversity of voices, some very private and often in a reticent vein. His great committed poetry – despite a phase of Stalinism from the mid-40s – tends to the meta-political, the title of his superb epic *Canto General* giving the hint of rising up as well as uprising. Much of this was written in hiding from arrest in Chile and Latin America with radical and hurt memories of the Spanish Civil War strongly in his mind. He died of cancer at his house in Isla Negra in 1973 two weeks after the devastating military coup that had overthrown Salvador Allende. Over fifty books of his poetry have been published in English translation alone. In 1971 he was awarded the Nobel Prize.

AGOSTINHO NETO (1922-1979)   trained as a doctor in Portugal but was arrested on a number of occasions. Returning to Angola in 1959 he again was arrested and imprisoned in Portugal over a long period. International pressures forced the authorities to release him and he managed to escape house arrest,   returning to Angola where he led the MPLA to victory in its guerrilla war and was then elected the first President of an independent Angola, a post he held from 1975 until his death. His poetry and the collection *Sagrada Esperanca* in particular gave voice in direct and memorable language to the struggle against fascist colonial oppression: the hope in it is not sentimental and its expression identifies Angolan and African values of dignity and self-determination.

NGUYEN CHI THIEN (b.1933)   was born in Hanoi and grew up in Haiphong. From 1958 he was imprisoned almost without break in various 're-education' and prison camps until 1978. He returned to Haiphong where he found it impossible to be employed – but he did start to write down the poetry he had composed while in prison. In April 1979 he managed to get into the British Embassy in Hanoi where he left the manuscript of his poems and a letter asking that they be published abroad on behalf of all the "victims of dictatorship in Communist prisons." It seems that he was refused asylum and was arrested again immediately on leaving the embassy and that he was still being held in Hoa Lo Central Prison in Hanoi (according to information current in the late 1980s). His poetry has been translated in the United States.

BULAT OKUDZHAVA (b.1924)   of Armenian and Georgian background, Okudzhava was born in Moscow where his parents, both of whom were party officials, were arrested and purged in 1937. He himself fought in the war and later became a teacher, taking to full-time writing in 1956. A fine poet in his own right, a novelist also, he is best known for his songs and for bringing into existence the tradition of guitar poetry that was to prove so subversive of official language and music. His work attained great popularity from the '60s on, being widely circulated on clandestine tapes (as were the guitar-poems of Galich and Vysotsky). His songs have an intimate melancholy learned from "the great art of forgiveness and understanding", unorthodoxies that brought his career close at times to disaster with the Soviet regime. Some of his poems and songs and two of his novels have been translated into English.

DAN PAGIS (1930-1986)   was born in Bukovina (like Paul Celan) and as a boy was a prisoner in a concentration camp in the Ukraine. He escaped and survived and his poetry is one of survival suffused with grief and prophetic vision. He went in 1946 to Israel and learnt the Hebrew that became the language of his poetry, and taught in schools before becoming professor of Medieval Hebrew in Jerusalem. He was one of the foremost scholars of Judaic Spain and wrote superbly on that rich and destroyed culture. His own very fine poetry helped revolutionise the energy and language of modern Hebrew and his work, both the poetry (*Points of Departure*) and some of the scholarly criticism, has been consistently translated into English.

ANGEL PARDO   a Cuban poet imprisoned for many years under Castro. The poems we have included in this anthology are from a sequence written during and dated according to a prolonged hunger strike.

ALICIA PARTNOY (b.1955)   she was among the 30,000 Argentinians who were 'disappeared' through state terror after the military junta took power in 1976. Her stories and poems were smuggled out of prison and published anonymously. She was released after three years and forced to go into exile and has since lived in the United States where she has lectured extensively and presented testimony on human rights violations in Argentina. She is the author of *The Little School: Tales of Disappearance & Survival in Argentina* (1986), editor of a collection of exiled Latin American women's writing *You Can't Drown the Fire* (1988), and a bilingual edition of her own poems *Revenge of the Apple* was published in 1992. She lives with her husband, who was also imprisoned under the junta, and her two daughters in Washington D.C.

PADRAIC PEARSE (1879-1916)   born of an English father and an Irish mother, he was a poet and short story writer in both languages. He founded and ran two schools and was a radical educational thinker and journalist; he was deeply involved in the Gaelic League and the Irish Republican movement, was central in planning the Easter Rising and was elected the first President of the Provisional Government. Together with his younger brother and two fellow poets Thomas MacDonagh and Joseph Mary Plunkett he was among the leaders executed by the British after the Rising. Flawed themes of myth and martyrdom inevitably surround him and his name has been so over-used to represent extremes of good and evil that real sight of him has often been lost: but he was a complex and often ambiguous human being and both his life and his poetry were simply cut off in their midst. A new edition of his selected poems was published in 1993 in Dublin.

GYÖRGY PETRI (b.1943)   of a generation that grew to maturity after the 1956 Hungarian Uprising Petri at first published with the state publishing house but from 1982 he decided to preserve his integrity in samizdat and increasingly became an unperson in official eyes. His poetry – that of a major and unusual satirist – attacked the political system of the Warsaw Pact in a savage and vituperative language stemming from angered belief in personal freedom and raw disillusion with the ordinary rhetorics of justice. You could call him a medieval modernist if you believed in such terms, but the direction his raw satire will take under the new Hungarian democracy is not easy to foresee. One book of his has so far been published in English translation *Night Song of the Personal Shadow* in 1991.

JÁNOS PILINSKY (1921-1981)   his life and his poetry – and the two are very close – were moulded by his radical catholicism and his experience of the death camps at the end of the war and took their fruition after the communist takeover in Hungary when he was banned from publishing for ten years. Agnes Nemes Nagy, a close friend and fellow poet, wrote that he was "deeply deviant, rare and improbable... a persecuted legend." His popularity at home grew as did his reputation abroad: he remains an extraordinary phenomenon in Hungarian poetry, doing after the war perhaps what Jozsef had done (but in a very different way) before – leaving no gap between the poet and his subject and in this way writing a poetry that can speak 'after' Auschwitz through now to us here. English translations of his work include *Crater, The Desert of Love* and *66 Poems* as well as the prose *Conversations with Sheryl Sutton*.

VASKO POPA (1922-1991)   one of a generation of European poets 'caught in mid-adolescence by the war' (Ted Hughes' words), he was imprisoned by the Nazis in 194.. He is recognized as the most important post-war Serbian poet and has been translated into many languages, including the Penguin Modern European Poets series in 1969 and a forthcoming *Complete Poems* in English. His poetry developed out of a literary surrealism and moved towards the elemental mythic reality of Serbian folklore. From his first collection published in 1953, he wrote in cycles that brought together disparate elements with an unexpected coherence that has an almost healing quality. His death in the midst of rich writing was seen as a great loss by those who recognized in him a unique and wonderful poet. The poems we have included are from those of his prison experience.

AMRITA PRITAM (b.1919)   novelist and poet of international renown, longtime editor of the Punjabi journal *Nagmani* and widely translated into Hindi and English, as well as many other languages. Her awards include those of both Jnanpith and the Sahitya Akademi and reflect her popularity as well as the range of her work. Her hatred of partition and fratricidal strife is clear in her elegy for Waris Shah (from the volume *Laammiyaan Vaataan* of 1948) and women's struggles against injustice and oppresion are central themes of her writings. Perhaps she is best known as a poet and her short, intense prose works tend towards the language of poetry. She has retained her popularity – an autobiography was published in 1976 and has been translated into English – yet remains a very private person. Certainly she is the most translated Indian woman writer, although she remains relatively little known in this country.

PUTU OKA SUKANTA (b.1939)   born in Bali he began writing when he was sixteen, developing mainly as a poet and fiction writer, but also with active involvement in the Indonesian theatre. He was imprisoned for ten years during the 1960s and 1970s and this experience crystallized earlier concerns in his work which explored the function, dynamic and place of individuals within their own culture and societies. In the 1980s he visited Sri Lanka and Bangladesh to take part in Popular Theatre Workshops and made a reading tour of Australia. He has been living in Djakarta, continuing to write and also practising acupuncture (a skill he learnt whilst in prison), though recently his clinic was shut down by the government for political reasons.

SAMIH al-QASIM (b.1939)   is a Palestinian from a Druze family in Galilee. Imprisoned many times for his political actions (and indeed for the integrity of his poetry) he has remained all his life in Israel refusing either to leave his homeland or to dovetail to authority. He is a very prolific poet – the 1948 Palestinian war having traumatised him into the knowledge that the "only way I can assert my identity is by writing poetry". A member of the Israeli Com- munist Party, he lives in Haifa where he works as a journalist and runs the Arabesque Press andthe Palestinian Folk Arts Centre. A substantial selection of his work in included in the anthology *Victims Of A Map* compiled and translated by Abdullah al-Udhari.

MIKLÓS RADNÓTI (1909-1944)   a twin whose mother and brother died during his birth, Radnoti was raised by relatives. Educated at the University of Szeged, he visited Paris on various occasions. The last year of his life was spent in various labour camps. He was transported by the Nazis to work in the Bor mines in Serbia and after a forced march he was shot by his guards late in 1944. When his body was exhumed from its mass grave a small stained notebook was found. It contained the last of the great poems he had been writing since the middle 1930s. Murdered as a Jew and for his anti-fascism, Radnoti in fact had matured slowly as a poet, steeping his verse in traditions as open as Apollinaire's and as potently structured as Vergil's until his own poetry burst out under the pressures of Hungarian fascism in classic avant-garde words shoring up freedom.

SHAMSUR RAHMAN (b.1929)   a graduate of Dhaka University he began writing poetry before he was twenty, although his first volume was not published until 1960. The mass protest of the Language Movement (February 1952) exerted a powerful influence on his work as did even more so the Bangladeshi uprising for independence and subsequent invasion of his country by Pakistan in 1970-71. The volume he wrote from his occupied city was smuggled into India and published from Calcutta as *From The Prison Camp* in 1972. Throughout the 1970s his output was prolific and he came to be recognised as one of the two or three foremost poets of contemporary Bangladesh. Volumes of his poetry have been published in English translation in Dhaka and Calcutta but his work, in common with most Bangladeshi and Bengali writers, is still little known in Britain or America.

IRINA RATUSHINSKAYA (b.1954)   was born in Odessa. She studied physics there and began writing poetry and became involved with human rights issues. She was arrested by the authorities in 1982 and sentenced for her poetry to seven years hard labour in the "strict regime" labour camp of Barashevo where she was held in the Small Zone, a special unit for women political prisoners. There and in punishment isolation cells she was subjected to beatings and force-feeding. In the camp she wrote poems onto bars of soap and then memorised them or copied them onto strips of paper which were then smuggled out. Following intense pressure and international concern at the harsh conditions of her imprisonment she was released after four years and allowed to emigrate. Four volumes of her poetry have been translated into English, as well as a volume of short stories and two prose memoirs and she lives in London at present with her husband and two children.

ADRIENNE RICH (b.1929)   through over forty years Adrienne Rich has come to be respected as one of the great writers of modern America. Over fifteen separate books of her poetry have ben published as well as a number of selected and collected volumes. Her very influential essays were collected in *Blood, Bread, And Poetry* and the classic *Of Woman Born* a feminist study of motherhood.She has been honoured with many awards, both national and international and has been translated into many languages. Her most recent books are *Collected Early Poems 1950-1970* and *What Is Found There: Notebooks On Poetry And Politics*. Increasingly through her life and work she has sought to bring language and politics, and particularly sexual politics, into exact and radical correspondence, to the great enrichment of both.

OKTAY RIFAT (1914-1988)   grew up in Istanbul and Ankara. In 1941 he initiated Turkish poetry into modernism with the poets Orhan Veli and Melih Cevdet Anday but his own poetry evolved through various voices to a unique synthesis. He led a highly uneventful and private life with little overt political activity though with clear commitments which gained voice in his poetry. He once wrote that 'poetry, socialism and shying away from lies are the pillars of my personality.' His combination of lyrical power and shared memory come together in the title of a book from 1966: *Freedom Has Hands*. And in 1993 he was finally published in English when the book *Voices Of Memory* came out in London, published by Rockingham Press.

GOPALPRASAD RIMAL (1918-1973)   the first revolutionary in Nepali poetry, both in the sense of his commitment and in his abandonment of metre, he was imprisoned on several occasions and was highly critical of the Rana government. Many of Rimal's poems are framed as dialogue between a mother and her suffering children and it's clear that they should be seen in terms of Nepal and the oppression of the people by the state, even where the poet held back from overt identification. In his last years Rimal (like Devkota) spent a long period in the asylum at Ranchi and, disillusioned with the outcome of the revolution of 1950-1, he wrote no further poetry between 1960 and his death over twelve years later. He remains even so a distinctive voice in Nepali poetry.

YANNIS RITSOS (1909-1990)   one of the most prolific and celebrated poets of modern Greece, he published his first book in 1934. His mother and older brother died from tuberculosis and as a young man he was in and out of sanatoria. During the war he joined the Greek Democratic Left and in the civil war period (1948-53) was imprisoned in a number of concentration camps due to his socialist sympathies. Again under the junta of the Colonels (1967-74) he was exiled and imprisoned and later also put under house arrest. He wrote a startling range of poetry from sequences of short lyrics to long narratives and chorales and dramatic monologues and despite prison and uncertain health he published over 100 books of poetry in his lifetime. More than twenty book-length translations have appeared in English (notably the *Selected Poems 1938-1988* published in New York) and he himself translated into Greek such poets as Hikmet, Jozsef, Blok and Nicolas Guillen. One of the great poets of modern Europe he died in Athens in November 1990.

TADEUSZ RÓZEWICZ (b.1921) the trauma of the war and the German occupation of Poland (his brother was executed by the Gestapo, his fellow poets, Stroinski and Baczynski among them, died in the Warsaw Rising), formed his attitudes to poetry and its language: "How easy it was to create poetry while it still existed". From his first volume *Anxiety* in 1947 Rozewicz sought in a conscious crafting of banal truths to recreate a practice of poetry. This in itself could be seen to be fundamentally dissident – or fundamentally honest. However he is not a political dissident constantly in trouble with his government : his is a moral preoccupation, to express simply what is never simple. Besides his many volumes of poetry he is a foremost writer in Polish experimental theatre and a prolific essayist. Widely translated (into English by Adam Czerniawski who calls him clearly "one of the great poets of our time") his presence in Polish poetry remains seminal to its language.

NELLY SACHS (1891-1970) influenced by the German and Jewish mystics and later by Rilke and Holderlin, Nelly Sachs lived in isolation when the Nazis came to power, only escaping to Stockholm in 1940. Her mature voice is "great and mysterious" as Hans Magnus Enzensberger says and does not "dissolve in the weak solution of interpretation". Her poetry accrues like a single book, written in German about the genocide of the Jews, and its greatness is enveloping and goes in its language and its essence far beyond any one self. She received a Nobel prize in 1966 and died in Stockholm, not having returned to Germany. A large selection of her work was translated in 1970 but little attention has been paid (in English) to her work in recent years.

K. SATCHIDANANDAN (b.1946) born in central Kerala, he has been Professor of English at Christ College, Irinjalakuda for twenty five years and is now editor of Sahitya Akademi's journal *Indian Literature* in New Delhi. He has published fifteen collections of his own work in Malayalam as well as various translations into Malayalam from the poetry of Neruda and Zbigniew Herbert and the plays of Yeats and Brecht among others. His own poetry has been translated into many languages both in India and beyond and he is also a highly respected critic. He has taken part in many poetry festivals around the world and been awarded a number of prizes. *The Times of Torment* - an excerpt of which is included in this anthology - was written after his arrest in July 1980 when he had led a march protesting police oppression of the Dalit (*Untouchable*) community in his home town.

SARVESHWAR DAYAL SAXENA (1927-1984) born in Basti, Uttar Pradesh he joined All India radio after graduating from Allahabad University, and later worked on the literary journals *Dinman* and *Parag*. His early poetry was part of the modernist tendency within Hindi verse, and he also wrote plays, novels and short fiction. But after 1975 his work, clearly affected by the trauma of the Emergency period (1975-1977), became far more critical of authority and he sought to bring his language closer to popular experience without losing its previous inner balance and he came to emphasise freedom and struggle. His work is translated in a number of anthologies of Hindi and Indian poetries.

JORGE DE SENA (1919-1978)   is one of the foremost poets, scholars and cultural historians of twentieth century Portugal. Trained as a civil engineer and critical of the Salazar
regime, he quit Portugal for Brazil in 1959 and lectured in Portuguese literature at Sao Paulo.
After the coup d'etat he went to the USA and was subsequently Professor of Portuguese at
the University of California. Throughout his life he translated (from Cavafy, Emily Dickinson,
Faulkner, Whitman, Blake and many other English writers) and he is a figure of world literature, both through the quality and range of his own writing and for his wonderfully extensive
comparative knowledge. And in all his writings there shines through a profound attachment
to humanity and to human dignity, whether in his re-evaluations of Camões and Pessoa or in
his observation and critique of contemporary human suffering. His work is now widely available in English, though not as well known as perhaps it should be.

SIPHO SEPAMLA (b.1932)   was born in Krugersdorp and became a teacher. He published four books of poetry before the *Selected Poems* of 1984 and he has also published three
novels:*The Root Is One* (1979), *A Ride on the Whirlwind* (1981) and *Third Generation* (1986). His
poetry is powerfully urban, depicting the experience of black South Africans living under
apartheid together with a celebration of resilience and the will to self-determination. In the
'80s his books were frequently banned, basically because he said things as things were. Since
the late '70s he has worked with the Federation of Black Arts community organisation in
Johannesburg, the city in which he lives.

BHUPI SHERCHAN (1936-1989)   born into a wealthy family from a remote part of Nepal
to a minority ethnic group whose cultural orientation was essentially Tibetan, Sherchan studied in Banaras and in 1960 went to live in Kathmandu. His early poetry, written under a
pseudonym, made little impact but a volume first published in 1969 and often reprinted (*A
Blind Man On A Revolving Chair*) has had a huge influence on contemporary Nepali poetry,
with its mix of passionate anger and satire and the clarity of its language. During the 1960's
he was imprisoned for his activities in radical politics and he never fully recovered from the
damage done to his health at this time.

SIAMANTO (1878-1915)   born in Akn in Western Armenia, Siamanto was educated in
Istanbul and at the Sorbonne and travelled widely before settling in Istanbul. There in 1915 he
was among the intellectual leaders murdered by Turkish forces at the start of the Armenian
massacres. His ceremonial style, the polyphony and rhythms of his language and a real pes-
simism, that reflects the bitter history of Armenia and the pogroms that occured during his
lifetime, while affirming the strength and grace of Armenian culture, made him one of the
most beloved writers of his day and the richness of his work has been widely recognised by
Armenians ever since. A book of his poetry in English translation is due to be published in
the United States later this year.

TAKIS SINOPOULOS (1917-1988)   growing up in the dictatorships of the '30s and living through the terrible years of war, foreign occupation and bitter civil war from 1939-1949
(when he served as a doctor with front-line units) his poetry - like that of many twentieth century Greek poets - is haunted by his country's recent history. His great elegy *Deathfeast* looks
back precisely to the civil war period in a slow river of litanies and survival. Significantly,
though, it was written during the brutal dictatorship of the military junta (1967-1975). For
most of the post-war years Sinopoulos lived in Athens and worked as a general practitioner.

Through a sequence of poetry and prose-poem collections he came to be seen as a leading poet of his generation, continually raising and testing language against the paranoia and brutalities of political dictatorship.

JOSE MARIA SISON (b.1939)   graduating from the English department of the University of the Philippines in Manila, Sison was instrumental in founding the new Communist Party in his country and in establishing a poetry that rejected the prevailing tradition and drew inspiration from the committed writings of Jose Rizal and Amado V. Hernandez. After martial law was declared in 1972 he carried on his political involvement clandestinely. In 1977 he was captured and imprisoned, suffering torture and solitary confinement, and only escaped death through international pressure on his behalf. He was finally released in 1986 with the downfall of President Marcos. His long poem 'Fragments of a Nightmare' deals by means of acute political awareness and an absolute lack of self-pity with the issue of torture in prison and was published, together with his other prison poems, before he was released. At present he lives in Utrecht in Holland.

WOLE SOYINKA (b.1934)   one of the world's great contemporary writers, poet and playwright, novelist and cultural critic, Soyinka was born in a village in Nigeria and has written superbly about his childhood. In 1967 he was arrested by the Nigerian government and kept in solitary confinement for twenty-two months for his writings in sympathy with secessionist Biafra. He wrote about this experience in the prose *The Man Dies: Prison Notes* and the volume of poetry *Shuttle In The Crypt*. He was awarded the Nobel Prize in 1986 and has been the subject of very considerable critical attention. In recent years he has again been harrassed and threatened by his government but has remained wholly outspoken in his criticism. In late 1994 he managed to leave Nigeria. His most recent book of poems is *Mandela's Earth*, published in 1989 with later reprints.

VASYL STUS (1938-1985)   like many poets of his generation Stus became active in the human rights movement in the Ukraine and in 1972 was charged with "anti-Soviet agitation and propaganda." Sentenced to five years in a labour camp he was repeatedly denied medical attention and his manuscripts were routinely confiscated as the KGB tried to destroy his life and his culture. In exile he was assigned to mine work in appalling conditions and constantly harrassed. Released for a brief period he was rearrested in 1980 and tortured under interrogation before being sent for a further ten years to a strict-regime camp in Perm. Here he was again persecuted and abused to the point where he died in September 1985. It is testimony to the strength of his life and dissent that his poetry was not killed but remains part of the civic and cultural revival of the Ukraine.

ABRAHAM SUTZKEVER (b.1913)   was born in Vilna but his childhood was spent in Siberia and returning to his birthplace he became a leading presence in the culture of its Ghetto. He managed to live through the Nazi occupation, writing poetry in Yiddish to defy the brutality and working on an underground press. He joined a partisan group that broke through to the forests and later he was airlifted to Russia. His ghetto poems are extraordinary acts of art and defiance. After the war he testified at the Nuremberg trials and from 1948 has lived in Jerusalem, editing the Yiddish literary journal *Di goldene keyt*. He is recognised as a great virtuoso poet, defying the damage done to his culture, and uniting the destroyed past with the creative present. There are at present three books of his poetry in English translation.

TITSIAN TABIDZE (1895-1938)   a member of the *Blue Horns* group that took shape around 1916 and developed a genuinely original lyricism from its roots in European symbolism, Tabidze emerged after 1922 as a great lyric poet. His finest work was written in the second half of the 1920s but the increasingly totalitarian atmosphere of the '30s led his work to silence and exhaustion. He became close friends with Boris Pasternak who translated him superbly into Russian. He was murdered during the Stalin Purges, as were his fellow poet Paolo Yashvili and the novelist Mikheil Javakhishvili. They were all rehabilitated in 1954. Titsian Tabidze is one of the masters of the Georgian language, its lyric and its music.

VICTORIA THEODOROU (b.1928)   was born in Crete and studied at the University of Athens. She was imprisoned for five years during the civil war in various island concentration camps for her involvement in the Greek resistance. The book-length group of poems *Picnic* is her account of the lives of the hundreds of women political prisoners who chose to be exiled rather than sign "declarations of repentance" and the poems reflect their intense commitment. She wrote a very moving prison journal also that has been published in English translation. Since the 1950s she has lived in Athens and has continued writing, one of the many fine Greek women poets of the post-war period whose work is only now just beginning to be known in English: her work is in three anthologies of Greek women poets published in America.

TO HUU (b.1920)   born in Hue in Central Vietnam he began writing early and became recognised as one of the finest modern Vietnamese poets. His work has always had affiliations with the peasantry and with revolutionary movements but without the doctrinaire effects this often involves. He was arrested in 1939 and confined in a number of prisons before escaping in 1942. His poems were smuggled out of prison and passed around by word of mouth. He was president of the Hue Insurrectionary Committee during the 1945 revolution and involved with the government of Resistance between 1946 and 1954. His work is direct and simple and with great musical resource. It combines militancy with tenderness and the theme of independence. A book of his was published in English in 1978 (in Hanoi) but his work is hardly known in the English speaking world.

MARINA TSVETAYEVA (1892-1941)   a poet from a young age, and early a friend of Osip Mandelstam, she was by nature drawn to the anti-Bolshevik side during the Civil War, as was her husband Sergei Efron. She survived the hunger years in Moscow – when one of her children died – before emigrating in 1922 to Berlin and Prague and then Paris, where she lived for over 12 years. Her poetry is prolific both in lyric cycles and in long, intense narrative sequences. Always outspoken (she was moved to praise Mayakovsky in Paris) she was an outsider even in emigration. In summer 1939, almost fatefully she followed her husband back to the Soviet Union and, despite the support of a very few friends, the arrest of her husband, neglect by her fellow writers and the trauma and poverty of wartime evacuation led to her stark and tragic decision to take her own life in the town of Yelabuga in 1941.

U SAM OEUR (b.1936)   born in Svey Rieng province, U attended the Iowa Writers Workshop before returning to Cambodia in 1968 where he was elected Secretary General of the Khmer League for Freedom. With the takeover by the Khmer Rouge in 1975 he was interned but managed to survive four years in the concentration camps of Pol Pot (his childhood on a farm helped him adapt to the brutal rigours of forced agricultural labour) and the periods of terror that followed. Remaining in Cambodia, continually harrassed by the government and assumed by many of his friends to be dead, the poetry he was writing is extraordinary testimony to these terrifying years. In 1992 he was able to return to Iowa where he is collaborating with his long-time friend and translator Ken McCullough on a bilingual edition of the poems, a small group of which were published as the chapbook *Sacred Vows* in 1994.

USMAN AWANG (b.1929)　　joined the Malaysian police force straight from school but resigned in 1951 after which time he worked as a journalist and editor. His poetry and short stories began to be published in the early 1960's since when he has published prolifically and come to be recognised as one of the finest South East Asian writers, committed both to his literature and his people. His work is important both for his experimentation with traditional forms and for his identification with the people. If his reputation has yet to travel to the West it is international elsewhere. He has also written many plays adapting Malay theatrical traditions to contemporary issues. His poetry is included in various anthologies and one book has been published in English translation in Kuala Lumpur *Greetings to the Continent* 1982.

ARMANDO VALLADARES　　was tried for "offences against the powers of the state" and imprisoned in Cuba for a total of 21 years before being released in 1982. He refused to conform to the authorities' rehabilitation programme, protested the wearing of prison uniform, spent time in solitary confinement and was denied visits from his family and access to letters. In 1974 he contracted polyneuritis as the result of vitamin deficiency and lost the use of his legs. Valladares only began writing poetry while in prison and the publication abroad of smuggled texts contributed to his delayed freedom. In addition to his poetry he has written an intense prose account of his prison experience and this has been published in Spanish and in English translation.

CÉSAR VALLEJO (1892-1938)　　the youngest of eleven children, born in the Peruvian Andes, both of his grandmothers were pure Quechuan. Conflict and anguish were always close to both his life and his language. Briefly in prison in Trujillo he published *Black Heralds* and *Trilce* before leaving for Paris in 1923 where poverty and an increasingly heterodox commitment to communism mapped his life. The poetry of his last years – published only after his death – has a quite unique linguistic density and a torsion that treats pain with an implicit understanding that is both gentle and violent. As great a poet as Neruda, it is Vallejo who most nearly puts the consciousness of modern Latin America into words. By now very widely translated (Clayton Eshleman has translated the whole of the posthumous poetry into English) Vallejo's art has come to be recognised and praised as it rarely was during his lifetime.

JORGE VALLS ARANGO (b.1933)　　born near Havana, studied philosophy and in 1952 when Batista carried out his coup d'etat Valls was involved as a student in the struggle against his dictatorship. Persecuted and imprisoned he went into exile but after his return – and with Castro now in power – he was arrested, in 1964, and sentenced to twenty years in prison. Refusing to accept political indoctrination in return for better treatment he served out the full sentence. At times on the verge of complete psychological collapse, it was in part his poetry and the need to write that allowed him to survive. He once said that "of every hundred lines we wrote, only one got out of prison" and what did survive was smuggled out with great difficulty. In 1983 he was awarded the Rotterdam Poetry Festival Prize(as were a number of poets in this book). He was released in June 1984 following an international campaign and now lives in New York.

NIKOLA VAPTSAROV (1909-1942)   born in Bansko in Bulgaria he trained as a mechanic and his work brought him in contact with appalling factory conditions. He joined the Communist party in 1934 and was active in the anti-fascist and then anti-Nazi resistance. His son died in his absence in 1936. *Motor Songs* was published in 1940, the year in which he was also arrested for the first time. Interned in 1941 he was arrested again in March 1942 and tortured until he was hardly recognisable. In July of that year he was shot. (There is some parallel with another great revolutionary Bulgarian poet, Geo Milev, who was shot in the tragic days of April 1925). Vaptsarov's poetry, much of it collected after his death, still probably awaits thorough and effective translation into English though two selections have, fortunately, been published.

DANIEL VAROUJAN (1884 -1915)   educated in Istanbul, Venice and Ghent he was a teacher in Istanbul in 1915 when he was rounded up with other poets and intellectuals and imprisoned and then murdered: up to two million Armenians were massacred by Turkish forces during the genocide of the next five years. His poetry contains some of the richest, most complex and sensual imagery in Armenian literature: it was and remains extraordinary for its range and vertiginous energies and for the way he lets classical incantation through his own contemporary language. But his final and posthumously published book *Songs of Bread*(1921), written in prison before his death is remarkable for its lyric evocation of a pastoral Armenian calm. It is from this collection (rescued from his jailers by an Armenian priest) that the poem here included comes. Sadly no collection of his work has yet appeared in English.

DAVID VOGEL (1891-1944)   born in Satanov in southwest Russia, he lived in Vienna from 1912 to 1925 and thereafter in Palestine, Berlin and Paris. He was arrested as an enemy alien in France, released and in 1944 arrested again by the Nazis and almost certainly died in a concentration camp. His collected poems were edited by Dan Pagis and published in 1966 and again in 1971 under the title *Before The Dark Gate* and a selected English translation appeared in 1976. His translator A.C.Jacobs has described his poetry as complex and startling, and certainly it has a lucid beauty that is very real and very rare. One of his novels, *Married Life*, is also available in English.

VLADIMIR VYSOTSKY (1938-1980)   became an immensely popular poet, actor and balladeer and was probably the nearest equivalent in the USSR to a media superstar. He joined the Taganka Theatre under Lyubimov in its heyday of the 1960s and remained until his death: his most memorable performances were in the role of Hamlet. He also played in many films. His poems were songs which he sang inimitably in a deep gravelly voice that caught in its edges the tension of people's lives and he was in the subversive tradition of guitar poetry for which Galich and Okudzhava were also famous. Much in the public eye but little published in his lifetime, instead he relied on *magnitizdat* for a popularity the authorities could do little about. Though never imprisoned he was undoubtedly harrassed and intimidated. This and his heavy drinking probably contributed to his early death at the age of forty-two.

ROBERT WALKER (1958-1984)   was born in Port Augusta into a big Aboriginal family where human dignity was not considered an arrogance and intolerance was to be overcome. After his father died he moved to Adelaide with his family and underwent schooling. Imprisoned for minor offences he protested his treatment and in August 1984 he was taken from his cell in the middle of the night by prison officers and severely beaten. He died almost immediately. Despite the Coroner's verdict of death by misadventure it is clear that he died at the hands of the police. A book of his poetry and prose had been published in his lifetime as *Up! Not Down Mate* (1981).

ALEKSANDER WAT (1900-1967)   in a quite extraordinary life – that was nonetheless firmly rooted in Polish-Jewish history, and not untypical of our century – Wat moved in his work from a raw Dadaist experimentation through commitment to and then disillusion with communism in the 1930s and was arrested in Moscow in 1940, having left Poland to escape Nazi occupation. He was in the Lubianka and other prisons and for three years lost all contact with his wife and young son after they had been deported to Soviet Central Asia. Returning to Poland together in 1946 Wat was branded a 'hostile element' and suffered a stroke. Able to publish with the thaw and also to travel abroad for the sake of his health, his unique work is the achievement of old age – the spoken prose of *My Century* and poems in free verse melting together metaphysics and buffoonery – that make him a great poet and witness for our century.

WEN YIDUO (1899-1946)   following a traditional Chinese education Wen became influenced by Western literature while still a student and all his life he sought to cling to both traditions: the qualities of his writing often arise from the tensions of oscillating between the two. After three years in Chicago and New York he returned to China, writing in the vernacular on the one hand and researching the classics on the other. The poverty and sufferings accentuated by the Sino-Japanese war convinced him that the political and social order in China had to be changed: he was assassinated following an impassioned speech denouncing the government. Together with Dai Wangshu and other poets (they were none of them weighed down by dogma) Wen foreshadows the modernism of the best of recent Chinese poets. In his lifetime he published *Red Candle* (1923) and *Dead Water* (!928) and he has been translated in many anthologies and one separate volume,

ERROL WEST (b.1947)   born in Launceston, Tasmania in the traditional lineage of the Emeratta tribe, his people and culture having been almost entirely wiped out by 1900. He received only five years of formal education in a variety of schools, moving as his parents followed the cycles of seasonal work. Later he qualified as a primary school teacher and at present he is Chairman of the National Aboriginal Education Committee. Although his work has not yet (to the editors' knowledge) been collected in one volume, the richness of his language, a poetry of long lines and dense clarity that emerges from sureness of spirit and tradition and a personal history of collective survival, seems to link him to a number of other poets throughout this book.

OSCAR WILDE (1854 -1900)   born into the Anglo-Irish ascendancy and with every prospect of an exalted career his natural wit, brilliance and exuberant high spirits led him to a successful life of writing and lecturing and a dazzling entry to high society. His apotheosis as the cynical and ceaselessly entertaining critic of the age came however with the acclaim he received in the theatre with *Lady Windermere's Fan* and *The Importance of Being Earnest*. But following a failed libel action against Lord Queensberry, he was tried and imprisoned for two years in 1895 'for acts of gross indecency with other male persons' and was declared bankrupt. It was as if his society and the legal system (in the formidable person of Sir Edward Carson) were taking their revenge for his bravado. His years in prison destroyed his health and his spirit. After his release he went to live in Paris where in 1898 he wrote *The Ballad Of Reading Gaol* and where two years later he died of cerebral meningitis.

YANG LIAN (b.1955)   was born in Switzerland but grew up in Beijing. His poetry has an international quality and yet it is deeply Chinese and if it is influenced by western forms and sensibilities it more so plummets back to the root strands of his own culture. His poetry is dense and subtle and evasive, "a gymnasium for the intuition" in his translator's lovely words. He himself has described his poetry as "ruthless" and says "each of my poems is a mandala." Banned from publishing in China since 1983 and in exile from China since June 1989 (the time of the massacre in Tiananmen Square) much of his shorter work has been translated into English (indeed often in various versions) but Yang has also been writing for some years an epic poem in numerous cantos and hopefully this will see the light of day. Although he belongs to the school of so-called *menglong* poets (such as Bei Dao, Gu Cheng or Duo Duo) Yang has created a more complex poetic universe than his contemporaries.

YI YUKSA (1904-1944)   a descendant of Yi Hwang(1501-1571), the great Neo-Confucian philosopher of the Yi dynasty, Yi Yuksa received a traditional education. In 1925 he joined the anti-Japanese secret society *Uiyoltan* and, implicated in the bombing of a bank, was imprisoned from 1927-1930. His cell number was 264 (pronounced *iyuksa* in Korean) and from this he took his pen name. He did not start to write poetry until after his return from China in 1933, having graduated from Peking University. Arrested again by Japanese forces in 1943, he died in prison in the following January. Not prolific – thirty- four poems were published posthumously by his friends in 1946 with frequent reprints – Yi Yuksa is nonetheless one of the most influential modern Korean poets.

CAN YÜCEL (b.1926)   son of Turkey's finest Minister of Education, Hasan Ali Yucel, and educated in Istanbul and England, after which he worked in the external service of the BBC. He was imprisoned on his return to Turkey in 1970 for translating works by Che Guevara and Mao but released after two years in a general amnesty. A man of immense knowledge and cultural awareness his own work embraces lyricism, warmth and irony in a voice inspired with the will to live and he is a superb translator from Shakespeare and modern English poets. At present living in Istanbul he has now become one of Turkey's outstanding poets.

SA'DI YUSUF (b.1934)   was born in Basra and educated in Baghdad. A former member of the Iraqi Communist Party, he was forced to leave Iraq in 1964. He taught in Algeria and was in Beirut at the time of the Israeli invasion of Lebanon in 1982. He now lives in Cyprus and is unable to return to Iraq. His first book was published in 1953, and his Collected Works in 1979, with many individual volumes both between and since. His poetry speaks in simple and direct terms of everyday experience, abounding with their intimacies, and much of his achievement is held in the ways he has matched the content and forms of these experiences and in the ways he has made poetry out of them.

NIKOLAI ZABOLOTSKY (1903-1958)   born into a family of peasant origin he was a founder member of the *Oberiu* group of experimental poets in 1920s Leningrad and his early poetry, published in 1929 as *Scrolls*, has a surrealistic fragmentary quality. (Kharms and Vvedensky, other founders of the group, later died in prison). Zabolotsky was arrested and tortured in 1938 and lived through eight years of labour camp and exile. He retained a dignity and reserve throughout his life and his late poetry became lyrically attuned to nature. Unpublished for many years in Soviet Russia his work has in recent years had print runs of a million copies and in Britain two volumes of critical biography published in 1994 and a forthcoming *Selected Poems* should bring his work the wider attention that he deserves as one of the major poets of post-revolutionary Russia.

BENJAMIN ZEPHANIAH (b.1958)   grew up in Handsworth, Birmingham with a childhood spilt between Jamaica and Britain. He spent time in approved schools and prison and it was while serving a prison sentence that (like Jimmy Santiago Baca and some of the Irish political prisoners) he became a poet. He spends much time now visiting schools, youth clubs, universities and other prisons giving readings and doing workshops. Social and racial injustice have always been concerns at the heart of his poetry, and his poety has always been galvanised by music and street talk and performance. He has published *The Dread Affair* (1985), *City Psalms* (1992) and other pamphlets, recorded many albums and had his plays widely performed and is recognised as a master of performance art.

-------------------- **AFTERWORD** --------------------

£1.00 from every copy of this book sold will be given to the Medical Foundation for the Care of Victims of Torture, the London based charity which since it was established in 1986 has helped more than 8,000 men women and children from 65 countries.

The book's editors have spent more than five years compiling this anthology; from the early days some of the poems collected have been read aloud by actors and actresses at Medical Foundation evenings. Survivors telling their stories is a fundamental aspect of the charity's life - yet few have the opportunity to give such permanent voice to their experience as poets do.

Sometimes poets and writers may be the only ones who have been able to express in the written word a particular suffering that many thousands have borne.For this reason and others, the Foundation welcomes the publication of Voices of Conscience.

Helen Bamber
(Director, Medical Foundation)
Richard McKane
(Interpreter,Medical Foundation;
co-editor, Voices of Conscience)

Acknowledgements

M. GOPALAKRISHNA ADIGA: From *Voices of Emergency: An All India Anthology of Protest Poetry of the 1975-77 Emergency* (edited by John Oliver Perry): 'A Common Man'. Translated by Sumatheendra Nadig and published by Popular Prakashan, Bombay, 1983. Reprinted by permission of John Oliver Perry. **ADONIS (ALI AHMAD SA'ID):** From *Modern Poetry of the Arab World* (edited by Abdullah al-Udhari): from 'The Desert'. Translated by Abdullah al-Udhari and published by Penguin Books, London, 1986. 'A Mirror for the Twentieth Century'. Translated by Abdullah al-Udhari and published by Penguin Books, 1986. [(First published in Arabic, Beirut, 1968; this translation first published, 1973), copyright (c) Adonis, 1968; translation copyright (c) Abdullah al-Udhari, 1973.] Both poems reprinted by permission of Abdullah al-Udhari and Penguin Books Ltd. **MARJORIE AGOSIN:** From *Zones Of Pain*: 'Torture' and 'The most unbelievable part'. Translated by Cola Franzen and published by White Pine Press, Fredonia, New York, 1988. Reprinted by permission of White Pine Press. **AI QING:** From *Selected Poems of Ai Qing*: 'Dayanhe – My Wet-Nurse'. Translated by Eugene Chen Eoyang and published by Indiana University Press (Bloomington) and Foreign Languages Press (Beijing), 1982. Reprinted by permission of Eugene Chen Eoyang. **MILA AGUILAR:** From *A Comrade Is as Precious as a Rice Seedling*: 'To a Foreigner'. Published by Kitchen Table: Women of Color Press, Brooklyn, 1984. Reprinted by permission of Kitchen Table; permission from author pending. From *The Guerrilla Is Like a Poet*: 'Pigeons for My Son'. Published by Cormorant Books, Dunvegan, Ontario, 1988. Permission from author pending. **ANNA AKHMATOVA:** From *Anna Akhmatova: Selected Poems*: 'Terror, Rummaging Through Things in the Dark' and from 'Requiem: Poems 1935-1940'. Translated by Richard McKane and published by Bloodaxe Books, Newcastle upon Tyne, 1989. Reprinted by permission of Richard McKane. From *20th Century Russian Poetry*: 'The Seventh (Incomplete) Northern Elegy'. Translated by Richard McKane and published by Kozmik Press, London, 1990. Reprinted by permission of Richard McKane. **NIZAMETDIN AKHMETOV:** From *The Poetry of Perestroika*: 'Back Beyond the Burnt Out, Disfigured Day'. Translated by Richard McKane & Helen Szamuely and published by Iron Press, Cullercoats, Tyne & Wear, 1991. Reprinted by permission of Richard McKane. 'My Miracle Blue' translated by Richard McKane and Helen Szamuely. Printed by permission of Richard McKane. **GÜLTEN AKIN:** 'The Prison Yard' translated by Ruth Christie. Printed by permission of Ruth Christie. **ANONYMOUS:** 'The Arsenal Prison Psychiatric Hospital Poems' translated by Richard McKane. Printed by permission of Richard McKane. **PAT ARROWSMITH:** From *Nine Lives*: 'English Political Prisoner'. Published by Brentham Press, St Albans, Herts, 1990. Reprinted by permission of the publisher. **KOFI AWOONOR:** From *Until the Morning After*: 'On Being Told of Torture' and from 'The Wayfarer Comes Home'. Published by The Greenfield Review Press, Greenfield Centre, New York, 1987. Reprinted by permission of Kofi Awoonor. **GENNADY AYGI:** From *Veronica's Book*: 'Song from the Days of your Forefathers'. Translated by Peter France and published by Polygon, 1989. Reprinted by permission of Peter France and Polygon. **JIMMY SANTIAGO BACA:** From *Immigrants in Our Own Land & Selected Early Poems*: 'I Will Remain', 'Against' and 'The New Warden'. Copyright (c) 1982 by Jimmy Santiago Baca. Published by New Directions, New York, 1990. Reprinted by permission of New Directions Publishing Corp. **REZA BARAHENI:** From *God's Shadow (Prison Poems)*: 'The Doves', 'Barbecue', 'Hosseinzadeh, the Head Executioner', 'What is Poetry?' and 'F.M.'s Autobiography'. Translated by the author and published by Indiana University Press, Bloomington, 1976. Reprinted by permission of the author. **BRENDAN BEHAN:** From *The Flowering Tree: Contemporary Irish Poetry with Verse Translations*: 'Loneliness'. Translated by Ulick O'Connor and published by Wolfhound Press, Dublin, 1991. Reprinted by permission of Ulick O'Connor. **BEI DAO:** From *The August Sleepwalker*: Declaration' and 'An End or a Beginning'. Translated by Bonnie S. McDougall and published by Anvil Press Poetry, London, 1988. From *Old Snow*: 'A Picture'. Translated by Bonnie S. McDougall and published by Anvil Press Poetry, London, 1992. All poems reprinted by permission of Anvil Press Poetry Ltd. **SHERKO BEKAS:** From *Anthology of Contemporary Kurdish Poetry*: from 'Small Mirror'. Translated by Kamal Mirawdeli and published by Kurdistan Solidarity Committee and Yashar Ismail, London, 1994. Reprinted by permission of Kamal Mirawdeli. **HORST BIENEK:** From *Selected Poems: Johannes Bobrowski and Horst Bienek*: 'The Silos of Torment' and 'Our Ashes'. Translated by Ruth and Matthew Mead and published by Penguin Books, London, 1971. Permission from translator pending. **BO YANG:** From *Poems of a Period*: 'To My Daugher Jiajia on the Eve of My Release from Jail'. Translated by Stephen L. Smith & Robert Reynolds and published by Joint Publishing (Hong Kong) Company Limited, 1986. Copyright (c) Joint Publishing (H K) Co. Ltd., 1986. Reprinted by permission of the publisher. **KAMAU BRATHWAITE:** From *Middle Passages*: 'Stone'. Published by Bloodaxe Books, Newcastle upon Tyne, 1992. Reprinted by permission of Bloodaxe Books Ltd. **TOMÁS BORGE:** From *Poets of the Nicaraguan Revolution* : 'Letter to Ana Josefina'. Translated by Dinah Livingstone and published by Katabasis, London, 1993. Reprinted by permission of Dinah Livingstone. **BERTOLT BRECHT:** From *Bertolt Brecht: Poems 1913-1956*: 'When Evil-Doing Comes Like Falling Rain', translated by John Willett. 'To Those Born Later', translated by John Willett, Ralph Manheim, and Erich Fried. Published by Eyre Methuen, London, 1976, 1979. (Most recently published by Mandarin Paperbacks, 1994.) Reprinted by permission of Reed Books. **BREYTEN BREYTENBACH:** From *and death white as words*: 'Letter to butcher from abroad'. Translated by Andre B. Brink and published by Rex Collings (London) in association with David Philip (Cape Town), 1978. Permission from author pending. **EDITH BRÜCK:** From *Against Forgetting*: 'Equality, Father'. Translated by Ruth Feldman and published by W.W. Norton & Company, 1993. Reprinted by permission of Ruth Feldman. From *Voices Within the Ark: The Modern Jewish Poets*: Why Would I have Survived?'. Translated by Anita Barrows and published by Avon Books, 1980. Reprinted by permission of Anita Barrows. **DENNIS BRUTUS:** From *Salutes & Censures*: 'Hanged'. Published by Fourth Dimension, Enugu, Nigeria, 1984. Reprinted by permission of Dennis Brutus. **MARÍA EUGENIA BRAVO CALDERARA:** From *Prayer in the National Stadium*: 'And I Cried', translated by Dinah Livingstone, and 'On Exiles and Defeats', translated by Cicely Herbert. Published by Katabasis, London, 1992. Reprinted by permission of Katabasis. **ION CARAION:** From *The Error of Being*: 'Hallucination', 'Nobody's Who I Have' and 'The Porch with Mud Saints'. Translated by Marguerite Dorian and Elliott B. Urdang and published by Forest Books, London, 1994. From *Ion Caraion: Poems*: 'At the Rotten Sea'. Translated by Marguerite Dorian and Elliott B. Urdang and published by Ohio University Press, Athens, Ohio, 1981. All poems reprinted by permission of Marguerite Dorian and Elliot B. Urdang. **ERNESTO CARDENAL:** From *Poets of Nicaragua*: 'Somoza Unveils the Statue of Somoza in Somoza Stadium'. Translated by Steven F. White and published by Unicorn Press, Greensboro, 1982. From *Flights of Victory*: 'The Women of Cuá Arrived'. Translated by Marc Zimmerman and published by Orbis Books, Maryknoll, NY, 1985. Reprinted by permission of Curbstone Press. From *Nicaragua with Love*: 'A Museum in Kampuchea'. Translated by Jonathan Cohen and published by City Lights, San Francisco, 1986. Reprinted by permission of City Lights Books. **MARTIN CARTER:** From *Poems of Succession*: 'I Come from the Nigger Yard', 'This Is the Dark Time My Love', and 'Letter 1'. Published by New Beacon Books, London, 1977. Reprinted by permission of New Beacon Books. **OTTO RENÉ CASTILLO:** From *Tomorrow Triumphant*: 'Police Jail', translated by Stephen Kessler, and 'Apolitical Intellectuals', translated by Francisco X. Alarcón. English Translations (c) 1984 by Night Horn Books. Published by Night Horn Books, San Francisco, 1984. Reprinted by permission of the publisher. **C.P. CAVAFY:** From *Selected Poems*: 'Waiting for the Barbarians'. Translated by Edmund Keeley and Philip Sherrard and published by Princeton University Press, Princeton, New Jersey, 1992. Reprinted by permission of Princeton University Press. **PAUL CELAN:** From *Selected Poems*: 'Death Fugue', 'Tenebrae', 'Psalm' and 'Corona'. Translated by Michael Hamburger and published by Penguin Books, London, 1990. (A new and slightly enlarged edition to be published by Anvil Press Poetry, London.) Reprinted by permission of Michael Hamburger and Anvil Press Poetry. **AMARJIT CHANDAN:** From *Poems from Prison*: 'Who Will Not Want It'. Translated by Nirupama Dutt. From *Being Here*: 'Name Any Saz'. Translated by the author with Amin Mughal & John Welch and published by The Many Press,

London, 1993. Poems reprinted by permission of Amarjit Chandan. **EGHISHE CHARENTS:** From *Land of Fire: Selected Poems of Eghishe Charents* (edited by Diana Der Hovanessian and Marzbed Margossian): 'Dantesque Legend (IV & V)' and 'For Avedik Issahakian'. Translated by Diana Der Hovanessian and published by Ardis Publishers, Ann Arbor, Michigan, 1986. Reprinted by permission of Diana Der Hovanessian. **FRANK MKALAWILE CHIPASULA:** From *When My Brothers Come Home: Poems from Central and Southern Africa:* 'A Hanging'. Copyright (c) 1985 by Frank Chipasula. Published by Wesleyan University Press, Middletown, Connecticut, 1985. Reprinted by permission of University Press of New England. **JOSÉ CRAVEIRINHA:** From *A Horse of White Clouds: Poems from Lusophone Africa:* 'Cell 1' and 'Black Protest'. Translated by Don Burness and published by Ohio University Press, Athens, Ohio, 1989. Reprinted by permission of Don Burness. **ANGEL CUADRA:** From *The Poet in Socialist Cuba:* 'This Man' and 'Brief Letter to Donald Walsh (In Memoriam)'. Translated by Catherine Rodríguez-Nieto and published by University Press of Florida, 1994. Reprinted by permission of University Press of Florida. **DAI WANGSHU:** 'A Severed Finger' translated by John Cayley. Printed by permission of John Cayley. **ROQUE DALTON:** From *Roque Dalton: Poems:* 'The Consolations of Soul Saving' and 'Hitler Mazzini: Comparison Between Chile in 1974 and El Salvador in 1932'. Translated by Richard Schaaf and published by Curbstone Press, Willimantic, Connecticut, 1984. Reprinted by permission of Curbstone Press. From *Clandestine Poems:* 'Like You'. Translated by Jack Hirschman and published by Curbstone Press, Willimantic, Connecticut. Reprinted by permission of Jack Hirschman and the publisher. **MAHMOUD DARWISH:** From *Modern Poetry of the Arab World* (edited by Abdullah al-Udhari): 'Victim No. 48'. Translated by Abdullah al-Udhari and published by Penguin Books, London, 1986. [(First published in Arabic, Haifa, 1967; this translation first published, 1986), copyright (c) Mahmoud Darwish, 1967; translation copyright (c) Abdullah al-Udhari, 1973.] 'Earth Poem'. Translated by Abdullah al-Udhari and published by Penguin Books, 1986. [(First published in Arabic, Beirut, 1977; this translation first published, 1986), copyright (c) Mahmoud Darwish, 1977; translation copyright (c) Abdullah al-Udhari, 1986.] Both poems reprinted by permission of Abdullah al-Udhari and Penguin Books Ltd. From *Victims of a Map:* 'A Gentle Rain in a Distant Autumn'. Translated by Abdullah al-Udhari and published by Al Saqi Books, London, 1984. Reprinted by permission of Abdullah al-Udhari. **ROBERT DESNOS:** From *The Random House of Twentieth Century French Poetry* (edited by Paul Auster): 'Epitaph'. Translated by Kenneth Rexroth and published by Random House, Inc., New York, 1982. Reprinted by permission of New Directions Publishing Corp. **LAXMIPRASAD DEVKOTA:** From *Nepali Visions, Nepali Dreams:* 'Quatrain'. Translated by David Rubin and published by Columbia University Press, New York, 1980. Copyright (c) Columbia University Press, 1980. Reprinted by permission of the publisher. From *Himalayan Voices: An Introduction to Modern Nepali Literature* (edited by Michael James Hutt): 'Mad'. Translated by Michael James Hutt and published by University of California Press, Berkeley, 1991. Copyright (c) 1991 The Regents of the University of California. Reprinted by permission of the publisher. **ERNESTO DÍAZ RODRÍQUEZ:** From *La Campana del Alba/The Bell of Dawn:* 'The Little One'. Published by Editorial Playor, Madrid. **BLAGA DIMITROVA:** From *Poetry East, Number Twenty-nine* (edited by Richard Jones): 'Blinded, they march on...'. Translated by Ludmilla Popova-Wightman & Elizabeth Socolow and published by Poetry East, Chicago, Spring 1990. Reprinted by permission of Poetry East and Ludmilla Popova-Wightman. **MAK DIZDAR:** From *Contemporary Yugoslav Poetry* (edited by Vasa D. Mihailovich): 'The Blue River'. Translated by Vasa D. Mihailovich and published by the University of Iowa, Iowa City, 1977. Copyright (c) University of Iowa, 1977. Reprinted by permission of the publisher. **LEILA DJABALI:** From *African Women's Poetry:* 'For My Torturer, Lieutenant D . . .' . Translated by Anita Barrows and published by Heinemann Educational Books, Oxford, 1995. Reprinted by permission of Anita Barrows. **TAHAR DJAOUT:** From *Sulphur 34* (edited by Clayton Eshleman): 'March 15, 1962.' Translated by Pierre Joris and published by Sulphur, Ypsilanti, Michigan. Reprinted by permission of Pierre Joris. **ARIEL DORFMAN:** From *Last Waltz in Santiago:* 'First Prologue: Simultaneous Translation' and 'Corn Cake'. Translated by Edith Grossman with the author and published by Viking Penguin Inc., New York, 1988. Reprinted by permission of Wylie, Aitken & Stone and the author. **PAUL ÉLUARD:** From *Paul Eluard: Selected Poems:* 'Liberty'. Translated by Gilbert Bowen and published by John Calder (Publishers) Ltd [London] & Riverrun Press Inc [New York], 1987. Reprinted by permission of The Calder Educational Trust, London. **FAIZ AHMED FAIZ:** From *The Rebel's Silhouette:* 'The Rain of Stones Is Finished'. Translated by Agha Shahid Ali and published by Peregrine Smith Books, Layton, Utah, 1991. Reprinted by permission of Agha Shahid Ali. From *The Penguin Book of Modern Urdu Poetry:* 'A Prison Nightfall' and 'Do Not Ask of Me, My Love'. Translated by Mahmood Jamal and published by Penguin Books, London, 1986. Reprinted by permission of Mahmood Jamal. From *The True Subject: Selected Poems of Faiz Ahmed Faiz:* 'Prison Daybreak'. Translated by Naomi Lazard and published by Princeton University Press, Princeton, N.J., 1988. Reprinted by permission of Naomi Lazard and Princeton University Press. **JERZY FICOWSKI:** From *A Reading of Ashes:* 'The Seven Words', 'I did not manage to save ...', 'The Assumption of Miriam...' and 'The Silence of the Earth'. Translated by Keith Bosley with Krystyna Wandycz and published by The Menard Press, London, 1981. Reprinted by permission of Keith Bosley. **ALAIDE FOPPA:** From *Lovers and Comrades: Women's Resistance Poetry from Central America* (edited by Amanda Hopkinson): 'Prayer I'. Translated by Amanda Hopkinson and published by The Women's Press, London, 1989. Reprinted by permission of Amanda Hopkinson and The Women's Press. **ERICH FRIED:** From *100 Poems Without a Country:* 'Paradise Lost'. Translated by Stuart Hood and published by John Calder (Publishers) Ltd., London. Copyright (c) this translation Stuart Hood 1978. Reprinted by permission of The Fried Estate and The Calder Educational Trust, London. **KEVIN GILBERT:** From *Inside Black Australia: An Anthology of Aboriginal Poetry:* 'Kiacatoo'. Published by Penguin Books Australia Ltd., Ringwood Victoria, 1988. Reprinted by permission of the publisher. **NATALYA GORBANEVSKAYA:** 'Memory of Pyarvalka' and 'And tomorrow you'll not even find a trace' translated by Daniel Weissbort. Reprinted by permission of Daniel Weissbort. **GU CHENG:** From *Poetry East, Number Thirty* (edited by Richard Jones): 'A Generation'. Translated by Sam Hamill and published by Poetry East, Chicago, Fall 1990. Reprinted by permission of Sam Hamill and Poetry East. From *Gu Cheng: Selected Poems:* 'An Ending'. Translated by John Cayley and published by Renditions Paperbacks, Hong Kong, 1990. Copyright (c) The Chinese University of Hong Kong 1990. Reprinted by permission of John Cayley. **DHRUBA SEN GUPTA:** From *Dissenting Voices:* 'The Charge – Treason'. Translated by Rati Bartholomew, Anjan Ghosh and Radha Kumar. Published by Peoples Union of Civil Liberties and Democratic Rights (Delhi State), 1977. Reprinted by permission of Rati Bartholomew. **JOY HARJO:** From *In Mad Love and War:* 'For Anna Mae Pictou Aquash...' and 'We Must Call a Meeting'. Copyright (c) 1990 by Joy Harjo. Published by Wesleyan University Press, Middletown, Connecticut, 1990. Reprinted by permission of University Press of New England. **JAVIER HERAUD:** From *Our Word: Guerrilla Poems from Latin America:* 'Flies'. Translated by Edward Dorn & Gordon Brotherston and published by Cape Goliard Press, 1968. Reprinted by permission of Gordon Brotherston. From *Latin American Revolutionary Poetry:* 'In Praise of Days/Destruction and Eulogy to Darkness'. Translated by Robert Márquez and published by Monthly Review Press, New York, 1974. Reprinted by permission of Monthly Review Press. **ZBIGNIEW HERBERT:** From *Report from the Besieged City:* 'The Trial' and 'Damastes (Also Known as Procrustes) Speaks'. Translated by John & Bogdna Carpenter and published by Oxford University Press, Oxford, 1987. Translations (c) by John and Bogdna Carpenter 1987. Reprinted by permission of Oxford University Press. **AMADO V. HERNANDEZ:** From *Rice Grains:* 'A Man's Share of the Sky'. Translated by E. San Juan Jr. and published by International Publishers, New York, 1966. (The poem later reprinted in *The Guerrilla Is Like a Poet: An Anthology of Filipino Poetry*, Cormorant Books, Dunvegan, Ontario, 1988.) Reprinted by permission of E. San Juan, Jr. **MIGUEL HERNÁNDEZ:** From *Selected Poems: Miguel Hernández and Blas de Otero* (edited by Timothy Baland and Hardie St. Martin): 'Lullaby of the Onion'. Translated by Robert Bly and published by Beacon Press, Boston 1972. Copyright (c) 1972 by Timothy Baland and Hardie St. Martin. Reprinted by permission of Beacon Press. **NAZIM HIKMET:** From *Poems of Nazim Hikmet:* 'Angina Pectoris' and 'On Living'. Translated by Randy Blasing & Mutlu Konuk and published by Persea Books, New York, 1986. Copyright (c) 1994 by Randy Blasing and Mutlu Konuk. Reprinted by permission of Persea Books. From *Modern Turkish Poetry:* 'Sunday'. Translated by Richard McKane and published by The Rockingham Press, Ware, Herts, 1992. Reprinted by permission of Richard McKane. From *Nazim Hikmet: A Sad State of Freedom:* 'Poems to Piraye' and 'Advice for Someone Going into Prison'. Translated by Richard McKane and published by Greville Press Pamphlets, Emscote Lawn, Warwick, 1990. Reprinted by permission of Richard McKane. **HO CHI MINH:** From *Prison Diary:* 'The Stocks', 'Tungzheng', 'Transferred to Tianbao on "Double Ten" Day', 'Overnight Stop at Lungquan', 'Scabies', 'Good-bye to a Tooth' and 'Cold Night'. Translated by Dang The Binh and published by Foreign Languages Publishing House, Hanoi, 1978. (Later published as *The Prison Poems of Ho Chi Minh* by Cormorant Press, Dunvegan, Ontario, 1992). **VLADIMÍR HOLAN:** From *Mirroring: Selected Poems of Vladimír Holan:* 'To the Enemies'. Translated by C.G. Hanzlicek & Dana Hábová and published by Wesleyan University Press, Middletown, Connecticut, 1985. Copyright (c) 1985 by C.G. Hanzlicek and Dana Hábová. Reprinted by permission of University Press of New England. **GYULA ILLYÉS:** From *Poetry East, Number Twenty-nine* (edited by Richard Jones): 'One Sentence on Tyranny'. Translated by Bruce Berlind and published by Poetry East, Chicago, Spring 1990. Reprinted by permission of Bruce Berlind and Poetry East. **ANTÓNIO JACINTO:** From *A Horse of White Clouds: Poems from Lusophone Africa:* 'Monte Gracioso'. Translated by Don Burness and published by Ohio University Press, Athens, Ohio, 1989. Reprinted by permission of Don Burness. **LINTON KWESI JOHNSON:** From *Tings an Times: Selected Poems:* 'Sonny's Lettah'. Published by Bloodaxe Books, Newcastle upon Tyne, 1991. Reprinted by permission of Bloodaxe Books Ltd. **ATTILA JÓZSEF:** From *Attila József: Selected Poems and Texts:* 'A Breath of Air!' and 'The Seventh'. Translated by John Bátki and published by Carcanet Press, Manchester, 1973. Reprinted by permission of John Bátki. **KATSETNIK 135633:** 'Melech Shteier (Poem for Burning)' and 'At the Moment's End' translated by Anthony Rudolf. Printed by permission of Anthony Rudolf. **PARVIZ KHAZRAI:** 'The Art of Miracle' translated by Joan MacDougall and the author. Printed by permission of Parviz Khazrai. **KIM CHI HA:** From *Cry of the People and other Poems:* 'The Yellow Dust Road'. Translated by an international group of Kim Chi Ha's friends and associates and the editorial staff of Autumn Press. Published by Autumn Press, Hayama, Kanagawa-ken, Japan, 1974. **ETHERIDGE KNIGHT:** From *The Essential Etheridge Knight:* 'Hard Rock Returns to Prison from the Hospital' and 'The Idea of Ancestry'. Copyright (c) 1986 by Etheridge Knight . Published by the University of Pittsburgh Press, Pittsburgh, 1986. Reprinted by permission of the University of Pittsburgh Press. **KO UN:** From *The Sound of My Waves: Selected Poems by Ko Un:* 'Sunlight' and 'When May Is Gone'. Translated by Brother Anthony of Taizé & Young-Moo Kim and published by Cornell University East Asia Series, Ithaca, New York, 1993. Reprinted by permission of Brother Anthony of Taizé. **RACHEL KORN:** From *Generations: Selected Poems:* 'A New Dress'. Translated by Ruth Whitman and published by Mosaic Press/Valley Editions, Oakville, Ontario, 1982. Reprinted by permission of Mosaic Press. **ABDELLATIF LAÂBI:** 'Hunger Strike' translated by Jacqueline Kaye. Printed by permission of Jacqueline Kaye. **PRIMO LEVI:** From *Collected Poems:* 'Shemà'. Translated by Ruth Feldman and Brian Swann. 'Gedale's Song' and 'Song of Those who Died in Vain' translated by Ruth Feldman. Published by Faber and Faber Ltd, 1988, 1992. Reprinted by permission of Ruth Feldman, Brian Swann, Mrs. Primo Levi and Faber & Faber Ltd. **SAUNDERS LEWIS:** From *Saunders Lewis: Selected Poems:* 'The Carcass' and 'A Word to the Welsh'. Translated by Joseph P. Clancy and published by the University of Wales Press, Cardiff, 1993. Copyright (c) by Mair Saunders of the original Welsh poems. Reprinted by permission of the University of Wales Press. **LIAO YIWU:** From *Sonoma Mandala Literary Review (Vol. 19):* 'Slaughter, Part IV'. Translated by Michael Day and published by Sonoma Mandala Literary Review, Rohnert Park, California, 1992/93. **EOGHAN MacCORMAIC:** From *H Block: A Selection of Poetry from   Republican Prisoners in Long Kesh:* 'Aquaintance Renewed'. Published by South Yorkshire Writers, Sheffield, 1991. From *Seneca Review:* 'A Reflection Across the Yard'. Published by Seneca Review, Vol. XXIII, Nos 1 & 2, Winter, 1993. Poems reprinted by permission of Eoghan MacCormaic. **OSIP MANDELSTAM:** From *The Moscow Notebooks:* 'Eyelashes Sting with Tears' and 'The Flat Is Quiet as Paper'. Translated by Richard and Elizabeth McKane and published by Bloodaxe Books, 1991. Reprinted by permission of Richard and Elizabeth McKane. From *Osip Mandelstam: Selected Poems:* '341' and '385'. Translated by Clarence Brown & W. S. Merwin and published by Oxford University Press, Oxford, 1973. Copyright (c) Clarence Brown 1973. Reprinted by permission of Oxford University Press. **JACK MAPANJE:** From *The Chattering Wagtails of Mikyu Prison:* Scrubbing the Furious Walls of Mikuyu' and 'To the Unknown Dutch Postcard-Sender (1988). Published by Heinemann Publishers (Oxford) Ltd., 1993. Reprinted by permission of Heinemann Publishers (Oxford) Ltd. **CZESLAW MILOSZ:** From *Czeslaw Milosz: The Collected Poems 1931-1987:* 'Dedication' and 'The Sun'. Translated by the author and published by Penguin Books, London, 1988. Reprinted by permission of Penguin Books. **JANICE MIRIKITANI:** From *Awake in the River:* 'Awake in the River'. Published by Isthmus Press, 1978. Reprinted by permission of Janice Mirikitani. **MITTA VASLEYE:** From *An Anthology of Chuvash Poetry:* 'Message to friends'. Translated by Peter France and published by Forest Books (London) and UNESCO, 1991. Reprinted by permission of Forest Books. **RITA MPOUMI-PAPPAS:** From *Greek Women Poets:* 'Krinio' and 'Maria R.'. Translated by Eleni Fourtouni and published by Thelphini Press, New Haven, Connecticut, 1978. Reprinted by permission of Eleni Fourtouni. **SUBHAS MUKHOPADHYAY:** 'Why he didn't come back' and 'The petition' translated by Sibani Raychaudhuri and Robert Hampson. Printed by permission of Sibani Raychaudhuri. **ÁGNES NEMES NAGY:** From *Selected Poems by Ágnes Nemes Nagy:* 'To Freedom'. Translated by Bruce Berlind and published by University of Iowa Press, Iowa City, 1980. Reprinted by permission of Bruce Berlind. **KISHWAR NAHEED:** From *We Sinful Women: Contemporary Feminist Poetry* (edited by Rukhsana Ahmad): 'We Sinful Women'. Translated by Rukhsana Ahmad and published by The Women's Press, 34 Great Sutton Street, London EC1V 0DX, 1990. Reprinted by permission of The Women's Press Ltd. **AHMED FOUAD NEGM:** From *Index on Censorship, Vol.9, No. 2:* 'Prisoner's File'. Translated by Janet Stevens & Moussa Saker and published by Index on Censorship, London, 1980. Reprinted by permission of Index on Censorship. **AGOSTINHO NETO:** From *Sacred Hope: Poems by Agostinho Neto:* 'In Exhaustion He Thus Clamoured'. Translated by Marga Holness and published by Journeyman Press Limited (London) and UNESCO, 1988. Reprinted by permission of Marga Holness. **PABLO NERUDA:** From *Canto General:* 'Letter to Miguel Otero Silva, in Caracas (1948)'. Edited & translated by Jack Schmitt and published by University of California Press, Berkeley, 1991. Copyright (c) 1991 Fundacion Pablo Neruda, Regents of the University of California. Reprinted by permission of the publisher. **NGUYEN CHI THIEN:** From *Index on Censorship, Vol 11, No. 3:* 'I Kept Silent'. Translated by Nguyen Huu Hieu and published by Index on Censorship, London, 1982. Reprinted by permission of Index on Censorship. From *Flowers from Hell:* Sundry Notes. Translated by Huynh Sanh Thong and published by Yale South East Asia Studies, New Haven Connecticut, 1984. Reprinted by permission of Huynh Sanh Thong. **BULAT OKUDZHAVA:** From *Contemporary Russian Poetry:* 'Letter to My Mom'. Translated by Gerald S. Smith and published by Indiana University Press, Bloomington and Indianapolis, 1993. Permission from publisher pending. **DAN PAGIS:** From *Points of Departure:* 'Written in Pencil in the Sealed Railway-Car' and 'Testimony'. Translated by Stephen Mitchell and published by The Jewish Publication Society, Philadelphia, 1981. Copyright (c) 1981. (Later published as *Variable Directions: The Selected Poetry of Dan Pagis,* North Point Press, San Francisco, 1989.) Reprinted by permission of The Jewish Publication Society and Stephen Mitchell. **ANGEL PARDO:** From *Behind Bars at Boniato:* ' Fracture', 'Take Me with You', 'Rays of Faith' and 'Globule in the Void'. Translated by Barbara E. Joe and published by Editorial Sibi, Miami, 1989. **ALICIA PARTNOY:** From *Revenge of the Apple:* 'To My Daughter (Letters from Prison)'. Translated by Richard Schaaf, Regina Kreger and Alicia Partnoy and published by Cleis Press, Pittsburgh, 1992. Reprinted by permission of Cleis Press. **PADRAIC PEARSE:** From *Collected Poems:* 'The Rebel'. Published by New Island Books, Dublin, 1993. Reprinted by permission of the publisher. **GYÖRGY PETRI:** From *Night Song of the Personal Shadow: Selected Poems:* 'To Be Said Over and Over Again', 'To Imre Nagy' and 'Cemetery Plot No.301'. Translated by Clive Wilmer & George Gömöri and published by Bloodaxe Books, 1991. Reprinted by permission of Bloodaxe Books Ltd. **JÁNOS PILINSKY:** From *János Pilinsky: The Desert of Love:* 'Passion of Ravensbrück' and 'Harbach 1944'. Translated by János Csokits & Ted Hughes and published by Anvil Press Poetry, London, 1988. Reprinted by permission of Anvil Press Poetry Ltd. **VASKO POPA:** 'Man's Job', 'The Cherry Tree in the House of Death' and 'Wolves' Tenderness' translated by Anne Pennington. 'United Apples' translated by Francis Jones. All poems printed by permission of Francis Jones. **AMRITA PRITAM:** From *Blood into Ink: South Asian and Middle Eastern Women Write War* (edited by Miriam Cooke and Roshni Rustomji-Kerns): 'To Waris Shah'. Translated by Kiron Bajaj & Carlo Coppola and published by Westview Press, Boulder, Colorado, 1994. Reprinted by permission of Westview Press. **PUTU OKA SUKANTA:** From *The Song of the Starling:* from 'Time', and 'Walking along the path'. Translated by Keith Foulcher and published by Wira Karya, Kuala Lumpur, 1986. Reprinted by permission of Keith Foulcher and Wira Karya. **SAMIH AL-QASIM:** From *Modern Poetry of the Arab World* (edited by Abdullah al-Udhari): 'The Clock on the Wall'. Translated by Abdullah al-Udhari and published by Penguin Books, London, 1986. [(First published in Arabic, Beruit, 1971; this translation first published, 1984). Copyright (c) Samih al-Qasim, 1971; translation copyright (c) Abdullah al-Udhari, 1984.] Reprinted by permission of Abdullah al-Udhari and Penguin Books Ltd. From *Victims of a Map:* 'End of a discussion With a Jailer'. Translated by Abdullah al-Udhari and published by Al Saqi Books, London, 1984. Reprintd by permission of Abdullah al-Udhari. **MIKLÓS RADNÓTI:** From *Forced March: Selected Poems:* 'Fragment', 'A La Recherche' and 'Forced March'. Translated by Clive Wilmer & George Gömöri and published by Carcanet New Press Limited, Manchester, 1979. Reprinted by permission of Clive Wilmer and George Gömöri. **SHAMSUR RAHMAN:** From *Poems from Bangla Desh* (selected by Tambimuttu): *The Voice of a New Nation:* 'Mother'. Translated by Pritish Nandy and published by The Lyrebird Press, London, 1972. Reprinted by permission of Editions Poetry London. From *Take Me Home Rikshaw:* 'Signs of Fear'. Translated by Farida Majid and published by The Salamander Imprint, London, 1974. **IRINA RATUSHINSKAYA:** From *Pencil Letter:* 'I will live and survive'. Translated by David McDuff and published by Bloodaxe Books, Newcastle upon Tyne, 1988. Reprinted by permission of Bloodaxe Books Ltd. **ADRIENNE RICH:** From *Your Native Land, Your Life:* 'North American Time'. Copyright (c) 1986 by Adrienne Rich. Published by W.W Norton & Company, New York. Reprinted by permission of Adrienne Rich and W.W Norton & Company, Inc. **OKTAY RIFAT:** From *Voices of Memory: Selected Poems of Oktay Rifat:* 'The Embrace'. Translated by Ruth Christie and published by Rockingham Press, Ware, Herts, and Yapi Kredi Yayinlari, Istanbul, 1993. Reprinted by permission of Ruth Christie. **GOPALPRASAD RIMAL:** From *Himalayan Voices: An Introduction to Modern Nepali Literature* (edited by Michael James Hutt): 'A Mother's Dream'. Translated by Michael James Hutt and published by University of California Press, Berkeley, 1991. Copyright (c) 1991 The Regents of the University of California. Reprinted by permission of the publisher. **YANNIS RITSOS:** From *Gestures:* 'Awaiting His Execution' and 'Soldiers and Dolls'. Translated by Nikos Stangos and published by Cape Goliard Press, London, 1971. Reprinted by permission of Nikos Stangos. From *The Fourth Dimension: Selected Poems of Yannis Ritsos:* 'The Blackened Pot'. Copyright (c) 1977 by Yannis Ritsos. Translated by Rae Dalven and published by David R. Godine, Publisher, Inc, Lincoln, Massachusetts, 1977. Reprinted by permission of the publisher. **TADEUSZ RÓZEWICZ:** From *Tadeusz Rozewicz: They Came To See a Poet:* 'The Survivor' and 'In the Midst of Life'. Translated by Adam Czerniawski and published by Anvil Press Poetry, London, 1991. Reprinted by permission of Anvil Press Poetry Ltd. **NELLY SACHS:** From *O the Chimneys:* 'A Dead Child Speaks'. Translated by Ruth & Matthew Mead and published by Farrar, Straus & Giroux, New York, 1967. (Originally from *Fahrt ins Staublose*. Copyright (c) Suhrkamp Verlag Frankfurt am Main, 1961.) Reprinted by permission of Suhrkamp Verlag. From *Voices Within the Ark: The Modern Jewish Poets:* 'O the Chimneys'. Translated by Keith Bosley and published by Avon Books, New York, 1980. Reprinted by permission of Keith Bosley. **K. SATCHIDANANDAN:** From *Times of Torment:* 'Poetry and the Police'. Translated and printed by permission of the poet. **SARVESHWAR DAYAL SAXENA:** From *Voices of Emergency: An All India Anthology of Protest Poetry of the 1975-77 Emergency* (edited by John Oliver Perry): 'Red Cycle'. Translated by Rati Bartholemew and published by Popular Prakashan, Bombay, 1983. Reprinted by permission of Rati Bartholomew. **JORGE DE SENA:** From *The Poetry of Jorge de Sena:* 'Letter to My Children on the Shooting of Goya'. Translated by Jean R. Longland and published by Mudborn Press, Santa Barbara, California, 1980. Reprinted by permission of Mudborn Press, Mécia de Sena, and Jean R. Longland. **SIPHO SEPAMLA:** From *The Soweto I Love:* 'Tell Me News'. Published by Rex Collings, London, 1977. Reprinted by permission of Sipho Sepamla. **BHUPI SHERCHAN:** From *Himalayan Voices: An Introduction to Modern Nepali Literature* (edited by Michael James Hutt): 'This Is a Land of Uproar and Rumor'. Translated by Michael James Hutt and published by University of California Press, Berkeley, 1991. Copyright (c) 1991 The Regents of the University of California. Reprinted by permission of the publisher. **SIAMANTO:** From *Anthology of Armenian Poetry* (edited by Diana Der Hovanessian and Marzbed Margossian): 'The Dance'. Translated by Diana Der Hovanessian and published by Columbia University Press, New York, 1978. Reprinted by permission of Diana Der Hovanessian. From *Armenian Poetry Old and New:* 'Handful of Ash'. Translated by Aram Tolegian and published by Wayne State University Press, 1979. Reprinted by permission of Mrs. Aram Tolegian and Wayne State University Press. **TAKIS SINOPOULOS:** From *Selected Poems:* 'Death Feast'. Translated by John Stathatos and published by Wire Press (San Francisco)/Oxus Press (London), 1981. Copyright (c) by the estate of Takis Sinopoulos of the original Greek poem. Translation copyright (c) John Stathatos. Reprinted by permission of John Stathatos. **JOSE MARIA SISON:** From *The Guerrilla Is Like a Poet: An Anthology of Filipino Poetry:* from 'Fragments of a Nightmare' and 'The Guerrilla Is Like a Poet'. Published by Cormorant Books, Dunvegan, Ontario, 1988. (Originally from *Prison and Beyond*, published by the Free Jose Ma. Sison Committee, Manila, 1984.) Reprinted by permission of Jose Maria Sison. **NOÉMIA DE SOUSA:** From *When Bullets Begin to Flower:* 'The Poem of João'. Translated by Margaret Dickinson and published by East African Publishing House Ltd, Nairobi, Kenya, 1972. Permission from publisher pending. **WOLE SOYINKA:** From *A Shuttle in the Crypt:* 'To the madmen over the wall'. Published by Rex Collings/Eyre Methuen, London, 1972. Reprinted by permission of Wole Soyinka. From *Mandela's Earth and other Poems:* 'Your Logic Frightens Me, Mandela'. Published by André Deutsch Limited, London, 1989. Reprinted by permission of Wole Soyinka and André Deutsch Limited. **VASYL STUS:** From *The Idler, No. VII, Vol. II:* from 'Elegies'. Translated by Marco Carynnyk and published by The Idler, Toronto, May 1986. Reprinted by permission of Marco Carynnyk. **ABRAHAM SUTZKEVER:** From *Burnt Pearls: Ghetto Poems of Abraham Sutzkever:* 'For a Comrade'. Translated by Seymour Mayne and published by Mosaic Press/Valley Editions, Oakville, Ontario, 1981. Reprinted by permission of Seymour Mayne and Mosaic Press. From *Voices Within the Ark: The Modern Jewish Poets* (edited by Howard Schwartz and Anthony Rudolf): 'A Cartload of Shoes'. Translated by Hillel Schwartz & David G. Roskies and published by Avon Books, New York, 1980. Reprinted by permission of David G. Roskies. **TITSIAN TABIDZE:** From *Modern Poetry in Translation, No. 18:* 'Poem-Landslide'. Translated by Donald Rayfield and published by Modern Poetry in Translation, London, Winter 1974. Reprinted by permission of Donald Rayfield. **VICTORIA THEODOROU:** From *Greek Women Poets:* 'Picnic.3'. Translated by Eleni Fourtouni and published by Thelphini Press, New Haven, Connecticut, 1978. Reprinted by permission of Eleni Fourtouni. **TO HUU:** From *Blood and Flowers:* 'The State of a Prisoner's Soul'. Translated by Elisabeth Hodgkin & Mary Jameson and published by Foreign Languages Publishing House, Hanoi, 1978. **MARINA TSVETAYEVA:** From *Selected Poems of Marina Tsvetayeva:* from 'Poems to Czechoslovakia'. Translated by Elaine Feinstein and published by Oxford University Press, Oxford, 1994. Reprinted by permission of Elaine Feinstein. **U SAM OEUR:** From *Sacred Vows:* 'Exodus', 'The Loss of My Twins' and 'The Krasang Tree at Prek Po'. Translated by Ken McCullough & U Sam Oeur and published by the Zephyr *Limited Edition* Chapbook Series, Iowa City, Iowa. Reprinted by permission of Ken McCullough and U Sam Oeur. **USMAN AWANG:** From *The Puppeteer's Wayang: A selection of modern Malaysian poetry* (edited by Muhammad Haji Salleh): 'Little Girl' and 'Father Utih'. Translated by Adibah Amin and co-published by In Print Publishing Ltd. (Brighton) and Dewan Bahasa dan Pustaka Malaysia (Kuala Lumpur), 1992. Reprinted by permission of In Print Publishing Ltd; permission from author pending. **ARMANDO VALLADARES:** From *Index on Censorship, Vol. 11, No. 2:* 'Planted in My Chair' and 'Wings Will Grow One Day'. Published by Index on Censorship, 1982. Reprinted by permission of Index on Censorship. **CESAR VALLEJO:** 'A Man Goes by with a Loaf on his

Shoulder' translated by Anthony Edkins. Reprinted by permission of Anthony Edkins. **JORGE VALLS ARANGO:** From *Donde Estoy No Hay Luz Y Esta Enrejado/Where I am There Is No Light and It Is Barred:* 'Sweet Fish'. Translated by James E. Maraniss & Emilio E. Labrada with Louis Bourne and published by Editorial Playor, Madrid, 1984. **NIKOLA VAPTSAROV:** From *Poetry East, Number Twenty-nine* (edited by Richard Jones): 'Last Words Found in His Pockets'. Translated by William Pitt Root and published by Poetry East, Chicago, Fall 1990. Reprinted by permission of William Pitt Root and Poetry East. **DANIEL VAROUJAN:** From *Anthology of Armenian Poetry* (edited by Diana Der Hovanessian and Marzbed Margossian): 'Sowing'. Translated by Diana Der Hovanessian and published by Columbia University Press, New York, 1978. Reprinted by permission of Diana Der Hovanessian. **DAVID VOGEL:** From *Voices Within the Ark: The Modern Jewish Poets* (edited by Howaed Schwartz and Anthony Rudolf): 'Days Were Great as Lakes' and 'In Fine, Transparent Words'. Translated by A.C. Jacobs and published by Avon Books, New York, 1980. Copyright (c) All rights for the original Hebrew version are reserved by the author. Reprinted by permission of David Vogel. **VLADIMIR VYSOTSKY:** 'Throw Meat to the Dogs' translated by Richard McKane. Reprinted by permission of Richard McKane. **ROBERT WALKER:** From *Inside Black Australia: An Anthology of Aboriginal Poetry:* 'Life is Life' and 'Solitary Confinement'. Published by Penguin Books Australia Ltd, Ringwood Victoria, 1988. Reprinted by permission of the publisher. **ALEKSANDER WAT:** From *Aleksander Wat: Selected Poems:* 'Before Breughel the Elder'. Translated by Czeslaw Milosz & Leonard Nathan and published by Penguin Books, London, 1991. Reprinted by permission of Penguin Books. **WEN YIDU:** From *Twentieth Century Chinese Poetry: An Anthology:* 'Quiet Night'. Translated by Kai-yu Hsu and published by Cornell University Press, 1970. (Originally published by Doubleday & Company, Inc, 1963.) Reprinted by permission of Doubleday & Company, Inc. **ERROL WEST:** From *Inside Black Australia: An Anthology of Aboriginal Poetry:* 'There is no one to teach me the songs that bring the Moon Bird' and 'I feel the texture of her complexion with both hand and heart'. Published by Penguin Books Australia Ltd, Ringwood Victoria, 1988. Reprinted by permission of the publisher. **OSCAR WILDE:** From *The Ballad of Reading Gaol:* 'The Ballad of Reading Gaol (V & VI)'. Published by Journeyman Press, London, 1991. Public Domain. **YANG LIAN:** From *Non-Person Singular:* '1989'. Translated by Brian Holton and published by The Wellsweep Press, London, 1994. Reprinted by permission of Brian Holton and Wellsweep Press. **YI YUKSA:** From *The Silence of Love: Twentieth Century Korean Poetry* (edited by Peter H. Lee): 'Deep-Purple Grapes'. Translated by Peter H. Lee and published by The University Press of Hawaii, 1980. Reprinted by permission of the publisher. **CAN YÜCEL:** From *The Poetry of Can Yücel: A Selection:* 'Poem 25' & 'The Latest Situation in Chile' translated by Feyyaz Kayacan Fergar and 'Arithmetic' translated by Esra Nilgun Mirze & Richard McKane. Published by Papirüs Yayinlari/Papirüs Publications, Istanbul, 1993. All poems reprinted by permission of Richard McKane. **SA'DI YUSUF:** From *Modern Poetry of the Arab World:* 'Hamra Night'. Translated by Abdullah al-Udhari and published by Penguin Books, 1986. Reprinted by permission of Abdullah al-Udhari and Penguin Books. **NIKOLAI ZABOLOTSKY:** 'In a Field Somewhere Near Magadan' and 'A Woodland Lake' translated by Daniel Weissbort. Printed by permission of Daniel Weissbort. **BENJAMIN ZEPHANIAH:** From *The Dread Affair:* 'Dis policeman keeps on kicking me to death'. Published by Arrow Books Limited, London, 1985. From *Inna Liverpool:* 'Strange Truth'. Published by AK Press, Edinburgh, 1992. Poems reprinted by permission of Benjamin Zephaniah.

IRON Press was formed in Spring 1973, initially to publish the magazine IRON which more than two decades, and more than 1,500 writers on, survives as one of the country's most active alternative mags – a fervent purveyor of new poetry, fiction and graphics. £12.00 gets you a subscription. Try our intriguing book list too, titles which can rarely be found on the shelves of mega-stores. Fortified by a belief in good writing, as against literary competitions or marketing trivia, IRON remains defiantly a small press. Our address is at the front of this book